S0-ACS-134

THEORETICAL AND CONCEPTUAL ISSUES IN HISPANIC MENTAL HEALTH

THEORETICAL AND CONCEPTUAL ISSUES IN HISPANIC MENTAL HEALTH

Edited by
Robert G. Malgady
Orlando Rodriguez

KRIEGER PUBLISHING COMPANY
MALABAR, FLORIDA
1994

Original Edition 1994

Printed and Published by
KRIEGER PUBLISHING COMPANY
KRIEGER DRIVE
MALABAR, FLORIDA 32950

Library of Congress Cataloging-In-Publication Data

Theoretical and conceptual issues in Hispanic mental health/edited
by Robert G. Malgady, Orlando Rodriguez.
p. cm.
Includes bibliographical references and index.
ISBN 0-89464-839-X
1. Hispanic Americans—Mental health. 2. Hispanic Americans—Mental health services. 3. Hispanic Americans—Cultural assimilation—Psychological aspects. I. Malgady, Robert G.
II. Rodriguez, Orlando, 1942–
RC451.5.H57T48 1994
362.2'08968073—dc20 93-38655
CIP

10 9 8 7 6 5 4 3 2

BACHRACH

To the proposition guiding the lifetime work of Lloyd H. Rogler:
the scientific study of society is itself a major cultural value.

CONTENTS

FOREWORD

Somewhere in his masterful writings, the French sociologist Emile Durkheim penetratingly observed that desires far exceed increases in prosperity when traditional cultural norms lose their controlling function. In mutual stimulation, the desires and the prosperity spiral upward, the two progressively feeding on each other until the unfortunate person experiencing all of this is hurled into the painful bewilderment of anomia.

For one fleeting moment, I felt that the rich symbolic rewards of the events leading to the publication of this book honoring my work might afflict me with a touch of anomia. Success, as is often said, is hard to take. I need not have worried. I never came close to the distress of anomia. Two persons lucidly imbedded in my memory, both sociologists, kept me from such distress: my father, Charles C. Rogler, and my former research collaborator and colleague, August B. Hollingshead. Both were accomplished but profoundly humble men, and to both puffery and hyperbole were anathema. Both believed that the pride of accomplishment always had to be tempered by recognizing the vast work that inevitably remains to be done.

I don't know whether or not it makes philosophical sense or any other kind of sense, for that matter, to thank persons who are now deceased. But I shall do it anyhow: Charlie and Sandy, my thanks to you.

My thanks also to the many persons who contributed to the production of this volume, in particular the editors and the authors of chapters. I have read the chapters and like them. Somehow, I also feel that Charlie and Sandy would have enjoyed them too.

Lloyd H. Rogler

INTRODUCTION

Robert G. Malgady and Orlando Rodriguez

In the Spring of 1992, the National Institute of Mental Health sponsored a *Festschrift* to honor the lifetime achievements of Lloyd H. Rogler, Albert Schweitzer Professor of Humanities and Professor of Sociology at Fordham University. The *Festschrift* was hosted by president of Fordham University, Father Joseph O'Hare. At this conference, leading researchers throughout the United States, distinguished in a wide array of mental health disciplines, were invited to present their own original theoretical discussions related to themes within the framework of Professor Rogler's research on Hispanic populations.

Professor Rogler's lifetime achievements are aptly summarized in an excerpt from a statement written by Father Joseph O'Hare, nominating him for the National Medal of Science in recognition of his pioneering achievements in interdisciplinary research advancing our understanding of the role of culture in human societies and in the development of exemplary research institutes and training programs accruing to the benefit of future generations of researchers in the social and behavioral sciences:

> Born and raised in Puerto Rico and of Puerto Rican parentage on his mother's side, Lloyd H. Rogler began his work as a social and behavioral scientist in the most economically impoverished neighborhoods of San Juan, observing how families coped with daily experiences of psychological distress. His three and a half decades of work have culminated in widely recognized contributions spanning an interdisciplinary mix of psychiatry, psychology, and sociology. His work is also known in behavior genetics, anthropology, and psychiatric epidemiology. For eighteen years he has occupied the Albert Schweitzer Professorial Chair at Fordham University, which is endowed by the Regents of the State of New York.

> The total impact of his interdisciplinary work is evident at various levels. Through the findings of pioneering research which has led to new visions and perspectives, and the creative but rigorous theoretical statements designed to integrate the products of myriad research projects, he has made notable contributions to the scientific conduct of psychiatry, psychology, and sociology. His research foreshadowed developments in the study of stressful life events, family structure and dynamics, professional and folk therapies, mental illness and idiomatic expressions of distress, transcultural psychiatry, intergenerational change and continuity in the behavior of immigrants, and organizational responses and adaptations to different sociocultural environments. He showed that the interdisciplinary complexity of such topics required the versatile use of the entire armamentarium of methods in the social and behavioral sciences, from historical analyses and ethnographic documentations to experimental designs and epidemiological surveys. His efforts to integrate the scientific literature to show points of convergence and new directions for research are recognized as seminal: frameworks for organizing mental health relevant research and for posing critical questions; inductively ordering the research and clinical meanings of culturally sensitive mental health treatment; outlining the meaning of culturally sensitive research and how such research should evolve; delineating the interconnections between migration experiences and psychological distress; and, formulating the parameters within which acculturative forces shape migrant adaptation. Thus, his unusually significant achievements derived from studying the emergence and transmission of culture in human populations, as well as the multitudinous influences stemming from culture, have contributed new visions to scientific thought in the social and behavioral sciences.

Accordingly, the *Festschrift* speakers chosen to honor Professor Rogler's lifelong work consisted of a cadre of eminent anthropologists, sociologists, epidemiologists, psychologists, and psychiatrists, all experts in Hispanic research with a fundamental concern for the role of culture in their particular discipline. Similarly, their state-of-the-art presentations, which compose the chapters of this book, encompass two major themes: culture and the process of acculturative change and the role of culture in mental health evaluation and treatment. First, acculturation is discussed as a psychological process involving cognitive, attitude, and behavior change. Acculturatively induced stress is linked to the development of mental health problems and disorders. Next, the later chapters turn directly to the relevance of culture and acculturation to mental health services, including the manifestation of symptomatology, the diagnosis of psychiatric disorder, and the effectiveness of psychotherapeutic intervention.

THEME I: CROSS-CULTURAL AND ACCULTURATIVE ISSUES IN HISPANIC MENTAL HEALTH

The six chapters in the first section of this book provide distinct perspectives on the concept of acculturation as viewed from anthropology, psychology, sociology, psychiatry, and epidemiology. All six chapters deal with the theme of acculturation and its relation to mental health. Acculturation is broadly conceived in the interplay of social, political, economic, and psychological forces having an impact on individuals before and after they cross cultural borders. This section focuses on different aspects of the concept of acculturation, such as biculturality, and moves from Hispanics in general to particular Hispanic or Latino nationalities. Thus, this section includes a critical conceptual and methodological review of the literature on the relationship between acculturation and mental health among diverse Hispanic groups, as well as discussions of cultural norms in Cuban and Cuban-American mental health treatment, the prevalence and risk factors of depression among Mexican-American children, and the effects of migration on the mental health of Mexican women.

In chapter 1, Professor Alan Harwood broadly examines from an anthropological perspective the assumptions of traditional acculturation theory in light of contemporary patterns of world migration, information dissemination, and technology transfer, arguing against the idea that migrants' cultures of origin are separable from the host culture. Because of such influences as international mass media exchange; U.S. military installations around the globe; and educational, health care, and manufacturing influxes from the United States, many migrants today arrive with a functional knowledge of English and American ideas and values. Harwood suggests that contemporary people acquire cosmopolitan cultural orientations in their countries of origin and do not necessarily perceive these orientations as distinctly "American" or alien from their own culture. Besides the permeation of elements of American culture far beyond its borders, within the United States any ethnic group's presumed values, beliefs, and other cultural characteristics develop in interaction with other groups in the context of the host society culture and economic opportunity structure. Professor Harwood departs from traditional attempts to define objective (or even subjective) criteria to differentiate cultural groups. Rather, he suggests that it is more important to understand what members of these groups think separates them from others and what changes they think it takes to become "American." Accordingly, studying these perceptions in relation to the perceptions of other groups, to objective social and economic conditions and to the way individuals orient their lives with respect to these multiple perceptions, will yield fruitful insights into the mental health status of ethnic minorities.

In chapter 2, Professor Amado Padilla narrows the scope of discussion to the theoretical construct of biculturalism and its mental health implications for Hispanics, while focusing on dual culture socialization among children and adolescents. Padilla contrasts early sociological literature, associating biculturalism with social marginality, with the consensus today that biculturalism promotes psychosocial functioning. Over the years, Padilla has assumed a definitive role in the development of the concept of acculturation in the field of psychology. In this chapter, he shares his current thinking on the topic. He defines biculturalism as both behavioral competence and positive affect toward two cultures. The literature surrounding bicultural development is reviewed from four perspectives: immigrant children and adolescents, second generation offspring of immigrants, later generation ethnic children and adolescents, and mixed ethnic heritage youngsters. Each of these situations, Padilla contends, presents different socialization contexts and challenges for parents and offspring in the development of biculturalism. Although the primary focus of the literature reviewed by Padilla pertains to Hispanics, he presents a general model of biculturalism and thus integrates literature with other ethnic groups into his analysis. An important assumption derived in this analysis is that the maintenance of ethnic identity and bicultural orientation is often imposed on individuals depending on their physical features that mark them as "outsiders" to the majority group. Padilla concludes that ethnic loyalty and biculturalism can serve as positive coping responses in a prejudicial society and, regardless of the reasons for bicultural socialization, he advocates the benefits of bicultural competence.

In chapter 3, Dr. Dharma Cortes provides a conceptual and methodological overview of the literature on the relationship of acculturation to mental health among diverse Hispanic populations, highlighting several issues that may explain disparate empirical findings in this area.

Cortes examines the way acculturation and mental health outcomes have been conceptually defined and psychometrically assessed in empirical research, describing some points of incongruence between concept and operational definition. She also provides insight into the complexity of the correspondence between conceptual models of acculturation and mental health and the wide diversity of studies on this topic. She concludes with suggestions for how current research strategies ought to be modified such that the two highly complex processes—acculturation and mental health—can be interrelated without oversimplifying them.

In chapter 4, Professor Pedro Ruiz discusses from a psychiatric point of view the historical and demographic characteristics of the Cuban-American migration to the United States during the 20th century, focusing attention on the periods during which this migration led to major acculturative processes. Ruiz extracts the preventive role in terms of mental health disturbance and maintenance from elements within the norms and patterns of Cuban culture, both in Cuba and in the United States. He discusses the role of folk religious practices, linked with socioeconomic status, in relation to psychiatric intervention techniques and practices. Professor Ruiz concludes with clinical issues pertaining to mental health and illness with the framework of the Cuban-American migratory process.

In chapter 5, Professor Robert Roberts explores conceptual, methodological, and substantive issues surrounding our understanding of the epidemiology of depression among a very understudied group, adolescents of Mexican origin. Roberts bases his observations upon the results of three pilot studies conducted in New Mexico, comparing large samples of Mexican origin and non-Hispanic white students. His conceptual focus involves assessing the phenomenology (dimensionality) of depressive symptomatology in the two groups and the patterns of correlation between depression and putative psychosocial risk factors. His methodological focus is on the psychometric properties of various measures of depression, as compared between the two groups. His substantive focus provides descriptive estimates of the burden of depression within the two ethnic groups based on several epidemiological techniques.

In chapter 6, Professor Nelly Salgado de Snyder considers a topic that has been traditionally ignored in the literature: the active role of women in international migration. Even less attention has been given to women who stay behind in the small villages of developing countries, such as Mexico. Salgado de Snyder argues that, in spite of evidence documenting that migration across international boundaries may affect the people who go and those who stay behind similarly, more research is needed on the wives of male migrants who stay behind caring for family and household until their spouses return. In order to understand the mental health implications of the migration process among the women involved, she maintains, it is important to know the psychological and social dynamics of women who live on both sides of the border. This chapter reviews some of the psychosocial issues and dynamics related to mental health that have an impact on the lives of Mexican women who directly or indirectly are affected by international migration. Salgado de Snyder organizes her presentation according to a psychosocial stress model that consists of potential stressors, external resources, coping responses, and outcomes.

THEME II: CULTURAL ISSUES IN MENTAL HEALTH EVALUATION AND TREATMENT OF HISPANICS

The four chapters in the second section of this book, contributed by psychologists and psychiatrists, are concerned with the role of Hispanic culture in the assessment and treatment of psychopathology. They examine how culture and language affect the process of psychiatric diagnosis and psychological assessment among Hispanic patients, how psychotherapeutic treatment modalities can be modified to become culturally sensitive, how posthospitalization aftercare is affected by cultural factors, and how the cultural diversity of Hispanic populations poses particular hurdles for the delivery of mental health services.

In chapter 7, New York City Mental Health Commissioner Luis Marcos confronts the daily reality of a rapidly growing Spanish-dominant population in the United States, juxtaposed with an insufficient number of Spanish-speaking mental health professionals. Marcos reviews and systematizes the literature on the effects of the language barrier on the psychiatric examination of limited-English-speaking Hispanic patients, focusing on three language dimensions: dominance, independence, and attitude. Marcos concludes that the areas of the mental status examination most commonly affected by the language barrier include the patient's attitude, motor activity, speech and stream of talk, affect, and sense of self. Marcos also finds evidence to indicate that mental health clinicians who are unfamiliar with the implications of the language barrier for assessment of mental disorders may risk misevaluation of the patient's psychiatric condition.

In chapter 8, Professors Jose Szapocznik, William Kurtines, and Daniel Santisteban explore how the interplay among theory, research, and application has fostered breakthroughs in the treatment of Hispanic youngsters' behavioral problems. They demonstrate how research conducted in a multicultural context and with a multicultural focus can facilitate the simultaneous study of general clinical issues and specific cultural factors that play a critical role in understanding and treating clinical problems. These issues are presented in the context of an ongoing program of psychotherapy research that targets for intervention Hispanic behavior problem youth and their families, primarily Cuban Americans. Their presentation includes findings and breakthroughs in structural family therapy, the measurement of family functioning, the development of culturally appropriate interventions, the role of attrition as a measure of treatment outcome, the role of cultural variables in treatment outcome, and the investigation of theoretically postulated mechanisms in behavior change.

In chapter 9, Drs. Giuseppe Costantino and Carmen Rivera describe a program of culturally sensitive treatment outcome research involving Puerto Ricans across the lifespan. Four treatment modalities are presented. Storytelling of Puerto Rican *cuentos* or folktales was developed as a treatment modality to promote modeling of adaptive behavioral functioning among young children. Older children are exposed to visual Thematic Apperception Test-like stimuli developed to provoke conflict regarding a particular therapeutic target behavior. The pictures portray interactions among Hispanic family members and embody cultural themes that the adolescents discuss and enact through role playing. The adolescent treatment modality is based on role modeling of heroic male and female characters in Puerto Rican history. Finally, their adult program of culturally sensitive treatment is based on a psychoeducational approach, with seriously mental ill patients and their families. Costantino and Rivera illustrate in detail procedures for adapting standard therapeutic techniques, such as modeling therapy and psychoeducational intervention, to become culturally and age appropriate for their clientele.

In chapter 10, Professor Malgady proposes three hurdles to be surmounted in research regarding mental health evaluation and treatment of Hispanic populations. The first is a general question concerning whether or not a consideration of Hispanic culture is consequential to the delivery of effective clinical services. The cross-cultural mental health assessment and treatment outcome literature indicates an affirmative answer. The second question is whether or not further modifications of clinical services are warranted in accordance with the distinctive subcultural character of diverse Hispanic nationalities. To surmount this hurdle, it is argued that two kinds of research are required: studies of the generalizability to multiple Hispanic groups of culturally sensitive techniques found to be effective with one or another Hispanic nationality and studies directly comparing multiple Hispanic groups to assess subcultural moderating effects on evaluation and treatment techniques. An affirmative answer to the second question poses a third hurdle: whether or not it is practical for the mental health service system to respond to the consequences of the diversity of Hispanics and other ethnic groups. The conclusion is that the potential grocery list of multiethnic *x* multiple subcultural modifications of standard assessment batteries, diagnostic criteria, and treatment modalities would pose not only an unenviable validation task, but also would be economically prohibitive to implement. Thus, research and resources should target the commonalities, not the diversity, of cultural groups as they affect mental health evaluation and treatment.

THEME I:

CROSS-CULTURAL AND ACCULTURATIVE ISSUES IN HISPANIC MENTAL HEALTH

CHAPTER 1

ACCULTURATION IN THE POSTMODERN WORLD: IMPLICATIONS FOR MENTAL HEALTH RESEARCH

Alan Harwood, PhD

Professor of Anthropology, University of Massachusetts at Boston

In a recent and already widely cited article, Rogler, Cortes, and Malgady (1991) critically surveyed 30 studies exploring the relationship between acculturation and mental health status among Hispanics. Their efforts uncovered "problems and limitations in the treatment of the two concepts" and in the ways the two constructs were interconnected. The authors concluded that a "continuing multiplication of research framed according to current assumptions and practices is not likely to advance substantially our knowledge of this topic. New directions are needed" (Rogler, Cortes, & Malgady, 1991, pp. 585–586).

In this paper I respond to this call by Rogler and his collaborators by making two suggestions. One of them arises out of the fact that important aspects of contemporary immigration no longer fit a key assumption of traditional acculturation theory. In addition, I contend that interethnic relations and acculturation are more dynamic and fluid than even the most current acculturation theories take into account. In light of these limitations in present theory, I propose a shift in research direction from etic to emic investigations of acculturation and interethnic phenomena as a necessary preliminary to a new conceptualization of acculturation and the development of new methods for collecting data on this important phenomenon.

The second suggestion I propose in this essay concerns the mental health side of the research agenda, although as an anthropologist I feel less comfortable in commenting on this subject than on matters of ethnicity and acculturation. My point, however, is similar to the first. I contend that acculturation research in relation to mental health status has erred methodologically by studying acculturation almost exclusively as an objective phenomenon. What we must probe more fully, I suggest, are people's emotional assessments of and reactions to the complex interethnic situations they face. In this regard I advocate a change in research direction to a phenomenological approach.

TOWARD A MORE DYNAMIC VIEW OF ACCULTURATION

In the past decade or so, useful theoretical and empirical work on the concept of acculturation has clarified and extended its original formulation in the 1930s (Herskovits, 1938; Linton, 1940; Redfield, Linton, & Herskovits, 1936; Stonequist, 1937; Social Science Research Council Summer Seminar, 1954). In particular, a host of investigators, by developing such concepts as integration, multidimensionality, acculturational stress, biculturalism, and transculturalism, has expanded our view of the range of adaptations that people from one culture can make to another (Berry, 1980; Berry, Trimble & Olmedo, 1986; Clark, Kaufman, & Pierce, 1976; Padilla, 1980; Pierce, Clark, & Kaufman, 1978–79; Ramirez, 1984; Szapocznik & Kurtines, 1980; Szapocznik, Kurtines, & Fernandez, 1980). More recently, Oetting and Beauvais (1991) contended that most of these recent formulations have erred, too, in viewing identification with one culture as necessarily interdependent with identification with other cultures. They also criticize most contemporary theories for assuming unidirectionality in the acculturative process, a point also made by Rogler, Cortes, and Malgady (1991), which has prompted my rethinking of this subject.

Yet none of these reformulations of traditional acculturation theory has gone far enough, I contend. They still ignore important aspects of contemporary acculturational phenomena. In this regard, one key but outmoded assumption of prevailing acculturation theory is that migrants' cultures of origin are, by and large, distinct and analytically separable from the receiving culture. Developing out of the immigration experience of the 19th and early 20th centuries, the focus of research is on immigrants' acquisition of the receiving society's culture and the relationship of this process to the migrant's original culture, all the while treating the two as separate phenomena. The 1954 formulation by the Social Science Research Council Summer Conference, for example, articulates this position by defining acculturation as "culture change that is initiated by the conjunction of two or more *autonomous* cultural systems" (1954; p. 974; emphasis mine). This assumption of autonomy or separateness pervades not only older models of acculturation (many of which have been cited above) but also more recent multidimensional (Berry, 1980; Berry, Trimble, & Olmedo, 1986; Olmedo, 1979; Padilla, 1980), bicultural or transcultural (Ramirez,

1984; Szapocznik & Kurtines, 1980), and orthogonal models (Oetting & Beauvais, 1991).

In contrast to this view, I maintain that in the contemporary world it is no longer heuristic to assume such separateness between recipient and immigrant cultures. Present-day patterns of world migration, information dissemination, and technology transfer have brought about a situation in which people entering the United States today already participate to varying degrees in a global culture heavily infused with ideas, values, and skills that have accompanied the worldwide spread of industrial capitalism and United States political and economic influence since World War II.[1] The degree of "autonomy" or "separateness" of cultures is therefore no longer something one can assume; it requires empirical investigation.

People in remote parts of the contemporary world, in both rural and urban settings, learn "American" cultural standards from U.S.-made television programs (see, for example, Kottak, 1990, for a study of urban and rural Brazil). Cosmopolitan health care facilities, medicines (van der Geest & Whyte, 1988, 1989), processed foods, mass-produced clothing, and other manufactured goods have penetrated to all parts of the globe. In addition, the worldwide spread of factory work has challenged community values, time orientations, and family structures in ways similar to those already observable in industrialized nations. Compared to earlier periods, too, proportionately fewer immigrants arrive today without prior exposure to English. Educational systems, even in some of the world's poorest nations, now introduce children to English as the international lingua franca. English language instruction has also been provided to sponsored refugees, and U.S. military installations abroad foster at least rudimentary knowledge of the language among people living in the vicinity of camps.

In short, compared to earlier times, many contemporary immigrants have already acquired cosmopolitan cultural orientations in their countries of origin and have internalized them, not as alien accretions or "American" ways, but as part of their own culture. As a result, differences separating immigrants' cultures from American culture have diminished since the earlier decades of this century when acculturation theory developed. To become "Americanized" today (except for people from the most rural, least Westernized areas, very few of whom emigrate) entails less cultural reorientation than it did for earlier cohorts of immigrants whose cultures were much freer of modernizing and specifically U.S. influences.[2] Indeed, Portes and Rumbaut (1990, pp. 13–14) have even characterized contemporary immigration as

> a direct consequence of the dominant influence attained by the culture of the advanced West in every corner of the globe. . . . Immigrants do not come to escape perennial unemployment or destitution in their homeland. Most undertake the journey instead to attain the dream of a new life style that has reached their countries but that is impossible to fulfill in them.

It must be noted that this interpenetration of American capitalist culture with individual, national, and regional cultures has not proceeded equally in all parts of the globe. U.S. influences have varied greatly from country to country and across social classes within the same country. As a result, immigrants to the United States today are more diverse in their knowledge of American ways than ever before. We therefore cannot assume agreement either within an ethnic group or across groups about what behaviors or values are considered to be particularly "American." We must acquire this information from each individual and group independently.

Worldwide economic development has also led to increasing social differentiation within the nations of the world, a phenomenon that has led in turn to greater class and occupational diversity among immigrants than prevailing acculturation theories assume. In fact, many voluntary immigrants are precisely those who already participate in cosmopolitan culture. Thus, approximately one third of all immigrants to the United States in recent years are professionals, mainly from the Philippines, the Indian subcontinent, China, and areas of Asia to which Chinese people immigrated in earlier times (Vega & Rumbaut, 1991). In fact, nearly all recent immigrant groups are more heterogeneous with respect to education than those of former times. Portes and Rumbaut (1990, p. 7) have described the situation vividly:

> contemporary immigration features a bewildering variety of origins, return patterns, and modes of adaptation to American society. Never before has the United States received immigrants from so many countries, from such different social and economic backgrounds, and for so many reasons.

In sum, contemporary immigrants to the United States, compared to those of earlier periods, are both highly diverse and already acquainted in varying degrees with American or global cosmopolitan culture. These features of the modern reality of immigration are not taken into account in traditional acculturation theory, which tends to regard the immigrants of each ethnic group as relatively homogeneous internally, yet quite separate culturally from American standards for behavior. But surely for coethnics of different class and educational backgrounds the forces leading to acculturation are quite different, and therefore their acculturational experiences must also differ (cf. Gordon, 1964). Current acculturation theory and instruments have proven inadequate to the task of accounting for the actual diversity of contemporary acculturation.

In addition, the situations to which immigrants come are largely ignored by present-day acculturation theory and instruments. Multiethnic situations are simply much more dynamic than our present research armamentarium assumes. This quality of multiethnic situations is succinctly captured in the following quotation from the British sociologist Michael Banton (1981, p. 35).

> Ethnic identities are not primordial characteristics programmed into individuals, but have continually to be established from the actions of people as they choose to align themselves in one way or another and make use of shared notions about who belongs in what social category. It is not just that some members forsake the immigrant minority group, or pull it in a different direction, but that members of the majority are engaged in changing their group, too.

In this statement Banton calls attention to three important features that contribute to the dynamic of multiethnic situations: (1) the variability of ethnic social relations and ethnic cultural markers across time and space; (2) the fact that ethnicity is a quality of groups and of individuals who may in fact differ in the social uses to which they put their ethnic identity (see also Graves 1967); and (3) the importance of situation, particularly interactions with other cultural groups, for defining ethnic identity. Let us look at these features in greater detail.

Particular political and economic conditions (e.g., local stratification systems, local effects of the economic cycle, degree of cultural pluralism) help foster competition and/or cooperation among groups and, in doing so, influence the formation of ethnic identities and ethnic alignments. The existence of a global cosmopolitan culture does not neutralize these endogenous forces creating ethnic boundaries. These boundaries and their markers may vary at local, regional, and national levels of the economy and polity, depending on the other major competitors for jobs and/or power in the system (Barth, 1969; Keyes, 1981).

Moreover, at each level the ethnic designata and interests of the group may change. For example, on the most local level, competition and/or cooperation may arise for people of Puerto Rican ancestry between those who come from cities and those coming from the countryside or between people from Ponce and those from Mayaguez; on the regional level, the relevant ethnic identity may be Puerto Rican as contrasted to Cuban, Salvadorean, Haitian, U.S. black, or West Indian black; on the national level, Puerto Ricans may identify for some purposes as Hispanic in contrast to blacks and whites. People thus learn to expand or contract the scope of their ethnic identification depending on the situation (Alba, 1990; Light, 1981), and to do so, they may have to learn specific (sometimes new) ideas, values, and attitudes associated with these identities. Similar patterns of behavior have been observed not only in the United States but also in multiethnic situations in the African Copperbelt (Mitchell, 1956) and among eastern Europeans in northwestern Ontario (Stymeist, 1975), to cite just two cases. Lock (1990, p. 251) also provides a negative example of Greek immigrant women to Canada who, because they sustain old-world village and regional boundary concepts and sentiments, have neither learned nor accepted a new Greek-Canadian identity and refuse to affiliate with Greek cultural groups.

Thus, from the individual perspective, each person possesses a number of ethnic identities, each of which may be invoked (voluntarily or involuntarily) in different social situations. From the point of view of the ethnic group as a whole, however, its boundaries, as well as its defining properties, develop in political and economic relation to other groups in a local and national system. Interethnic circumstances thus change in time as the relative numbers and attitudes of other interacting groups also change. This phenomenon has been described for Malays in Malaysia (Nagata, 1981), and we have clearly seen it in the United States in the realignments that have occurred for white Euro-American, Mexican, Puerto Rican, and Asian ethnics in the wake of heavy immigration from South and Central America and southeast Asia in the past 15 years (Alba, 1990; Nielsen, 1985; Olzak, 1983).

Besides incorporating the existence of multiple nesting ethnic identities in our research paradigm, we must also acknowledge that individual migrants from the same place of origin can adopt different aspects of culturally provided ethnic identities under different conditions. For example, Japanese Americans may at times adopt an individualistic perspective and strive to achieve the economic success that several generations of their forebears have attained in the United States; at other times Japanese Americans may identify as a disparaged minority that is due reparation because of their history of internment during World War II. This situational adoption of what Taylor, Moghaddam, and their associates refer to as individualistic and collectivistic strategies of coping with perceived inequality (Taylor & Moghaddam, 1987) has also been reported among Haitian and Indian women in Montreal (Lalonde, Taylor, & Moghaddam, 1988).

In other words, the way one expresses ethnic identity, as well as the situations in which one expresses it, may both vary. Ethnic identity is not a unidimensional quality of persons; it is a characteristic of persons in relation to social situations. This fundamental fact about ethnic identity dramatically affects acculturation, as exemplified by Euro-Americans and Hispanics in inner-city areas who acculturate to African-American speech patterns in local situations where African Americans are in the majority, or by Indians and Pakistanis who acculturate to West Indian norms in certain sections of London where the latter are in the majority (Banton, 1983).

I must insert a word of caution here. Though Banton and I have stressed individual choice in this formulation, it is important to acknowledge that ethnic identification is in many ways *not* voluntary but imposed on the individual by the dynamic of interacting groups in a particular sociopolitical and economic situation. Yet the fundamental point is still appropriate: Ethnic boundaries and markers emerge from situations of economic competition and cooperation among various groups and are not simply an outpouring of a retained ancestral cultural heritage (cf. Rogler, 1972).

IMPLICATIONS FOR STUDYING ACCULTURATION EMPIRICALLY

What, now, can we conclude about methods for assessing acculturation after reviewing these characteristics of contemporary immigrants and interethnic relations? How do we begin to capture the dynamic, situational, and individualized character of ethnic identity, as well as the enormous social, economic, and educational diversity among contemporary immigrants, including their different degrees of exposure and prior assimilation to cosmopolitan or American cultural standards? In short, can we develop methods for understanding the relationship between acculturation and mental health that encompass the dynamism and diversity of modern acculturation?

I submit that we must augment the present etic focus of acculturation research with an emic one in which we examine how each individual perceives interethnic relations within his or her locale, region of the country, and nation as a whole. We need to understand what particular behaviors or skills the individual sees as being "American" or as being characteristic of his/her own ethnic group(s) or of other groups with which he/she interacts, or whether there are behaviors or skills that are seen as neutral with respect to these ethnic categories. We also need to hear how people *evaluate* the attributes of these groups and whether they in fact wish to acquire or manifest the attributes of "Americans" or any other group. Do immigrants come to the United States intending to use the money they will earn to retain and support their own indigenous way of life, or are they coming prepared to change? Discovering the situations in which the individual expresses and uses his or her multileveled ethnicities for social, political, and/or economic purposes should also be a major goal of contemporary research. In short, we need to design instruments that assess how individuals cognize their ethnic environment and the criteria by which they assess members of their reference group as being more or less acculturated. We then need to see whether there are agreements about such criteria among members of the same ethnic group, as well as whether members of the ethnic category share the same range of adaptive strategies.

INCORPORATING EMOTION INTO THE STUDY OF ACCULTURATION

Beyond the development of emic methods for assessing the manner in which each individual and ethnic group cognizes and evaluates the interethnic environment, more needs to be done to study normal emotional reactions to these environments. In introducing this second suggestion for a new research direction, I would like to review the life history of Eduardo, a Puerto Rican man from Holyoke, Massachusetts, as described by Tracy Kidder in his book *Among Schoolchildren* (1989, pp. 246–250).

> At age 14 Eduardo came to Massachusetts with his family and learned English by immersion as a student in the Westfield public schools. Remaining with relatives after his immediate family went back

> to the island, Eduardo got a job in a bicycle factory at age 16, then returned to the island when he was laid off. Back in his Cayey community, Eduardo was struck with the beauty of his homeland but also with the poverty of his people compared with North Americans, and so when his job at the bicycle factory became available again, Eduardo returned to Westfield.
>
> Eduardo finished high school, supporting himself by working in the factory and at times by picking tobacco. He became a machinist and later president of his union local, running on a platform critical of the policies of past union leadership. For a time he was a disk jockey on a Spanish-language station in Hartford and then met an "old-fashioned" woman from his home town in Puerto Rico, married, and settled down to raise a family in the Hispanic section of Holyoke.
>
> Today his friends include Puerto Ricans, South American Hispanics, and North American blacks and whites, with all of whom he appears to interact comfortably. Self-taught, he plays an excellent game of golf and frequently tees off with acquaintances at an exclusive local country club. Both Eduardo and his wife work, and though their income would permit the family to live elsewhere, they choose to remain in the Hispanic section of Holyoke. Politically, Eduardo is an Independentista who is critical of his fellow party members who receive welfare checks.

This description of Eduardo, which provides the kind of "objective" information that would be covered in most existing acculturation instruments, quite clearly identifies him as "bicultural." However, this account tells us nothing about Eduardo's own perceptions and feelings about his adaptation to the multiethnic world of Holyoke. What is Eduardo's mental state as a result of his apparently successful bicultural adaptation? Fortunately, Kidder's vignette provides some of these personal insights, and I think they point to issues that are pertinent, perhaps even central, to studying the relationship between acculturation and mental health status.

In a moment of introspection Eduardo tells some North American friends, "I feel I am a Puerto Rican American, and I feel, really, I am an American. You people took me over. *You* made me American, not me" (Kidder, 1989, p. 250). In interacting with Euro-Americans, Eduardo sometimes admits to thinking that they must be saying to themselves, "Goddamn Puerto Rican, what's he doing here?" On some occasions he ignores "dirty looks and slurs" against Puerto Ricans; at other times, he challenges them (Kidder, 1989, p. 250). In looking back to his early days in Westfield, after he had returned to work in the bicycle factory,

Eduardo recalls a New Year's Eve alone with nowhere to go. He asked himself, "What am I doing here? . . . Why not go back to the island?" In the period that followed, he reports repeatedly wondering, "Who am I? I know this body. But who is Eduardo?" (Kidder, 1989, p. 248). Even today he dreams of going back to his parents' farm in Cayey, but then thinks it is also nice "to see a little snow" (Kidder, 1989, p. 250).

These statements from Eduardo go beyond the objective evidence of his biculturality to get at what it means to him psychologically to be bicultural. In his words, "*You* made me American, not me," we hear a feeling of loss of a sense of agency. We sense from his statements an uncertainty about whether he really belongs in either world. We hear his ambivalent feelings about having succeeded in the Anglo world and the psychic price he feels he pays at times in both imagined rejections and real "dirty looks and slurs." We also learn of an extremely painful period of self-doubt during his acquisition of biculturality. I contend that this dimension of ongoing psychological experience must also be measured in order to understand relations between acculturation and mental health status. Biculturality, or any other adaptation to a multiethnic world, is not just an objective fact about a person; it raises a set of continuous emotional issues and adjustments for that person that are always relevant to their mental health status.

I therefore suggest that specific individual feelings concomitant with acculturation and the ways individuals handle these feelings be examined in our research agendas so that this information can be related to the etiology of serious mental health problems. Rather than attributing such problems vaguely to "acculturational stress," a phenomenological approach would document specific, ongoing emotional issues in acculturation that may predict certain specific mental health problems for individuals at a later time.

CONCLUSION

In their call for new directions in acculturation studies in mental health, Rogler and his colleagues challenge us to bring our theories and research more in line with the dynamism and diversity of interethnic relations in the United States today. To capture this dynamism and diversity, I am advocating several changes in approach. These changes would provide us with data on how people actually cognize their multiethnic environments, the markers they use for defining ethnic groups in these environments, and particularly what behavioral or cultural adaptations they actually display or deem necessary in order to achieve acceptance in these groups—and if indeed they desire such acceptance. The change in approach would also assess the feelings that arise out of people's adaptations to a multiethnic world. I submit that these kinds of understandings—of people's cognitions and evaluations of their multiethnic world and of their ongoing affective reactions to interethnic situations—provide a research direction that can clarify relationships between acculturation and mental health status in today's highly dynamic and diverse multiethnic environment.

ENDNOTES

1. Although I focus in this essay on United States immigration and world influence, the argument applies generally to interethnic relations in other First World nations.
2. In referring to "Toyotafication" and "Cocacolonization" of the world, Berry, Trimble, and Olmedo (1986, p. 296) allude to the development of a global culture, but they do not consider the feedback that this development has on the acculturation experience of immigrants.

REFERENCES

Alba, R.D. (1990). *Ethnic identity: The transformation of white America.* New Haven: Yale University Press.

Banton, M. (1981). The direction and speed of ethnic change. In C.F. Keyes (Ed.), *Ethnic change* (pp. 31–52). Seattle: University of Washington Press.

Banton, M. (1983). *Racial and ethnic competition.* Cambridge: Cambridge University Press.

Barth, J.W. (Ed.). (1980). *Ethnic groups and boundaries.* Boston: Little, Brown.

Berry, J.W. (1980). Acculturation as varieties of adaptation. In A.M. Padilla (Ed.), *Acculturation: Theory, models and some new findings* (pp. 9–25). Boulder, CO: Westview Press.

Berry, J.W., Trimble, J.E., & Olmedo, E.L. (1986). Assessment of acculturation. In W.J. Lonner & J.W. Berry (Eds.), *Field methods in cross-cultural research.* Beverly Hills, CA: Sage.

Clark, M., Kaufman, S., & Pierce, R.C. (1976). Explorations of acculturation: Toward a model of ethnic identity. *Human Organization, 35*, 231–238.

Gordon, M.M. (1964). *Assimilation in American life: The role of race, religion, and national origins*. New York: Oxford.

Graves, T.D. (1967). Psychological acculturation in a tri-ethnic community. *Southwestern Journal of Anthropology, 23*, 337–350.

Herskovits, M.J. (1938). *Acculturation: The study of culture contact*. New York: J.J. Augustin.

Keyes, C.F. (1981). The dialectics of ethnic change. In C.F. Keyes (Ed.), *Ethnic change* (pp. 3–30). Seattle: University of Washington Press.

Kidder, T. (1989). *Among schoolchildren*. New York: Avon Books.

Kottak, C.P. (1990). *Prime-time society: An anthropological analysis of television and culture*. Belmont, CA: Wadsworth.

Lalonde, R.N., Taylor, D.M., & Moghaddam, F.M. (1988). Social integration strategies of Haitian and Indian immigrant women in Montreal. In J.W. Berry & R.C. Annis (Eds.), *Ethnic psychology: Research and practice with immigrants, refugees, native peoples, ethnic groups and sojourners*. Amsterdam: Swets and Zeitlinger for the International Association of Cross-Cultural Psychology.

Light, I. (1981). Ethnic succession. In C.F. Keyes (Ed.), *Ethnic change*. Seattle: University of Washington Press.

Linton, R. (Ed.). (1940). *Acculturation in seven American Indian tribes*. New York: Appleton-Century.

Lock, M. (1990). On being ethnic: The politics of identity breaking and making in Canada, or *never* on Sunday. *Culture, Medicine and Psychiatry, 14*, 237–254.

Mitchell, J.C. (1956). *The Kalela dance: Aspects of social relationship among urban Africans in Northern Rhodesia*. Manchester: Manchester University Press.

Nagata, J. (1981). In defense of ethnic boundaries: The changing myths and charters of Malay identity. In C.F. Keyes (Ed.), *Ethnic Change*. Seattle: University of Washington Press.

Nielsen, F. (1985). Toward a theory of ethnic solidarity in modern societies. *American Sociological Review, 50*, 133–149.

Oetting, E.R., & Beauvais, F. (1991). Orthogonal cultural identification theory: The cultural identification of minority adolescents. *The International Journal of the Addictions, 25*, 655–685.

Olmedo, E.L. (1979). Acculturation: A psychometric perspective. *American Psychologist, 34*, 1061–1070.

Olzak, S. (1983). Contemporary ethnic mobilization. *Annual Review of Sociology, 9*, 355–374.

Padilla, A.M. (1980). The role of cultural awareness and ethnic loyalty in acculturation. In A.M. Padilla (Ed.), *Acculturation: Theory, models, and some new findings*. Boulder, CO: Westview Press.

Pierce, R.C., Clark, M., & Kaufman, S. (1978–79). Generation and ethnic identity: A typological analysis. *International Journal of Aging and Human Development, 9*, 19–29.

Portes, A., & Rumbaut, R.G. (1990). *Immigrant America: A portrait.* Berkeley: University of California Press.

Ramirez, M. (1984). Assessing and understanding biculturalism-multiculturalism in Mexican-American adults. In J.L. Martinez & R. Mendoza (Eds.), *Chicano Psychology*. New York: Academic Press.

Redfield, R., Linton, R., & Herskovits, M.J. (1936). Memorandum on the study of acculturation. *American Anthropologist, 38*, 149–152.

Rogler, L.H. (1972). *Migrant in the city: The life of a Puerto Rican action group*. New York: Basic Books.

Rogler, L.H., Cortes, D.E., & Malgady, R.G. (1991). Acculturation and mental health status among Hispanics: Convergence and new directions for research. *American Psychologist, 46*, 585–597.

Rogler, L.H., & Hollingshead, A.B. (1961). The Puerto Rican spiritualist as a psychiatrist. *American Journal of Sociology, 67*, 17–21.

Rogler, L.H., & Hollingshead, A.B. (1965). *Trapped: Families and Schizophrenia.* New York: Wiley.

Social Science Research Council Summer Seminar. (1954). Acculturation: An exploratory formulation. *American Anthropologist, 56*, 973–1002.

Stonequist, E.V. (1937). *The marginal man: A study of personality and culture conflict.* New York: Charles Scribner's Sons.

Stymeist, D.H. (1975). *Ethnics and Indians: Social relationships in a northwestern Ontario town.* Toronto: Peter Martin Associates.

Szapocznik, J., & Kurtines, W.M. (1980). Acculturation, biculturalism, and adjustment among Cuban Americans. In A.M. Padilla (Ed.), *Acculturation: Theory, models, and some new findings.* Boulder, CO: Westview Press.

Szapocznik, J., Kurtines, W.M., & Fernandez, T. (1980). Bicultural involvement and adjustment in Hispanic-American youths. *International Journal of Intercultural Relations, 4*, 353–365.

Taylor, D.M., & Moghaddam, F.M. (1987). *Theories of intergroup relations: International social psychological perspectives.* New York: Praeger.

Van der Geest, S., & Whyte, S.R. (Eds.). (1988). *The context of medicines in developing countries: Studies in pharmaceutical anthropology.* Dordrecht: Kluwer Academic Publishers.

Van der Geest, S., & Whyte, S. R. (1989). The charm of medicine. *Medical Anthropology Quarterly, 3*, 345–367.

Vega, W.A., & Rumbaut, R.G. (1991). Ethnic minorities and mental health. *Annual Review of Sociology, 17*, 351–383.

AUTHOR NOTES

Although I had not met Professor Rogler until the Festschrift honoring him in April 1992, his published research on schizophrenia in Puerto Rico served as the stimulus for my study of *espiritismo* in the South Bronx, New York City, and I have been long grateful to him for his fruitful lead. In addition to Professor Rogler, Glen Jacobs, Morris Lounds, Lee Strunin, and Margot Welch have all provided sound advice and sage comments on earlier drafts of this chapter. Responsibility for lingering deficiencies in the argument is of course my own.

Correspondence concerning this chapter should be addressed to: Professor Alan Harwood, Department of Anthropology, University of Massachusetts, Boston, MA 02125.

CHAPTER 2

BICULTURAL DEVELOPMENT: A THEORETICAL AND EMPIRICAL EXAMINATION

Amado M. Padilla, PhD

Professor of Education, Stanford University

This paper examines the theoretical construct of biculturalism from a socialization perspective and focuses on children and adolescents who come from environments that foster dual culture socialization. Before we are able to thoroughly discuss the issues in bicultural development, it is first important to address a few general issues about socialization. Over the years there have been numerous excellent state-of-the-art summaries of the relevant research literature on socialization (e.g., Maccoby and Martin, 1983). In these summaries, we see the importance given to the role of parents and other family members in the enculturation of children to the values, beliefs, and acceptable standards of behavior of a society. This is then followed by examination of the role played by peers and institutions such as the school in shaping the social character of the individual (Minuchin and Shapiro, 1983). On the basis of this literature, we are very well informed about how children acquire knowledge of their culture and how they achieve full membership in society.

There is a glaring problem with the socialization literature, however, that is seldom mentioned and which is at the heart of my discussion. The implicit assumption in the majority of socialization research is that children are socialized into a single culture; therefore, culture is not a relevant consideration in trying to understand the effects of socialization processes because if everyone is having nearly the same exposure to a culture, differences that occur between children and socializing agents are not due to culture per se. This is a view that does not take into account the intergroup diversity known to exist in our society today, nor the intragroup variability that can be found among individuals from the same cultural background but who differ by generation, education, or social class. The point of view taken in this paper is that there are many children and adolescents who are socialized into the values and standards of conduct of not one, but at least two cultures. Socialization to two cultural orientations may occur simultaneously as in the case of a child who receives one cultural orientation from one parent and another from the other parent, or socialization to one cultural perspective from parents and another from grandparents. Another way this dual socialization occurs early in a child's life is when one cultural orientation is followed at home and another at school. This "growing up" in two cultures is the theme of this paper.

In this paper, I first discuss why growing up in two cultures is a timely and very necessary topic of discussion in understanding developmental processes. Second, I present an overview of the theoretical issues that surround bicultural socialization. Finally, some empirical findings are presented that enable us to better understand the psychosocial issues involved in what transpires during bicultural socialization.

MONOCULTURALISM VERSUS MULTICULTURALISM

In recent years considerable attention has been given to the increasing trend toward multiculturalism in education and in the workplace in the United States. The need for multiculturalism has included debate on university campuses concerning curriculum reform to include ethnic and gender diversity (D'Souza, 1991). In addition, we have witnessed cultural awareness training in a number of organizations. At the professional level we are seeing special issues of journals ranging from the humanities to medicine devoted to multicultural themes. In psychology we have similarly seen special issues of our journals dedicated to cross-cultural counseling psychology, child development, and social psychology. The major concern has been with the accurate portrayal of diversity in all of its ramifications in every aspect of life. An interesting question regarding monoculturalism versus multiculturalism has to do with the motivation for multiculturalism in society.

One of the factors clearly contributing to the attention given to multiculturalism in recent years has to do with the changing demography that is taking place in the United States. Demographers have shown, for instance, that the influx of immigrants from Latin America and Asia between 1970 and the present represent the largest movement of people to this country since the turn of the century (Portes and Rumbaut, 1990). These newcomers are visible in every major urban center in the country and have significantly shifted the population distributions in several major states such as California, Florida, Illinois, and New York. Coupled with immigration is a higher fertility ratio for Hispanics and Asians compared to native-born Americans of all ethnic/racial backgrounds (e.g., whites and African Americans). This also contributes to the changing demography of the U.S. population (Portes and Rumbaut, 1990).

Social theorists are pointing to these groups as emerging "majority" populations. Because these newcomers are a youthful population, their impact is being felt most dramatically in our schools (Olsen, 1988). Further, there is open concern that these newcomers are not being absorbed (assimilated) into mainstream society as rapidly as immigrants at other times in this country's history. This has generated considerable debate in the social science literature and in the popular press. One side of the debate has centered on the issue of "absorption" into mainstream culture and has presented data to show that absorption of immigrants has never been easy and that recent immigrant groups are becoming "Americanized" at the same rate as earlier immigrants. The other side of the debate acknowledges the slow absorption of recent immigrants and seeks an explanation through an analysis of social barriers that prevent more rapid absorption.

One common index of social absorption into society is intermarriage, and there have been marked changes in intermarriage patterns in the past two decades. According to the Census Bureau, the number of interracial marriages has tripled from 310,000 in 1970 to 956,000 by 1988, and it is still rising (U.S. Bureau of the Census, 1991). However, while Japanese, Chinese, and American Indians marry outside their race at rates between 40% and 70%, less than 2% of African Americans marry out. The outmarriage rate for Hispanics in some locales is as high as it is between Asian and whites (Murguia, 1982). Although intermarriage has always been seen as a sign of reduced social distance between groups, sociologists are pointing to the acceleration of intermarriage as another factor contributing to the current demographic shift taking place in this country. With the exception of black-white intermarriage, little importance was given to intermarriage until the 1970s, which coincided with the emergence of ethnic awareness and concern for biculturalism (Grebler, Moore, & Guzman, 1970).

Today there is considerably more discussion concerning biculturalism among social and behavioral scientists than ever before. However, an examination of most of our basic textbooks in the social sciences does not reflect the growing literature on biculturalism. In what follows, I discuss what biculturalism means from a socialization perspective, who is likely to be socialized into two cultures, and what the ramifications of biculturalism are on the individual and society.

BICULTURAL SITUATIONS

A review of literature on biculturalism indicates that this was first noted in the sociological literature under the heading of dual culture personality. Accordingly, it is appropriate to begin this section with a historical analysis of the sociology of dual culture exposure. This literature, as I show, essentially takes up the question of whether two culture socialization is positive or negative for the individual involved.

The question of whether there are positive or negative consequences to growing up in two cultures is not new. The noted sociologist Robert E. Park was one of the first to study immigrants, children of immigrants, and mixed racial heritage individuals. His study led him to speculate on the negative consequences of dual culture exposure. In an early paper, Park (1928) put forth the idea of the "marginal" man to describe the person who found himself between and betwixt two cultures. The idea of marginality was subsequently popularized by a student of Park, E.V. Stonequist (1937), who authored a book entitled *The Marginal Man: A Study in Personality and Culture and Conflict.* The title of this book shows the focus that Stonequist gave to his sociological analysis of dual culture socialization. The conditions leading to marginality and the consequences of this status can be seen in the following excerpt from Stonequist:

> The individual who through migration, education, marriage, or some other influence leaves one social group or culture without making a satisfactory adjustment to another finds himself on the margin of each but a member of neither. He is a "marginal" man.
>
> The marginal personality is most clearly portrayed in those individuals who are unwittingly initiated into two or more historic traditions, languages, political loyalties, moral codes, or religions. (pp. 2–3)

In this quote, we see that Stonequist is primarily referring to situations that cause individuals to leave one cultural orientation for another and to do so "unwittingly." Further, according to Stonequist, individuals who are unable to adjust to the new culture then find themselves on the margin of both cultures. This analysis is important because it varies to a considerable extent from the contemporary analysis of the motivation, context, and outcome of dual culture socialization. The Park-Stonequist model is depicted in the top portion of Figure 1. We see in the figure the unidimensional movement from Culture A to

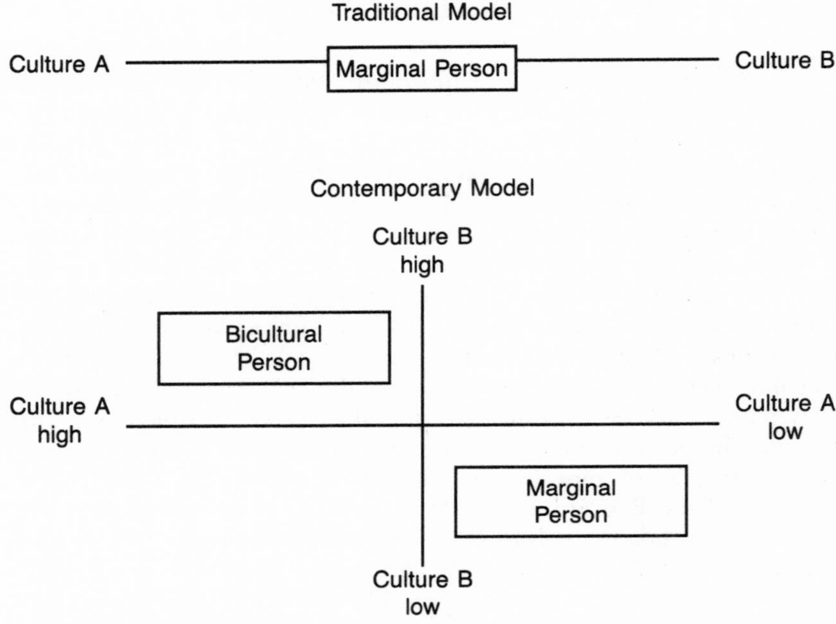

Figure 1. Two Views of Dual Culture Exposure.

Culture B discussed by Park and Stonequist and the marginal position between the two end points signifying the person who is caught in the middle between the two cultures.

The "marginal" person model advanced by Park and Stonequist was the generally accepted view until the late 1960s when social scientists began to make reference to biculturalism. According to this more contemporary view, it is possible to be a functioning member of two cultures without being in serious conflict about either. The lower portion of Figure 1 contrasts the position of the marginal and the bicultural person. According to the bicultural perspective, it is not so uncommon as earlier believed to be a functioning member of two cultural groups.

This new view has enriched our thinking about socialization processes and how individuals can participate to varying degrees as members of two cultural groups. Research in this area is exemplified in the work of such individuals as Wallace Lambert (1971); Jose Szapocznik, W. Kurtines, and T. Fernandez (1980); and William Cross (1980). These individuals have examined such phenomena as bilingualism, ethnic identification, acculturative stress, and importantly biculturalism.

The bicultural individual has been defined by Lambert (1977) as "a member of two cultural communities who not only possesses competent skills for dealing effectively with members of the two cultural groups, but who also maintains favorable attitudes toward the customs, beliefs, and values fostered by each group" (p. 21). In this definition we see two elements that are critical in understanding both biculturalism and marginality. Lambert emphasizes *behavioral competence* in two cultures and *positive affect* toward the two cultures. According to this view, we see a place for both biculturalism and marginality as seen in the lower portion of Figure 1. The bicultural person has behavioral commitment and competence in two cultures *and* positive affect toward both cultures. On the other hand, cultural marginality is more difficult to categorize and numerous different marginal situations can be described. One person may have behavioral competence in two cultures, but little affect toward either and thus feel marginalized to both. Another person may have a higher affect for one culture over another, but little behavioral competence in the high affect culture, and as a consequence be perceived as an outsider. Still a third individual may have behavioral competence in both cultures, but not feel much affect for either, preferring a third culture where he has some behavioral competence. The point is that there may be many categories that define a person's orientation to social groups. Nonetheless, an undeniable fact persists: Individuals can hold membership in different cultural groups without necessarily being marginalized.

This is different from the Park-Stonequist's model that also attributes personality characteristics to the marginal person. The characteristics noted by Park-Stonequist are shown in the right hand column of Table 1. The personality traits of the marginal person are in sharp contrast to the characteristics that have been attributed to the bicultural individual. According to researchers, the bicultural individual displays greater behavioral and cognitive flexibility to culturally diverse situations (Aellen & Lambert, 1969; Garza, Romero, Cox, & Ramirez, 1982; McFee, 1968; Valentine, 1971). The left hand side of Table 1 shows the personal characteristics attributed to the bicultural person.

According to the Park-Stonequist view, the marginal person feels isolated and closed off from members of either the culture of origin or the culture of the host group. Further, according to this view, the person suffers from self-hatred, low self-esteem, and feelings of inferiority. The

Table 1. Characteristics in the Literature Attributed to Bicultural and Marginal Individuals

The bicultural person	The marginal person
Confident	Self-hatred
Secure	Low self-esteem
Well adjusted	Anomie
Open to other people	Insecure
Socially/culturally tolerant	Closed to other people
Cultural translator/broker	Feelings of inferiority

marginal person is marked by negativity and character traits that predispose the individual to serious mental health problems.

For the "biculturalists," on the other hand, we see a much more positive image of the bicultural person. The bicultural person is seen to be well adjusted, open to others, and a cultural broker among people of different backgrounds. In the completely bicultural person, we see an individual who possesses two social *persona* and identities. The person is equally at ease with members of either culture and can easily switch from one cultural orientation to the other and do so with nativelike facility. Further, this comfort with two cultures also extends to interactions with individuals from cultures other than those in which the bicultural person has competence. This social flexibility is viewed by the biculturalists as an advantage and as one of the reasons for bicultural exposure.

When behavioral conflicts do occur among bicultural individuals, as they inevitably do, clinical researchers call for therapeutic interventions that strive to reaffirm the dual cultural background of their clients (LaFromboise, Coleman, & Gerton, 1993).

IDENTITY FORMATION

The concern for bicultural socialization is important because for young people, the question that frequently confronts them has to do with identity. They find themselves asking "Who am I?" Adolescence is a time when the crisis of identity is most paramount in the mind of the young person. Now the crisis of identity (Erikson, 1968) experienced by adolescents may be more problematic in at least the initial stages for those adolescents who have been socialized to two cultural orientations. This is especially true when one of the orientations belongs to a low prestige ethnic group.

I have frequently interacted with adolescents working through the crisis of whether they are Mexican, Mexican American, American, Chicano, Latino, or Hispanic. Too many labels for anyone. Yet each of these labels has a specific usage and it is not uncommon for an adolescent to use several of these labels depending on the situational context. Ethnic identifications create serious concerns for adolescents who often want to construct their own identities free of the ethnic and racial biases imposed on them by their parents, teachers, and other authority figures.

The significance of identity development during adolescence has been best summarized by Erikson (1968) who stated:

> identity includes, . . . all the successive identifications of those earlier years when the child wanted to be, and often was forced to become, like the people he depended on. Identity is a unique product, which now meets a crisis to be solved only in new identifications with age mates and with leader figures outside of the family (p. 87).

According to Erikson, the search for an identity during this period often leads adolescents to define, redefine, and even overdefine themselves and each other in terms of who they are. If the process of identification becomes too difficult, young persons may experience role confusion and rather than synthesize their sexual, ethnic, occupational, and typological identities, they feel compelled to decide conclusively for one identity or another. As we see, the identity crisis is difficult enough to overcome when just a single culture and language is involved. Imagine the crisis experienced by many adolescents as they attempt to resolve issues of identity when two cultural orientations are involved. I will have more to say about identity later, but before I get to this the more immediate task at hand is to describe the conditions that result in bicultural socialization.

SOCIALIZATION TO TWO CULTURES

There are four major conditions that have the potential for creating a situation of bicultural socialization. In discussing these conditions, we must keep in mind whether the exposure to two cultural orientations is done by the primary (parents and other family members) agents of socialization or by secondary (peers, school, and other institutions) agents. This is important because these socializing agents may emphasize different aspects of culture during socialization.

The four situations that lead to dual cultural exposure are

1. Immigrant children and adolescents
2. Offspring of immigrants
3. Later generation ethnics
4. Mixed ethnic heritage children

Immigrant Children and Adolescents

The reference here is to children and adolescents who immigrate and who become socialized to the host culture and society usually by native-born peers and the school. Children and adolescents who experience immigration to a new country must of necessity acquire the customs and behaviors of their adopted country. Because of their prior enculturation, these children are members of their culture of origin, and depending upon their age at the time of immigration, may experience considerable difficulty in adapting to their new surroundings because of the demand to learn the language and cultural practices of their hosts (Mena, Padilla, & Maldonado, 1987). The ease with which they are able to adapt depends frequently on the type of support and assistance they receive from their primary caretakers to make the transition to the new culture and the peer and institutional supports in place to assist these youthful newcomers to make the transition.

Most immigrant youth acquire the new culture in school and from peers. Many schools have special programs such as newcomer centers, English as a Second Language resource teachers, and bilingual education programs. The intent of these programs is to transition the young person to English as rapidly as possible and in some schools to provide personal and group counseling if necessary, especially with refugee youth. The overall objective of these efforts is "Americanization." Peers assist in this process via English language role modeling and youth culture orientation. Ultimately, the immigrants acquire the language and culture of the host group while also retaining their home culture to varying degrees.

In communities populated by immigrant groups, it is not uncommon to see children serving as translators and cultural brokers for their parents and other adult family members. Frequently, young bilingual children serve as translators between their parents and teachers, physicians, shopkeepers, etc. For the young person this is a situation of mandatory biculturalism because of the need to acquire the host culture in order to assist the parents. However, this situation, while advantageous on the one hand, also has a negative side. A heavy burden is placed on the child who must serve as a cultural and linguistic broker while still in the process of being socialized to the culture of the parents as well as of the host culture. For the parents there is also the potential danger of surrendering too much power to their children because of their reliance on children as cultural brokers.

Biculturalism, however, is not without other problems. In a very insightful paper, Betty Lee Sung (1985) described the bicultural conflicts experienced by Chinese immigrant children. The conflicts identified by Sung can be categorized along several dimensions:

- Immigrant Chinese parents do not encourage early independence in their children; socializing outside the family is discouraged until a much later age than other ethnic groups.
- Immigrant Chinese children find it hard to accept the lack of respect for authority—especially toward teachers—among their peers in school.
- The Chinese try to fit themselves into the scheme of things where the American way is based on individualism.

Although Sung discussed these and other cultural conflicts with Chinese immigrant youth, the actual categories are generalizable across many different immigrant groups. Further, although it is possible to readily identify the cultural conflicts, little counseling is available to parents or children to help them find strategies for minimizing these conflicts. Thus the transition to the new culture may be very difficult for immigrants of all ages, but for different reasons. Little support is available for immigrant parents or for the teachers of immigrant children in enabling them to mitigate the negative consequences of cultural marginality where youth are involved.

Offspring of Immigrants

Here we will address children and adolescents whose parents are immigrants and who still adhere to the cultural practices, values, traditions, and behaviors of their culture of origin. These parents expect the same cultural adherence from their American-born children at least part of the time. Children and adolescents in this situation usually have very demarcated boundaries in their socialization and in how they respond to their environment. These second-generation individuals, like their immigrant counterparts, frequently serve as the primary link for their parents with the host society. The major difference is that unlike the immigrants, second-generation adolescents frequently learn about the culture of origin in a social vacuum from the family with little environmental support. For example, children and adolescents may assume one cultural orientation in one environment (home) and a very distinct lifestlye in another environment. As one adolescent stated:

> At home with my parents and grandparents the only acceptable language was Spanish; actually that's all they really understood. Everything was like really Mexican, but at the same time they wanted me to speak good English. They also had very old fashioned customs and didn't want me to be American . . . or at least not too American. But at school, I felt really different because everyone was American, including me. Then I would go home in the afternoon and be Mexican again.

Like the individual above, second-generation youth often find themselves between "a rock and a hard place." Frequently, they are expected to maintain the culture of the parents while also given mixed messages about how "Americanized" they should become. Many immigrant parents will tell their offspring, "You're in America now and you must be an American!" However, at the same time, the young person will also be told by the parents not to forget who they are, meaning ethnic or culture membership. Often parents go so far as to warn their children to steer clear of serious relationships with members of different ethnic groups. For some youth, this creates a double bind and a form of forced biculturalism. As native-born Americans they are exposed to many of the social forces that would ensure their enculturation as Americans. However, they are pulled back toward the culture of their parents who expect their offspring to demonstrate loyalty to their cultural origins. How parents and other significant adults socialize children in bicultural contexts will determine the child's eventual level of competence in two cultures. No firmly established criteria exist for determining what the competencies are in determining biculturalism or how these competencies should be assessed. For instance, is proficiency in the language of the culture of origin a prerequisite in biculturalism? This is a debatable question with no established consensus. For many immigrant parents bilingualism is essential; otherwise, how can you truly understand parents or their culture. Other parents are less insistent on bilingualism and do not see it as essential in practicing other aspects of the culture.

We know from the work of sociolinguists that language shift occurs generally within one generation (e.g., Lopez 1978, 1982; Veltman, 1981). If we adhere strongly to a model that assumes that home language is critical to bicultural competence, then how is it possible to still talk about biculturalism with second-generation youth if they speak little or no Spanish, Vietnamese, Japanese, etc.? If the immigrant parents are not insisting on home language proficiency in the socialization of their children, then what is it about their culture that they are teaching and how? This question of cultural transmission is important and one clearly in need of more research.

An important consideration in this discussion is degree of social marginality in the same way we recognize levels of biculturalism. It is probably true that social marginality from the parents' culture occurs very easily for our second-generation youth, especially when the linguistic dimension is considered.

Child (1943) was one of the first psychologists to study second-generation offspring to determine their level of adjustment to their two cultures. In his study, Child investigated second-generation Italians in New England to see whether they identified as more Italian or more American. He noted that if the second-generation Italian adolescents were "too Italian," their relations with other non-Italian youngsters would be strained. However, if these second-generation Italians rejected their background completely, there was the danger of being cut off from the comfort and refuge given by the family and the community. Child found that the Italian-American adolescents could be subdivided into three groups: the first group rebelled against their Italian background, making themselves as American as possible; the second group rejected the American culture and fully adopted their Italian heritage; and those in the third group were withdrawn and unsure, refusing to think of themselves in ethnic terms at all.

Gardner and Lambert (1972) found similar trends among Franco-Americans in New England and Louisiana. Some oriented themselves toward their French background and tried to ignore their American roots; others were tugged more towards the American pole, negating the value of knowing French and in general rejecting their French background; and still others apparently tried not to think in ethnic terms at all, were ambivalent about their identity, and seemed to face a conflict of cultural allegiance. However, there was a fourth group who were successful at being both French and American simultaneously. These individuals adhered to a belief reinforced by their parents that it was socially desirable to know French. According to Gardner and Lambert, the cultural orientation and the appreciation of French-English bilingualism given to the young people by their family strengthened their resolve to be proficient in their two languages and cultures.

In sum, there is still much that we do not understand about the bicultural development of the second-generation individual. This individual is posed between the culture of the parents and the culture that comprises the environment that surrounds them. By definition they are enculturated into the parental culture, but how extensively depends entirely on the parents. Similarly, they are exposed to the host culture and to what extent they embrace it depends on the hold that the parents' culture places on them as well as on how they are accepted into membership in the host culture. We need longitudinal studies of how the roles of parents, peers, the school, and the workplace have an impact on members of the second or "bridge" generation as they develop competencies in one or both cultures and affective bonding toward their culture(s).

Later Generation Ethnics

In this section attention is on third or later generation children and adolescents whose parents and community hold strongly to their traditional culture while also adopting the culture of the host or dominant group. In this situation, varying forms of biculturalism are practiced by the primary socializing agents. There are many examples of this type of bicultural community in the United States. For example, Chicanos in the Southwest offer an excellent case study of an ethnic group that is constantly being infused by newcomers from Mexico while also having developed a specific culture of their own because of their long-standing residence within the borders of the United States. Many Chicanos are fourth- or fifth-generation native-born Americans who steadfastly identify with the Mexican culture and maintain many of the values, beliefs, and customs of Mexico. Importantly, Chicanos are frequently much more loyal to their ethnic heritage than they are knowledgeable of many of the cultural dimensions (e.g., history, art, literature, etc.) that underlie the ethnic group they identify with (Keefe & Padilla, 1987).

In the case of some Chicanos, dual culture socialization of children is carried out by the parents in their role as primary socializers because of the parents' commitment to their ethnic heritage as well as to the reality that they are also American. For reasons that differ across ethnic groups, the biculturally oriented later generation individual maintains his/her biculturalism by choice and sees it often as a benefit rather than a liability. For these individuals, being a "good" ethnic does not at all mean that one is a "bad" American. Involvement in ethnic community activities does not necessarily accompany a rejection of the majority American culture since ethnic involvement and national identity are not strongly correlated. This is consistent with Der-Karabetian's (1980) finding among Armenian Americans and Zak's (1973) finding with Jewish Americans and supports the bicultural hypothesis of acculturation. Thus, participation in Latino community affairs is associated with a stronger sense of bicultural ethnic belonging. Exposure to the dominant majority culture with eventual assimilation into it does not need to result in the rejection of one's ethnic and cultural heritage.

Some important considerations make this situation more problematic, however, than how I have described it so far. In an early paper on acculturation (Padilla, 1980), I drew a distinction between what I referred to as *cultural awareness* (CA) and *ethnic loyalty* (EL). Using this distinction, cultural awareness is the cognitive dimension that specifies the knowledge that a person possesses of their culture. In Padilla (1980) and Keefe and Padilla (1987), knowledge was defined as self-rated proficiency in Spanish and English; knowledge of the history, art, and music of both Mexico and the United States; and knowledge of current events that shape culture. In this model, a specific numeric index could be given to respondents on the basis of their responses on a questionnaire that locates individuals on a multidimensional space of Mexican and American cultural awareness. In this context, biculturality refers specifically to the extent of an individual's knowledge (or competence) about each of their two cultures. Ethnic loyalty, on the other hand, is the affective component of the model and is measured by assessing a respondent's behavioral preferences regarding language, other forms of cultural expression, leisure activities, and friendships. The rationale is that the affect one holds toward a social group will also dictate the preference one holds toward activities and members of the group.

In using this distinction, Susan Keefe and I (Keefe & Padilla, 1987) found that with Mexican Americans, it was possible to demonstrate how CA and EL change across generations. This is important, I believe, because most work on acculturation and subsequently biculturalism (and marginality) has concentrated on only immigrants or their immediate offspring. What we found was something that we hypothesized, but for which we had no data until we carried out this study. We found that cultural awareness decreases markedly between the first and second generation and continues to decrease, so that by the fourth generation our respondents knew little of the culture of their great-grandparents. Surprisingly though, our respondents showed little change in their loyalty to their ethnic heritage or in their social orientation to their ethnic background. This finding has been replicated with a different population of Mexican-American respondents in South Texas (Arbona, 1991; Montgomery, 1992; see Figure 2).

A major question of theoretical significance is why ethnic loyalty persists across generations in the face of decreasing or near total absence of cultural knowledge. In our work, Keefe and I created typologies based on our respondents' scores on CA and EL that would enable us to describe how respondents of different generations change in CA and how these individuals manifest loyalty to a social group that they have been removed from by as much as 75 years when their great-grandparents immigrated to the United States. Using a cluster analysis

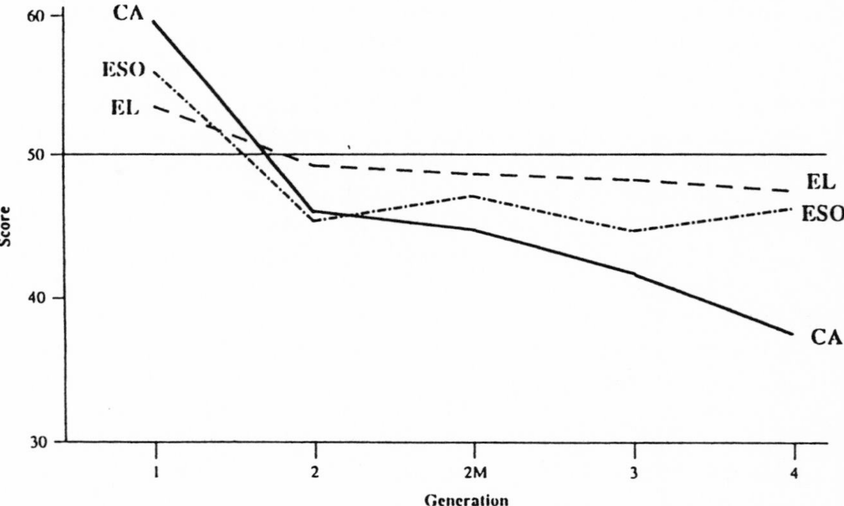

Figure 2. Cultural Awareness (CA), Ethnic Loyalty (EL), and Ethnic Social Orientation (ESO) by generation for Mexican-American respondents. (Adapted from Keefe and Padilla, 1987.)

technique, we identified five subgroups on the basis of their scores on CA and EL. We called these groups La Raza, Changing Ethnics, Cultural Blends, Emerging Americans, and New Americans. Table 2 shows the distribution by generation and educational level for each of these groups. Not surprisingly, the *Raza* category is composed primarily of first-generation immigrants who also possess little formal education.

The Cultural Blends and Emerging Americans are most associated with the description of biculturals we find in the literature. These individuals were primarily second- and third-generation Mexican Americans with between 9 to 12 years of education. Extensive interviews carried out with a subset of respondents revealed they held generally positive attitudes toward both Mexican and American culture and saw benefits in being participatory members of both cultures. These individuals professed varying degrees of proficiency in Spanish, but were mostly English-dominant speakers. They spoke about the benefits of knowing two languages and some wished they were more bilingual than they were. They also spoke about the richness of their biculturalism in being able to celebrate American holidays such as July 4th as well as Mexican holidays such as *Dia de los Muertos* (Day of the Dead).

On a less pleasant note, however, our informants did relate experi-

Table 2. Breakdown of Percentage of Cluster Types by Generation and Education. *Adapted from Keefe and Padilla (1987)*

Descriptive variables	La Raza (N = 94) %	Changing ethnics (N = 50) %	Cultural blends (N = 129) %	Emerging Americans (N = 78) %	New Americans (N = 19) %
Generation					
First	79	86	18	16	0
Second	12	14	58	63	22
Third	9	0	24	21	78
Total	100	100	100	100	100
Education					
0–8 grades	74	74	30	26	5
9–11 grades	16	14	33	23	37
12 grades	10	8	23	37	42
College	0	4	14	14	16
Total	100	100	100	100	100

ences of feeling singled out by members of the dominant group because of their ethnicity which made them feel uncomfortable. Our respondents related instances with stereotyping or discrimination that they had experienced directly or knew about because of friends or acquaintances. In a reexamination of our data, Keefe and I also observed two interesting and important findings. The first was that the higher our respondents scored on a measure of perceived discrimination, which was one of several subscales making up the Ethnic Loyalty dimension, the higher the respondents scored on overall EL. Further, regardless of how seemingly bicultural and/or Americanized our respondents appeared, they were still relatively insulated within their ethnic group. For example, few had intimate friends outside their ethnic group, and most had only limited social contacts with non-Mexican Americans. This was true even though the more acculturated or bicultural the informant was, the more likely they were to have co-workers from other ethnic groups.

On the basis of these findings, it is possible to advance a social integration model to explain phenomena such as acculturation, assimilation, marginality, and biculturalism. This model is depicted by a 2×2 matrix represented on one axis by the degree of similarity between cultures ranging from a hypothesized very similar to very dissimilar, and on the other axis by Shared Physical Attributes, again ranging from very similar to very dissimilar (see Figure 3).

Two quadrants are of particular interest in this discussion. The top left quadrant is marked by Minimal Stigma and Maximum Assimilation. In other words, those immigrants and their descendants from cultures that are similar to mainstream U.S. culture and who share physical attributes with "Americans" are the most easily incorporated into mainstream culture.

On the other hand, the bottom right quadrant represents quite a different picture. Here the more dissimilar the cultures and the more an individual resembles a "foreigner" or "outsider," the greater the social stigma and the more difficult assimilation is for these individuals. Unfortunately, we did not collect data on skin coloration or general physical characteristics of our respondents, so we have no way to confirm our general impression that those respondents who appeared more "Mexican" in their physical appearance also scored higher on our perceived discrimination index. However, such data does exist in a similar study of Chicano ethnicity. In this study, Arce, Murguia, and Frisbie (1987) hypothesized that Mexican Americans with a European physical appearance will have more enhanced life opportunities as measured by socioeconomic status than Mexican Americans with an

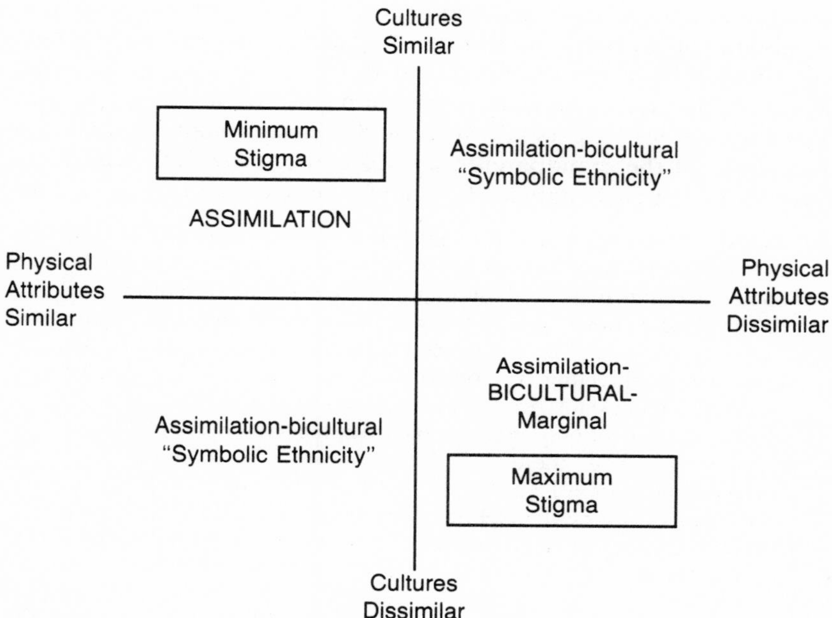

Figure 3. Interaction for predicting rate of incorporation into a new culture.

indigenous Native-American physical appearance. To test their hypothesis, Arce et al. examined the survey records of nearly 1,000 respondents who participated in the national Chicano survey. Since the survey was conducted in a face-to-face manner, the interviewer recorded the skin coloration and the physical features of their informants. When observed phenotype was correlated with indicators of socioeconomic status, the hypothesis was largely confirmed. Respondents and their parents who were classified as light/European in phenotype had more formal education, higher income, and a lower perception of past discrimination than did respondents classified as dark/Indian in phenotype. Finally, according to Arce et al., the darker and more Indian the phenotype, the greater the sociocultural and political attachment the individual has to being ethnic Mexican.

From this model, I will go a step further and suggest that for many individuals biculturalism is not only a preferred strategy, but in fact, it is a very suitable strategy for coping with discriminatory practices in society. This strategy allows a person to function with all the prerequisite knowledge and skills required to succeed in the dominant culture, but also provides a psychological safety net and retreat where the person can withdraw for the necessary nurturance and support following lapses of time in an unfriendly environment. Often the support received revalidates the person's esteem and reason for maintaining ties to the culture of the grandparents. This is expressed well by Charles, a successful chief civil engineer for a large construction firm in Seattle.

> At the job, I'm Mr. Ruiz and I spend most of my time trying to make sure that 100 or so guys who mostly hate my guts don't screw up. My company builds high rise buildings and it's important that every part of the job gets done right. I know the men don't always like taking orders from me. . . . on weekends I go to my brother's place in San Luis and am directing the construction of a community center. We work only on weekends because everyone has a full-time job. There I'm *Carlitos* and I'm the only engineer, but everyone has some kind of talent . . . I work harder there than I do the whole week, but it really refreshes me. I love the guys, we play loud Mexican music when we work, and I just love the feeling of being with my people, you know. Maybe I do it for the Mexican food . . . too. I just can't get that kind of food in Seattle.

To recap then, the model assumes that the level of assimilation depends on the degree of similarity between the newcomers' culture and that of the majority group, *and* most important, the greater the match in physical attributes, the greater the assimilation. Essentially, this is what I call the *principle of assimilation by invitation.* The model assumes that assimilation to some degree is inevitable regardless of the dissimilarity in cultures and physical attributes between the hosts and the newcomers. However, the model maintains that biculturalism, rather than marginality, is the preferred behavioral choice of the individual or group. Biculturalism offers the individual both the support of the group *and* coping responses that call forth specific ethnic related social behaviors. This is what I will refer to here as the *principle of ethnic protection.*

The themes embodied in these two principles are clearly illustrated in an autobiographical statement of a 19-year-old Chinese-American female.

The Case of Diane

> In my family, I am both the second and the third generation to be born in the United States. My paternal grandparents were born and

raised in China; however, my maternal grandparents were born in the United States.

The knowledge of the Chinese language and culture has gradually dissipated throughout the generations. Although both of my parents grew up in households where Chinese was spoken, they also grew up in an English-speaking community. Because of this, they focused more on the English language than Chinese. They have both retained enough knowledge of the language to be able to understand it, although neither of them can speak it very well.

Because my parents were raised in an American society, the American culture naturally became dominant over the Chinese culture. Both families grew accustomed to the American way of life, but they also managed to keep enough of the Chinese culture to remind them of their roots. Most of the Chinese customs, such as the celebration of Chinese New Year, were kept intact; however, the families also learned to celebrate traditional American holidays.

As I grew up, I was raised in a household that followed American culture. Although I knew that I was Chinese, I didn't think that there was any difference between myself and my friends. I never learned the Chinese language, and although I was taught some Chinese customs at an early age, it took me a few years before I understood them.

Personally, I have never denied that I am Chinese. However, like any young child, I didn't want to believe that I was any different than all of my friends. Since I was raised in an American society, I didn't really associate myself as being Chinese. I didn't acknowledge my cultural difference because I did not think that it was important. I wanted to believe that I was just like everyone else, because I wanted to fit in. Due to the innocence of childhood, my friends and I didn't recognize the fact that we were from separate ethnic backgrounds. It didn't seem to matter to us then.

The first time that I realized that I was part of an ethnic minority was when I entered elementary school. I noticed that there were only a few Asian students in the entire school. It struck me then that I was different, and I didn't like that feeling.

When I was in the first grade, I remember doing an exercise that was intended to teach us how to graph. We took an in-class poll on our hair color. When the teacher tallied the results, I realized that I was the only person in the entire class who had black hair. Although this fact may seem very trivial now, it was the first time that I felt that I wasn't like everyone else. I felt segregated, and I remember wishing that I weren't Chinese so that I could have brown or blond hair like the rest of the class.

I am currently working at a bank as a teller. I have been working at

> the same branch for over a year now, and I have come in contact with many different people. During this time, I have noticed that it is very common for a customer to inquire about my nationality. This happens quite frequently, usually about three times a week. After they know that I am Chinese, some people ask me if I speak the language. When I answer that question, they often ask me if I was born in this country. Sometimes they ask where my parents, and even my grandparents, were born and raised. At first, I did not mind being asked all of these questions. I figured that some of them were trying to strike up a conversation and others were genuinely interested in my background. However, I become irritated at times because I feel as if people are trying to find out too much about my personal life, which has nothing to do with the reason why they are at the bank. It becomes annoying when some customers lecture me by telling me that I should be ashamed because I do not know my own culture's language.
>
> I would like to point out that the customers who ask these questions are not mostly Orientals, as one might assume. I have had many customers of other nationalities who have also inquired. There are times when they acknowledge my ethnic difference without talking directly to me. I heard someone in the branch once who looked at the teller line and stated, "What is this, The United Nations?" This man was not only referring to myself, but also to another teller who is Filipino. Although he may not have meant to offend me, he did so by making me feel like I was different from the rest.
>
> As I have grown older I have come to realize how important my culture is to me. I am saddened that I have a great-grandmother who I have known all of my life who I have never been able to hold a conversation with because of our language barrier. There are times that I wish that I would have learned the language at any early age so that I could understand and communicate with my relatives.
>
> I am trying to learn more about my culture now. I dance with a Chinese group and study Chinese history. Although some people might call me a banana—yellow on the outside, and white on the inside—this is not true at all. I am as Chinese as I can be considering I was born in this country, as were my parents. I enjoy most things that are Chinese just as I do things American. Being Chinese and American at the same time makes me feel special, but it still bothers me when people ask me where I am from or make me feel different.

Here then is a case where a young woman is third-generation Chinese American. She speaks no Chinese and only knows some of the rudimentary aspects of Chinese culture, yet she clings to her bicultural identity. In large measure this is due to the fact that she is "stigmatized" as being different, an experience she first encountered in first grade and which persists even now as an adult where she works. The experience of being "different" reinforces the necessity of maintaining a bicultural identity. Further, as this case also demonstrates, our subject bemoans her loss of culture; for example, she has never had a conversation with her great-grandmother because of the language barrier that separates them. To compensate for the loss of Chinese across the generations, she has also become interested in Chinese history and has joined a Chinese dance group. These cultural activities provide her with the ethnic protection and social support she needs to maintain the integration of her identity as a person who is stigmatized as different.

In summary, this case illustrates several very important facts regarding the difficulty that some later generation ethnics have as they move both culturally and socially toward full Americanization. Diane was highly acculturated, but stigmatized because of her Oriental physical features. Although feeling no discomfort with her Chinese background, it was clear that she had been socialized by both her parents and teachers to be an American. Yet the social context of school and work had shown her that others perceived her differently and not as American, causing her great discomfort. To minimize this discomfort, she found solace in a reaffirmation of her Chinese ethnic heritage. However, the reaffirmation of ethnic and cultural origin is not sufficient as Diane learned. To be Chinese she had to learn more about her cultural background, which required formal instruction in history and participation in cultural activities.

Mixed Ethnic Heritage Children

This fourth category that produces dual culture socialization includes children and adolescents who are of mixed ethnic or racial heritage and where each parent adheres to at least some of their traditional cultural practices. As discussed in an earlier section, our multicultural society has given way to considerable intermarriage in the past 20 years. This is especially true in large metropolitan areas such as New York, Los Angeles, San Francisco where diverse racial, religious, and ethnic group members live and work together and where the opportunity to interact and learn about different cultures, as well as the opportunity to date and intermarry, is high (Murguia, 1982). The removal of social distance barriers between ethnic and racial groups is the desirable end point of a completely integrated and open society.

Further, intermarriage is often pointed to by social theorists as proof that an integrated society has been achieved. Thus it may seem strange to be speaking about bicultural socialization in this instance. However, it needs to be noted that intermarriage does not imply loss of one's culture or disinterest in socializing children into the culture of both parents nor does it automatically imply that the mixed-heritage children are easily incorporated into mainstream society. This country has long maintained in its treatment of African Americans that any amount of "black blood," regardless of the physical characteristics of the person, still makes the person black and the object of discrimination. Therefore, it has become commonplace to find adolescents of mixed-heritage backgrounds acknowledging their dual heritage.

Little literature exists on the offspring of mixed marriages despite the fact that numerous investigators who have studied exogamy have expressed concern for the emotional and psychological welfare of mixed-heritage children. The scant literature that does exist shows that children of interracial (e.g., African-American and white) marriages have received more attention from social scientists than have children of interethnic (e.g., Hispanic and white) marriages. In the discussion that follows, I will confine myself to only instances of exogamy involving ethnic/racial groups such as Hispanics, Asians, and Caucasians. Although there are increasing numbers of interethnic marriages involving Chinese and Japanese, Mexican and Filipinos, etc., these mixed ethnic arrangements are not the principal topic of concern here. Children of interethnic marriages must cope with a level of dual socialization that is different in many respects from that of children of endogamous unions. Mixed-heritage children at a very early age recognize that their parents differ not only in physiognomy but also culturally, linguistically, and often in terms of religious preference.

It has been noted by some authors (e.g., Gordon, 1964) that the offspring of mixed marriages often suffer from a variety of identity and adjustment conflicts, and that these children may hold a low self-image of themselves and lack a strong social network. Vander-Zanden (1963) suggests that children of mixed marriages develop an ambivalence toward both sociocultural groups. Further, Cleveland and Longaker (1972) propose that subjects exposed to two different sets of cultural values are targets for neurotic behavior if they fail to combine both sets of cultural values in satisfying coalescence.

Similarly, Murguia (1982) suggests that intermarriage encourages a movement away from a definite ethnic identity. He speculates that children of intermarriages are subject to more cultural diversity and if not properly handled may have difficulty in identifying with the lower status ethnic group. There is some support for these various positions. Let me illustrate by quoting from a case study of an 18-year-old woman who I will call Yolanda and who demonstrates an extreme form of rejection of her Mexican ancestry.

The Case of Yolanda

> The hardest thing I've ever encountered in my life was accepting my heritage. Up until this past summer, I had adamantly refused to admit that I was of Mexican descent, deciding instead to concoct an explanation which sounded like a recipe: one fourth Italian, one eighth French, and a pinch of Portuguese. For the longest time I took all precautions necessary to ensure that no suspicions ever arose about my *real* identity. In high school I bypassed the foreign language requirement by selecting French, cutting short my grandmother's hopes of conversing and gossiping in Spanish with me. At home, I made it clear that I would only tolerate loud *mariachi* music once a week, and on the condition that none of my "normal" friends were within earshot. Although I knew I was giving my family a stiff pain in the *nalga* (ass) with my quest for life as a "gringa," succumbing to the fact that I was part of the refried bean crowd seemed a fate worse than death.
>
> My mother attempted to enlighten me by telling me fascinating stories about my relatives and their accomplishments. She may as well have been speaking Chinese. It didn't matter to me that my ancestral uncle was a hero during the Mexican Revolution, or that my maternal grandfather was a celebrated poet in his hometown; Mexicans, *all* Mexicans, were voodoo in my book, and no mere legacy about their success could change my gripes towards them.
>
> I had it hardest during family parties. Whether I was at my aunt's house in Pasadena or my uncle's high-rise shack in San Fernando, that horrifying reality of being Mexican was trailing me everywhere. Unable to cut loose and *caramba* with my relatives, I would sit in the shadows and watch these strange people enjoy their life and their heritage, without any qualms or regrets.
>
> My father, who isn't Mexican, sympathized with me but didn't take my side.
>
> "You are who you are," he said. "Mexicans might have a bad name in society, but they are a good people. You should be proud of what's really you."
>
> Regarding this as a sign that the truth was closing in on me, I saucily told my father that I had no intention to ever be associated with

> anyone who sold oranges on freeway entrances, nor would I ever stoop low enough to bother acknowledging them as humans. I remember distinctly that the hate in my voice at that point was so intense, so fierce, I didn't even recognize it as my own. I saw a flash in my father's eyes—shock, pity, maybe even a small amount of contempt—and the sound of his voice as he said, "Don't go through life trying to be someone you're not just to please your friends. If you don't face up to the truth, you're going to be miserable the rest of your life."

As we see, Yolanda has developed a very strong sense of contempt for Mexicans and points out in numerous ways why she doesn't want to be identified with them. As a consequence, Yolanda has struggled through her adolescence with various identities, as suggested by Erikson, and in the process she discarded them all but, because she was not fair skinned and found herself being asked by her peers for an ethnic identity, she concocted an identity that resembles a recipe for stew ". . . one-fourth Italian, one-eighth French, and a pinch of Portuguese . . ." She also disrespectfully refers to her family as ". . . part of the refried bean crowd . . ."

Curiously in Yolanda's case, it was meeting a young Mexican man that shook her to the very essence of her being and that moved her to see Mexicans in a new light. In Yolanda's own words she said:

> He was a young Mexican who didn't look like one. I remember scrutinizing him critically, looking for Mexican symptoms. Where was his brown skin? Where were his gold front teeth? How come he wasn't wearing a hairnet? He didn't drive a lowrider and spoke perfect, flawless English. I refused steadfastly to believe his ethnic background until I introduced him to my mother; the introduction took four hours, with the two of them conversing heartily in Spanish and me sitting on the outskirts, cursing the three years I spent taking French. We went to Mexican parties together—with live *mariachi* bands—and he smiled at the people there, enjoying their company, their life, their heritage. And for the first time in my life, I was finally able to do the same.

Although I have not had any contact with Yolanda now for several years, I do speak to her mother from time to time who says that Yolanda has toned down her criticism of Mexicans and even seems to enjoy the company of her relatives. She is not Mexican, but neither is she something concocted from an ethnic cookbook as before.

The case of Yolanda is perhaps an extreme example of ethnic denial and hostility; however, the case does serve to highlight several important points about identity confusion resulting from mixed ethnic heritage when one ethnic group is held in low esteem by the mainstream society and this becomes incorporated into the fabric of the mixed-ethnic individual's feeling about this side of their heritage. Generally, the findings regarding mixed-heritage children are far more positive than that seen in the case of Yolanda. Some of the most exciting research on mixed-heritage individuals has recently been carried out by Walter and Cookie Stephan (Stephan & Stephan, 1991). In this research, the Stephans have also attempted to assess the psychological functioning of mixed-heritage individuals to test some of the notions advanced by the "marginalists" and "biculturalists." Recall that according to the marginalists, mixed-heritage individuals are at risk for developing marked feelings of marginalization from the cultures of their parents. On the other hand, the bicultural perspective is that mixed-heritage individuals are likely to develop traits that predispose them to greater openness to other cultural groups and at the same time feel positively toward both of their ethnic and cultural orientations. To test these contrasting positions, the Stephans have collected data in Hawaii and New Mexico. In Hawaii, the subjects consisted of single heritage Caucasians and Asian Americans, plus a group of mixed Caucasian-Asian heritage college students. In New Mexico, the single-heritage respondents were Caucasians or Hispanics, while the mixed-heritage subjects were mixed Caucasian-Hispanic college students. Subjects in both Hawaii and New Mexico were given a large battery of measures to assess psychosocial functioning of the mixed-heritage individuals compared to their non-mixed ethnic group counterparts. I will summarize only a few of the more salient findings that bear directly on the characteristics of the mixed ethnic groups.

On measures of "Attitudes toward Caucasians (C) and either Asian-Americans or Hispanics (A-A/H)," "Contact with Cs and A-A/Hs," and "Enjoyment of C culture and A-A/H culture," the mixed-heritage individuals fell midway between the non–mixed ethnic heritage comparison groups whether in Hawaii or New Mexico. Importantly, the mixed-heritage individuals projected the image of being the perfect cultural bridges between both ethnic and cultural groups.

Further, on three psychological measures—Anomie, Intergroup Anxiety, and Self-Esteem—there were no significant differences involving the mixed-heritage individuals and the comparison groups in either Hawaii or New Mexico. In fact, the only significant differences were on intergroup anxiety and self-esteem with the Hawaiian-Asian group expressing greater intergroup anxiety and lower self-esteem.

Finally, on a measure of psychophysiological symptoms (e.g., "Are you ever troubled with aches or pains in the head?"), there were no significant differences between any of the groups dispelling any belief that one group or the other was more prone to psychosomatic complaints.

Although I have touched on only the highlights of this study, the findings produced no support for the traditional "marginal" hypothesis (Park, 1928; Stonequist, 1937) that being socialized in bicultural homes has negative effects on personality formation and functioning. In fact, the findings suggest the opposite. That is, there are positive effects due to bicultural socialization in terms of insulation from the ethnocentrism of single-heritage groups and exposure to and liking for Hispanic or Asian-American culture.

CONCLUSION

In this paper, I have argued that there are important social and psychological reasons for a closer examination of dual-culture socialization. Socialization into the traditions and practices of two cultures is much more common than what our psychological literature suggests. Further, because of significant immigration, especially from Latin America and Asia, coupled with significant increases in exogamy (intermarriage) over the last 20 years, there is even more reason for redoubling of our attention on bicultural socialization, identity formation, and psychosocial functioning of children and adolescents.

Also important is that, although I have deliberately focused discussion in this paper on the bicultural socialization of Hispanic and Asian children and adolescents, it is vitally important to recognize that bicultural conflicts and eventual resolutions are commonplace with many other immigrant groups, later generation ethnic Americans, and mixed-heritage individuals of many different backgrounds. More research is called for in order to have a complete picture of dual-culture socialization processes and outcomes. Unless more attention is given to bicultural socialization, developmental psychology as a basic and applied branch of psychology will continue to be viewed by many as an incomplete description of the life experiences of many Americans whose life is enriched not by one, but rather by two cultures.

The models that are used to study this new diversity and biculturalism must also step aside from older models of "marginality" and examine new possibilities in the evaluation of lifestyles, syntheses of cultures, and psychological functioning. I have tried to show that socialization to two cultural orientations can be a painful experience for children and adolescents, but equally true is the richness and sense of fulfillment described to me by numerous young people I have interviewed about their joys and sorrows in possessing two cultural orientations and lifestyles.

I suggest that the variables of ethnicity *and* culture be given more importance in developmental research. Researchers need to incorporate strategies for obtaining demographic information about respondents' ethnic and cultural backgrounds. Simple questionnaires that force an individual to select white, Asian, African American, Hispanic, and American Indian are too simplistic and inadequate in assessing the multiplicity of ethnic, racial, and cultural backgrounds that constitute an individual's core identity and that determine how a person responds to different social contexts.

Similarly, generational status and acculturation is important in any cross-cultural study or investigation that seeks to determine how ethnicity may be important in some aspect of psychological functioning. I know that considerations of culture or ethnicity are troublesome in research or in providing psychological services, but important information may be missed when these variables are ignored. Sometimes also trying to get a handle on these complex and sensitive topics is difficult for the researcher not familiar with the ethnic or cultural group being studied and who is not knowledgeable about how these variables may in unexpected ways contaminate the outcomes of a study and result in misinterpretations of findings.

Also relevant to this discussion is that many of the crucial issues in dual-cultural socialization do not end with adolescence, but in fact extend through the entire lifespan of a person. Although the focus of this paper has not been on adult biculturalism as such, what research does exist on the topic is primarily with adults. For many individuals, the full ramifications of the presence or absence of biculturalism do not become significant until adulthood when the person leaves the protection of the family and community. For instance, in the case of Diane we see how this young woman became increasingly more uncomfortable with the incomplete development of her Chinese side and how she sought to establish a balance in order to counter the recognition that she was treated differently by some majority group members.

Finally, the argument is made in the paper that motives for biculturalism are different depending on generational status. For first-generation individuals, acculturation to "American" culture is a must for survival in the United States. For the second generation, on the other hand, biculturalism often occurs because of the demand to serve as a bridge between the culture of the parents and that of the majority group. Third and later generation individuals may feel the need to be bicultural because of perceived discrimination directed at them by nonethnics.

REFERENCES

Aellen, C., & Lambert, W. (1969). Ethnic identification and personality adjustment of Canadian adolescents of mixed English-French parentage. *Canadian Journal of Behavioral Sciences, 1*, 69–86.

Arbona, C., Flores, C.L., & Novy, D.M. (in press). Cultural awareness and ethnic loyalty: Dimensions of cultural variability among Mexican American college students. *Journal of Counseling Development.*

Arce, C.H., Murguia, E., & Frisbie, W.P. (1987). Phenotype and life chances among Chicanos. *Hispanic Journal of Behavioral Sciences, 9*, 19–23.

Child, I. (1943). *Italian or American? The second generation in conflict.* New Haven: Yale University Press.

Cleveland, E.J., & Longaker, W.D. (1972). Neurotic patterns in the family. In G. Handel (Ed.), *The psychosocial interior of the family.* Chicago: Aldine, pp. 159–185.

Cross, W.E. (1980). Models of psychological Nigrescence: A literature review. In R.L. Jones (Ed.), *Black psychology* (pp. 81–98). New York: Harper & Row.

Der-Karabetian, A. (1980). Two cultural identities of Armenian-Americans. *Psychological Reports, 47*, 123–128.

Domino, M., & Acosta, A. (1987). The relation of acculturation and values in Mexican Americans. *Hispanic Journal of Behavioral Sciences, 9*, 131–150.

D'Souza, D. (1991). *Illiberal education: The politics of race and sex on campus.* New York: The Free Press.

Erikson, H.E. (1963). *Childhood and society.* New York: W. W. Norton & Co.

Erikson, H.E. (1968). *Identity: Youth and crisis.* New York: W. W. Norton & Co.

Gardner, R., & Lambert, W. (1972). *Attitudes and motivation in second language learning.* Rowley, MA: Newbury House.

Ghaffarian, S. (1987). The acculturation of Iranians in the United States. *The Journal of Social Psychology, 127*, 565–571.

Gordon, A. (1964). *Intermarriage: Interethnic, interracial, interfaith.* Boston: Beacon.

Grebler, L., Moore, J.W., & Guzman, R.C. (1970). *The Mexican American People.* New York: The Free Press.

Hall, C.C.I. (1980). The ethnic identity of racially mixed people: A study of Black-Japanese. Unpublished doctoral dissertation, University of California at Los Angeles.

Keefe, S.E., & Padilla, A.M. (1987). *Chicano ethnicity*. Albuquerque, NM: University of New Mexico Press.

LaFromboise, T., Coleman, H.L.K., & Gerton, J. (1993). Psychological impact of biculturalism: Evidence and theory. *Psychological Bulletin, 114*, 395–412.

Lambert, W.E. (1977). The effects of bilingualism on the individual: Cognitive and sociocultural consequences. In P.A. Hornby (Ed.), *Bilingualism: Psychological, social, and educational implications* (pp. 15–27). New York: Academic Press.

Lopez, D.E. (1978). Chicano language loyalty in an urban setting. *Sociology and Social Research, 62*, 267–278.

Lopez, D.E. (1982). *Language maintenance and shift in the United States today: The basic patterns and their social implications. Volume III: Hispanics and Portuguese* (p. 135). Los Alamitos: National Center for Bilingual Research.

Maccoby, E.E., & Martin, J.A. (1983). Socialization in the context of the family: Parent-child interaction. In P.H. Mussen (Ed.), *Handbook of Child Psychology. Vol. IV: Socialization, Personality, and Social Development* (pp. 1–101). New York: Wiley.

McFee, M. (1968). The 150% man, a product of Blackfeet acculturation. *The American Psychologist, 70*, 1096–1107.

Mena, F.J., Padilla, A.M., & Maldonado, M. (1987). Acculturative stress and specific coping strategies among immigrant and later generation college students. *Hispanic Journal of Behavioral Sciences, 9*, 207–225.

Minuchin, P.P., & Shapiro, E.K. (1983). The school as a context for social development. In P.H. Mussen (Ed.), *Handbook for Child Psychology. Vol. IV: Socialization, Personality, and Social Development* (pp. 197–274). New York: John Wiley & Sons.

Montgomery, G.T. (1992). Comfort with acculturation status among students from South Texas. *Hispanic Journal of Behavioral Sciences, 14*, 201–223.

Murguia, E. (1982). *Chicano intermarriage: A theoretical and empirical study*. San Antonio: Trinity University Press.

Olsen, L. (1988). *Crossing the schoolhouse border: Immigrant students and the California public schools*. San Francisco: California Tomorrow.

Padilla, A.M. (1980). The role of cultural awareness and ethnic loyalty in acculturation. In A.M. Padilla (Ed.), *Acculturation: Theory, models, and some new findings* (pp. 47–84). Boulder, CO: Westview Press.

Park, R.E. (1928). Migration and the marginal man. *American Journal of Sociology, 5*, 881–893.

Portes, A., & Rumbaut, R.G. (1990). *Immigrant America: A portrait*. Berkeley, CA: The University of California Press.

Salgado de Snyder, N., Lopez, C.M., & Padilla, A.M. (1982). Ethnic identity and cultural awareness among the offspring of Mexican interethnic marriages. *Journal of Early Adolescence*, 2, 277–282.

Stephan, W.G., & Stephan, C.W. (1991). Intermarriage: Effects on personality, adjustment, and intergroup relations in two samples of students. *Journal of Marriage and the Family*, *53*, 241–250.

Stonequist, E.V. (1937). *The marginal man: A study in personality and culture conflict*. New York: Russell & Russell.

Sung, B.L. (1985). Bicultural conflicts in Chinese immigrant children. *Journal of Comparative Family Studies*, *16*, 255–269.

Sung, B.L. (1990). *Chinese American intermarriage*. New York: Center for Migration Studies.

Szapocznik, J., Kurtines, W., & Fernandez, T. (1980). Biculturalism and adjustment among Hispanic youths. *International Journal of Intercultural Relations*, *4*, 353–375.

Vander-Zander, J.V. (1963). *American minority relations*. New York: Ronald.

Veltman, C. (1981). Anglicization in the United States: The importance of parental nativity and language characteristics. *International Journal of the Sociology of Language*, *32*, 65–84.

Wilson, A. (1987). *Mixed race children: A study of identity*. London: Allen & Unwin.

Zak, I. (1973). Dimensions of Jewish-American identity. *Psychological Reports*, *33*, 891–900.

AUTHOR NOTES

Correspondence concerning this chapter should be addressed to: Professor Amado M. Padilla, School of Education, Stanford University, Stanford, CA 94305–3096.

CHAPTER 3

ACCULTURATION AND ITS RELEVANCE TO MENTAL HEALTH

Dharma E. Cortes, PhD

Research Associate,
Hispanic Research Center,
Fordham University

The study of the relationship between acculturation and mental health has proved to be a challenging proposition in social science research. Findings in the area are largely inconclusive with regard to the way the relationship operates. In this chapter, it is argued that research challenges in this area stem largely from the complexity of both constructs (i.e., acculturation and mental health) and the ways in which models of both acculturation and mental health outcomes have been assessed in empirical research. Thus, this chapter will examine measurement problems of acculturation and mental health, the correspondence between conceptual models of acculturation and mental health and the way they are or should be assessed in empirical research, current research efforts, and give suggestions for further research.

MEASUREMENT PROBLEMS

In a recent review of the literature on acculturation and mental health, Rogler, Cortés, and Malgady (1991) found that the great majority of studies confirm a link between the two. However, the direction of the relationship varied across the 30 studies they reviewed. Some studies reported a negative relationship between acculturation and mental health problems, suggesting that a breakup in primary networks, inability to speak the host society's language, and exposure to new customs and cultural practices lead to low self-esteem and to an increase in psychological symptoms (Escobar, Randolph, Puente, Spiwak, Asamen, Hill, & Hough, 1983; Escobar, Randolph, & Hill, 1986; Rogler & Cooney, 1984; Salgado de Snyder, 1987; Torres-Matrullo, 1976; Warheit, Vega, Auth, & Meinhardt, 1985).

Yet another set of studies indicated that acculturation was positively related to mental health problems (Buriel, Calzada, & Vázquez, 1982; Burnam, Hough, Karno, Escobar, & Telles, 1987; Caetano, 1987; Gilbert, 1987; Neff, 1986; Pumariega, 1986). This positive relationship implies that high levels of acculturation lead to an increase in mental health problems through internalization of the host culture's norms, beliefs, and stereotypical and prejudicial attitudes toward minority groups. Internalization of these norms, beliefs, and attitudes causes individuals to become estranged from their traditional culture and primary groups and to develop feelings of self-deprecation and ethnic self-hatred. Most of the studies indicating a positive relationship between acculturation and mental health problems focus on alcohol- and drug-related problems.

Finally, a third group of studies suggested a curvilinear relationship between acculturation and mental health (Ortiz & Arce, 1984; Szapocznik, Kurtines, & Fernández, 1980). In other words, a combination of elements from the culture of origin and those of the new culture lead to better mental health. Rogler and his collaborators (1991) attributed these inconsistent findings in the relationship between acculturation and mental health largely to problems in the measurement of acculturation and to the great diversity of definitions and indicators of mental health outcomes in the studies.

In their review of studies examining the link between acculturation and mental health, Rogler et al. (1991) concluded that the definitions and measurement instruments of acculturation and mental health outcomes, as well as the characteristics of individuals participating in those studies, were very heterogeneous. Acculturation has been conceptualized as one or more of the following: place of birth, length of residence in the United States, place of education, generational status, Spanish surname, language usage, ethnicity, degree of loyalty toward culture of origin, and by scores on psychometrically developed scales (Rogler et al., 1991). These scales include a variety of items tapping language usage in different social situations, language of media sources, food preferences, self-assessments of ethnic identity and distance between cultures, and ethnicity of friends, among others. Generally, they are based on a multidimensional model of acculturation, but since language appears to carry significant weight on the variance of acculturation, scales tend to focus solely on language (Marín, Sabogal, Marín, Otero-Sabogal, & Pérez-Stable, 1987) or have at least half of their items referring to language (Burnam, Telles, Karno, Hough, & Escobar, 1987; Szapocznik, Scopetta, Kurtines, & Aranalde, 1978). Not surprisingly, these scales yield high levels of internal consistency reliability, which is to be expected from a test based solely on language use and mastery. The problem is that this reliability is achieved at the expense of content validity. Moreover, it reduces the process of acculturation to acquisition of the host society's language. Although proficiency in the host society's language is instrumental to acculturation, the process also encompasses adaptation to values, the quality of interpersonal relations, food preferences, expected behavioral amenities, child rearing practices, and other elements of culture.

In addition to the language issue, the great majority of the current acculturation scales suffer from another limitation. They tend to force respondents to make a choice between levels of involvement in one culture to the exclusion of involvement in another. An example of this are items that provide the following choices for answers: mostly Hispanic, somewhat Hispanic, somewhat American, or mostly American. These choices do not allow for the expression of simultaneous involvement in both cultures. Even in those instances in which there are items offering an intermediate choice between the two cultures (i.e., about equally Hispanic and American), such choice does not necessarily provide a clear idea about level of biculturalism. Moreover, traditional acculturation scales do not enable the assessment of those instances in which a respondent might be highly or minimally involved in the two cultures under question. In sum, the way current acculturation scales assess levels of acculturation is based upon a zero-sum competitive process in which increments in American culture are accompanied by decrements of involvement in Hispanic culture (Rogler et al., 1991).

Similarly, the way in which mental health has been measured in studies relating it to acculturation has also been problematic. First of all, definitions of mental health status vary from one study to the other. These definitions include standard diagnostic categories from the *Diagnostic and Statistical Manual of Mental Disorders* (DSM-III), adjustment and adaptation scales, lists of specific symptoms, alcohol and drug abuse, perceptions of quality of life, suicide ideation and attempts, and standardized instruments assessing specific psychiatric symptomatology. In studies of acculturation and mental health, the latter has been so widely defined that researchers, like Berry and Kim (1988), recommend the use of a more general definition of mental health, one "that includes the notions of effective functioning in daily life and the ability to deal with new situations" (p. 208).

Problems with the conceptualization and assessment of mental health, however, go beyond issues of definition. In their analysis of the literature on acculturation and mental health, Rogler et al. (1991) questioned the validity of standard measures of mental health for minority groups such as Hispanics. They indicated that ". . . we do not know how well standard measures of mental health fit the realities of

Hispanic psychological distress or in what ways Hispanic people formulate their expressions of such distress" (p. 558). Furthermore, if acculturation is viewed as an endogenous variable affecting behavior, then the way Hispanics express psychological distress might vary by level of acculturation. On the one hand, low acculturated Hispanics would tend to manifest psychological distress through idiomatic expressions that are closer to their culture of origin. On the other hand, expressions of psychological distress among high acculturated Hispanics would resemble those of the mainstream host society. For instance, if standard measures of psychological symptomatology developed for groups other than Hispanics are used with low acculturated individuals, there might be instances in which these scales will overlook important components of these individuals' psychological distress that are closely linked to their culture of origin. Therefore, if it is argued that acculturation brings about psychological changes (e.g., high acculturated individuals behaving more like the dominant cultural group), this ought to be considered in the process of assessing their mental health problems.

MODELS OF ACCULTURATION AND MENTAL HEALTH

In looking at the literature on acculturation, there is a general consensus pointing to the complexity of the process of acculturation (Berry & Kim, 1988; Espin, 1987; Rogler et al., 1991). The same is true for the area of mental health. When these two complex processes are put together in models that attempt to explain how they can be linked, it is clear that the relationship is conditioned by numerous factors. Acculturation, for example, appears to be affected by a migrant's status (refugee, voluntary), timing, place of arrival, age, gender, cultural distance, and many other variables (Berry & Kim, 1988; Rogler et al., 1991; Szapocznik & Kurtines, 1980). Studies on mental health show it to be affected by variables such as socioeconomic status and sex roles (Kessler & Cleary, 1980; Dohrenwend, Dohrenwend, Gould, Link, Neugebauer, & Wunsch-Hitzig, 1980). Some propositions made by researchers in the field on what factors may affect acculturation and its relationship with mental health are now presented for illustrative purposes.

In proposing a multidimensional model of acculturation, Mendoza and Martínez (1981) indicated that people acculturate differently according to particular circumstances related to their migratory process, attitudes toward host society, plans to return, prejudice, and exclusion practices, among others. According to Portes and Rumbaut (1990), among the variables needed to be taken into account when studying acculturation are what they called *contexts of exit* and *contexts of reception.* Contexts of exit refer to the existing conditions in the place of origin that lead to the actual migratory movement. Contexts of reception, then, have to do with conditions encountered in the place of destination. On the basis of findings in research among refugees, Portes and Rumbaut (1990) argued that migrants' experiences prior to and immediately after the exodus from their country of origin are one of the strongest predictors of mental health problems. However, they argue that as length of residence in the place of destination increases, the ". . . contexts of exit gradually lose significance as contexts of reception gain salience" (p. 161). Thus, the relationship between the two contexts is not static but dynamic as it is affected by the temporal element.

Time appears to be related to acculturation and mental health in a curvilinear fashion. Some migrants experience mental health problems right after they arrive at the place of destination. These problems then decline as time goes by and they become accustomed to the new place of residence. In other instances, particularly when the migratory move is prompted by situations such as political persecution and civil war, arrival in a new country might be a source of joy and happiness. However, as time goes by and the person confronts situations such as discrimination, unfulfilled expectations, and other difficulties, mental health problems may develop.

Portes and Rumbaut (1990) also acknowledged the importance of considering the type of migrant when studying acculturation. Depending on whether the migrant is someone escaping from political persecution or someone voluntarily leaving the place of origin, the acculturation process would be different. Also, if mental health problems arise, the acculturation stage in which they appear would also differ. In other words, "acculturation per se is not the decisive variable in this situation because, depending on specific circumstances, it can lead to widely different outcomes" (Portes & Rumbaut, 1990, p. 175). Thus, in this proposition, the relationship between acculturation and mental health is conditioned by their interrelationships with other variables.

Szapocznik and Kurtines (1980) also recognized the importance of taking other factors into consideration when studying acculturation. The context in which acculturation takes place is one factor. They argued that if the context is monocultural, a unidimensional and unidirectional process of acculturation would lead to low levels of psychological distress. In a bicultural social context, however, individuals need cultural flexibility to operate successfully. Thus, according to Szapocznik and Kurtines (1980), how acculturation takes place and how it is related to mental health largely depends on the receiving sociocultural setting. The impact each culture has upon the larger social context also has an impact on migrants' acculturation and mental health. For example, if there is mutual influence among them, acculturation would entail the acquisition of elements from the cultures in contact. If one is dominant, acculturation would be toward the dominant culture.

In addition to the importance that context-related variables have upon acculturation, Szapocznik and Kurtines (1980) indicated that acculturation also varies as a function of age and gender. Younger individuals tend to acculturate faster than their older counterparts, and evidence also suggests that females may acculturate at a slower pace than males. In relating this model of acculturation to mental health, Szapocznik and Kurtines (1980) viewed family disruption or intergenerational conflicts as the result of an acculturation gap between generations. In a study conducted among Cuban Americans, they found that when there were significant differences in acculturation between parents and children, the latter showed a tendency to have drug abuse problems and problems of adjustment at school.

A much more comprehensive model of acculturation and mental health has been proposed by Berry and Kim (1988). This model's first proposition is that acculturation encompasses various levels of change: physical (e.g., new place to live, housing), biological (e.g., consumption of new food, exposure to new diseases), cultural (e.g., alteration of political, economic, technical, linguistic, religious, and social institutions), and psychological (e.g., adaptation). These changes, along with their respective impact on the individual's mental health, occur at different phases in the process of acculturation. The phases enumerated by Berry and Kim (1988) are: precontact, contact, conflict, crisis, and adaptation.

In order to assess the impact of acculturation on individuals' mental health, Berry and Kim (1988) indicate it is important to know their mental health status at the precontact stage and their goals at the contact stage. It is also important to clarify whether any conflicts (i.e., intergroup or psychological) occurred, as well as the kind of adaptation made by the individuals in question. In this model, then, mental health is the result of what happens at each phase.

Berry and Kim (1988) also argue that since individuals acculturate differently, the kind of acculturation an individual achieves will be related to specific mental health problems. For example, if a person becomes acculturated by giving up his/her cultural identity, mental health problems such as poor self-esteem might emerge. Those who maintain their cultural identity while entering the host society (integration) would confront few mental health problems. Migrants who adopt a separation mode of acculturation, that is, maintaining their cultural identity and not joining the larger group, would tend to face mental health problems. Finally, those who reject their cultural identity and that of the larger society would tend to have even more mental health problems due to their marginal status in both cultures. Therefore, according to this model, mental health status varies as a function of the mode of adaptation. Since people can acculturate in so many different ways, the relationship between acculturation and mental health would vary accordingly.

Berry and Kim's (1988) model suggests that mental health is conditioned by phases and modes of acculturation. In developing their model, they also argued that the type of migrant or acculturation group (i.e., voluntary, involuntary, ethnic groups, sojourners) has an effect on the relationship between acculturation and mental health. This implies that mental health status is also affected by social contacts, voluntariness, mobility, and permanence. The nature of the receiving society and its level of receptivity to other groups are also important factors contributing to migrants' mental health outcomes. On the one hand, pluralistic societies, networks of cultural and ethnic groups, would help in buffering acculturative stress. On the other hand, less tolerant societies might exclude low acculturated groups from participating in the mainstream society.

Finally, specific social, cultural, and psychological characteristics that may affect the mental health status of those individuals in the process of acculturation should be considered (Berry & Kim, 1988). These characteristics include degree of permanence in places of destination (i.e., nomadic versus sedentary), socioeconomic status at places of origin and destination, age, gender, social support, acceptance or prestige of migrant groups in the place of destination, degree of knowledge of host society's language and culture, cultural encounters, motives, attitudes toward acculturation, education, occupation, self-esteem, identity, achievement motivation, rigidity/flexibility, and cognitive style.

This brief examination of Berry and Kim's (1988) model of how acculturation can be related to mental health illustrates the complexity of the relationship and how both acculturation and mental health are affected by a large variety of other variables. The question to be posed is: How can this model be tested? Specifically, what research strategies can be implemented to take into account all the possible variables affecting acculturation and mental health? If the process is as complex as this model suggests, why is it that the great majority of studies assess the relationship between acculturation and mental health by merely administering a single acculturation scale and a measure of psychological distress? Moreover, if acculturation is affected by so many elements, why is the measure of acculturation frequently reduced to a small number of items on language usage? Clearly, our research strategies need to be modified.

CURRENT RESEARCH EFFORTS

In trying to shape acculturation research toward new directions, Rogler et al. (1991) have provided various suggestions. First, they proposed an acculturation model in which involvements in the culture of origin are independent of involvements in the host culture. Second, in considering the relationship between acculturation and mental health, Rogler and colleagues (1991) questioned the use of standard measurements of psychological symptomatology with groups other than those for which those measurements were designed.

Some research efforts have been made to deal with the measurement issues of acculturation and mental health (Cortés, Rogler, & Malgady, 1993; Rogler, Cortés, & Malgady, in press). Through the use of focus groups, an approach being reintroduced into the social sciences in the interest of minimizing researchers' preconceptions and maximizing respondents' contributions (Morgan, 1988; Stewart and Shamdasani, 1990), items were developed to assess acculturation and psychological distress among Puerto Ricans in New York City.

The discussions on acculturation among members of the focus groups were prompted by asking the participants to talk about what it meant to be Puerto Rican and how that meaning changes as the result of exposure to American culture. Themes coming out of those discussions centered on language preferences and usage, values, ethnic pride, food preferences, childrearing practices, and interpersonal relationships.

Acculturation items were developed from the themes emerging from the focus groups following the proposition that involvements in the culture of origin should be assessed independently from those with the host culture (Rogler et al., 1991). After administering those items to a sample of Puerto Ricans in New York City, factor analyses supported the contention that cultural involvements in both American and Puerto Rican cultures occurred independently from one another. Only food preferences (i.e., Puerto Rican vs. American) showed mutual exclusivity. This finding confirmed theoretical arguments suggesting that some behaviors that are altered in the process of acculturation are mutually inclusive and others are mutually exclusive (Mendoza & Martínez, 1981). Moreover, by measuring involvements in Puerto Rican culture independently from involvements in American culture, it was found that a considerable number of respondents were highly involved in both cultures. This information would have been lost in acculturation scales using the zero-sum competition approach.

With respect to the measurement of psychological distress, other focus groups were conducted, taking into account the realities of the group under study and how they express psychological distress. This time the focus was on an open-ended variant of a query used by Manson, Shore, and Bloom (1985) in their studies of Hopi Indians: "What are the things that can be wrong with the minds and spiritual lives of Puerto Ricans?" This question and variations used as follow-up questions revealed a rich vocabulary of psychological distress: *mal del cerebro* (sick in the brain), *mal de la mente* (sick in the mind), *nerviosidad* (nervousness), *espiritualmente débil* (spiritually weak), *sospechoso* (suspicious), *locura* (craziness), and *ido* (gone, usually accompanied by pointing to the head).

When asked about more general and more encompassing psychological afflictions commonly suffered by Puerto Ricans, participants referred to *enfogonamiento* (or anger) and *injusticia* (or injustice). Participants defined *enfogonamiento* as an incessant, free-floating anger in which the person repeatedly confronts the problem of suppressing hostile feelings so as not to provoke an untoward incident or blunder. *Injusticia* referred to the feeling that rewards are not distributed equably, that Puerto Ricans do not receive what they are entitled to.

Items tapping these two expressions of distress were developed and administered to a sample of Puerto Ricans in New York City that included individuals receiving psychological treatment at a mental health community center. In analyzing the impact these idiomatic expressions of distress have on predicting clinical diagnosis, they appeared to add to the variance already explained by standard measures of psychological distress, including the Diagnostic Interview Schedule (DIS) Somatization Scale and the Center for Epidemiological Studies Depression Scale (CES-D). Therefore, *enfogonamiento* and *injusticia* introduced information relevant to clinical diagnosis that was not taken into account in the standard measures of psychological distress, but which was relevant to understanding expression of symptoms when providing psychological services to Puerto Ricans.

The next step in these research efforts is to examine the relationship between acculturation and mental health. Very preliminary analyses suggest statistically significant relationships between these idiomatic expressions of distress and involvements in American and Puerto Rican cultures. More refined analyses taking into account other variables would provide a much clearer picture of the multiple linkages between cultural and psychological processes.

FURTHER RESEARCH

Considering the myriad variables that affect both acculturation and mental health in models of the relationship between the two, research must take them into account in the multiple measures of the two constructs. Current research reflects an oversimplification of the relationship between acculturation and mental health. For example, issues such as the nature of the migratory movement, time of migration, social mobility, socioeconomic status, differences between the two cultures in contact, length of time spent at place of destination, and availability of social support networks, among others, may moderate the way acculturation takes place. In other words, the relationship between acculturation and mental health appears to be influenced by many other variables. However, the great majority of studies disregard these interrelationships. Too often, the examination of the relationship between acculturation and mental health is reduced to the use of one acculturation scale, generally heavily loaded on language items, and a scale assessing psychological symptomatology. These research practices have resulted in the large number of inconsistent findings found in the area. Furthermore, the findings are, to a large extent, misleading in the sense that the relationship between acculturation and mental health is examined in a way that is different from the way it takes place in reality.

Taking into consideration how acculturation and mental health are affected by other variables and how this is overlooked by many researchers, it is not surprising to find instances in which it is difficult to establish a direct connection between acculturation and mental health outcomes. Researchers in the area of acculturation and mental health need to adopt more comprehensive models on how this relationship operates. Longitudinal approaches, for example, would allow us first to examine current propositions on how the process of acculturation is affected by so many other variables and eventually to how it is related to mental health. Acculturation measures, on the one hand, should move away from the overemphasis on language items since it is clear that acculturation encompasses more than acquisition of the host society's language. On the other hand, assessments of mental health outcomes should take into account cultural influences in the expression of psychological distress.

The intricate complexity of both constructs calls for extensive research in the area and the incorporation of more subjective approaches to study acculturation and mental health. It may even be necessary to reconsider how the relationship operates. In current research, the emphasis has been on viewing acculturation as being closely related to mental health outcomes. However, considering the many elements influencing acculturation itself, that might be an inadequate strategy to implement. Using Jessor's (1981) paradigm on distal (those that are removed from the immediate experience) versus proximal (those that are closer to the immediate experience) variables, which has been applied in psychological research, it can be argued that acculturation constitutes a distal variable thus requiring intricate connections leading to mental health outcomes. Within this paradigm, variables mediating between acculturation and mental health are then considered proximal variables because they mediate the linkage of distal variables to outcome.

The main issue in question in acculturation-mental health research is how two highly complex processes can be examined in actual research without oversimplifying them. Longitudinal approaches appear as a natural alternative and research strategies such as focus groups have shown their utility in the developmental stages of research in this area (Cortés et al., 1993). In sum, current research in the area of acculturation and mental health outcomes would benefit from innovative research strategies that reflect the complex dynamics between the two processes as they take place in reality.

REFERENCES

American Psychiatric Association. (1980). *Diagnostic and statistical manual of mental disorders* (3rd ed.). Washington, DC: Author.

Berry, J.W., & Kim, U. (1988). Acculturation and mental health. In P.R. Dasen, J.W. Berry, & N. Sartouris (Eds.), *Health and cross-cultural psychology: Toward applications* (pp. 207–236). Newbury Park, CA: Sage.

Buriel, R., Calzada, S., & Vázquez, R. (1982). The relationship of traditional Mexican American culture to adjustment and delinquency among three generations of Mexican American male adolescents. *Hispanic Journal of Behavioral Sciences, 4*, 41–55.

Burnam, M.A., Hough, R.L., Karno, M., Escobar, J.I., & Telles, C.A. (1987). Acculturation and lifetime prevalence of psychiatric disorders among Mexican Americans in Los Angeles. *Journal of Health and Social Behavior, 28*, 89–102.

Burnam, M.A., Telles, C.A., Karno, M., Hough, R.L., & Escobar, J.I. (1987). Measurement of acculturation in a community population of Mexican Americans. *Hispanic Journal of Behavioral Sciences, 9*, 105–130.

Caetano, R. (1987). Acculturation and drinking patterns among U.S. Hispanics. British Journal of Addiction, *82*, 789–799.

Cortés, D.E., Rogler, L.H., & Malgady, R.G. (1993). *Assessing biculturality among Puerto Rican adults in the United States*. Manuscript submitted for publication.

Dohrenwend, B.P., Dohrenwend, B.S., Gould, M.S., Link, B., Neugebauer, R., & Wunsch-Hitzig, R. (1980). *Mental illness in the United States*. New York: Praeger.

Escobar, J.I., Randolph, E.T., & Hill, M. (1986). Symptoms of schizophrenia in Hispanic and Anglo veterans. *Culture, Medicine, and Psychiatry, 10*, 259–276.

Escobar, J.I., Randolph, E.T., Puente, G., Spiwak, F., Asamen, J.K., Hill, M., & Hough, R. (1983). Post-traumatic stress disorder in Hispanic Vietnam veterans: Clinical phenomenology and sociocultural characteristics. *Journal of Nervous and Mental Disease, 171*, 585–596.

Espin, O.M. (1987). Psychological impact of migration on Latinas. *Psychology of Women Quarterly, 11*, 489–503.

Jessor, R. (1981). The perceived environment in psychological research. In D. Magnusson (Ed.), *Toward a psychology of situations: An interactional perspective* (pp. 297–317). Hillsdale, NJ: Erlbaum.

Kessler, R.C., & Cleary, P. D. (1980). Social class and psychological distress. *American Sociological Review, 45*, 463–478.

Manson, M., Shore, J. H., & Bloom, J.D. (1985). The depressive experience in American Indian communities: A challenge for psychiatric theory and diagnosis. In A. Kleinman & B. Good (Eds.), *Culture and depression: Studies in the anthropology and cross cultural psychiatry of affect disorder* (pp. 331–368). Berkeley: University of California Press.

Marín, G., Sabogal, F., Marín, B.V., Otero-Sabogal, R., & Pérez-Stable, E. (1987). Development of a short acculturation scale for Hispanics. *Hispanic Journal of Behavioral Sciences, 9*, 183–205.

Mendoza, R.H., & Martínez, J.L. (1981). The measurement of acculturation. In A. Barón (Ed.), *Explorations in Chicano psychology* (pp. 71–82). New York: Praeger.

Morgan, D.L. (1988). *Focus groups as qualitative research*. Newbury Park, CA: Sage Publications.

Neff, J.A. (1986). Alcohol consumption and psychological distress among U.S. Anglos, Hispanics, and Blacks. *Alcohol and Alcoholism, 21*, 111–119.

Ortiz, V., & Arce, C.H. (1984). Language orientation and mental health status among persons of Mexican descent. *Hispanic Journal of Behavioral Sciences, 6*, 127–143.

Portes, A., & Rumbaut, R.G. (1990). *Immigrant America: A portrait*. Berkeley: University of California Press.

Pumariega, A.J. (1986). Acculturation and eating attitudes in adolescent girls: A comparative study. *Journal of the American Academy of Child Psychiatry, 25*, 276–279.

Rogler, L.H., & Cooney, R.S. (1984). *Puerto Rican families in New York City: Intergenerational processes*. (Hispanic Research Center Monograph No. 11). Maplewood, NJ: Waterfront Press.

Rogler, L.H., Cortés, D.E., & Malgady, R.G. (1991). Acculturation and mental health status: Convergence and new directions for research. *American Psychologist, 46*, 585–597.

Rogler, L.H., Cortés, D.E., & Malgady, R.G. (in press). The mental health relevance of idioms of distress among Puerto Ricans in New York City. *Journal of Nervous and Mental Disease*.

Salgado de Snyder, V.N. (1987). Factors associated with acculturative stress and depressive symptomatology among married Mexican immigrant women. *Psychology of Women Quarterly, 11*, 475–488.

Stewart, D.W., & Shamdasani, P.N. (1990). *Focus groups: Theory and practice*. Newbury Park, CA: Sage Publications.

Szapocznik, J., & Kurtines, W. (1980). Acculturation, biculturalism and adjustment among Cuban Americans. In A. Padilla (Ed.), *Acculturation: Theory, models and some new findings* (pp. 139–159). Boulder, CO: Westview Press.

Szapocznik, J., Kurtines, W., & Fernández, T. (1980). Bicultural involvement in

Hispanic American youths. *International Journal of Intercultural Relations, 4*, 353–365.

Szapocznik, J., Scopetta, M.A., Kurtines, W., & Aranalde, M.A. (1978). Theory and assessment of acculturation. *Interamerican Journal of Psychology, 12*, 113–130.

Torres-Matrullo, C. (1976). Acculturation and psychopathology among Puerto Rican women in mainland United States. *American Journal of Orthopsychiatry, 46*, 710–719.

Warheit, G.J., Vega, W.A., Auth, J., & Meinhardt, K. (1985). Psychiatric symptoms and dysfunctions among Anglos and Mexican Americans: An epidemiological study. In J.R. Greenley (Ed.), *Research in community and mental health* (pp. 3–32). London: JAI Press.

AUTHOR NOTES

Correspondence concerning this chapter should be addressed to: Dr. Dharma Cortes, Hispanic Research Center, Thebaud Hall, Fordham University, Bronx, NY 10458.

CHAPTER 4

CUBAN AMERICANS: MIGRATION, ACCULTURATION, AND MENTAL HEALTH

Pedro Ruiz, MD

Professor and Vice Chair for Clinical Affairs, Department of Psychiatry & Behavioral Sciences, University of Texas/Houston Health Science Center

During the last several decades, a large number of Hispanic migrants have arrived in the United States. These Hispanic migrant groups came primarily from Mexico, Cuba, Dominican Republic, Nicaragua, and El Salvador. Moreover, all Hispanic countries from this hemisphere are well represented, in one way or another, in the ethnic minority mosaic of which the United States is now comprised. Despite many commonalities among Hispanic-American groups that reside in the United States, there are also wide differences among them (Ruiz, 1985).

By and large, Americans are not, as yet, fully aware of the intrinsic dissimilarities that are present in these various Hispanic-American groups. Among these differences, their ethnocultural characteristics appear to be the most prominent. These dissimilarities are even more pronounced and relevant when one focuses on the various types of migration and on the political ideologies surrounding these Hispanic migrant groups. Furthermore, nationality factors, geographic origins, educational backgrounds, socioeconomic levels, and religious beliefs are all key components contributing to the unique characteristics of these Hispanic migrant groups.

The mental health literature focusing on these ethnocultural manifestations in Mexican Americans is very rich and longstanding. Similarly, the mental health literature addressing Puerto Ricans is also fairly rich and longstanding. However, in regard to Cuban Americans it is rather scarce and recent. In this chapter, I focus on the most relevant ethnocultural aspects of the Cuban migration to the United States during this century, as well as the acculturation process of Cuban Americans. Additionally, emphasis will be given to the unique mental health characteristics of the Cuban Americans residing in this country.

THE CUBAN MIGRATION

Historically, Cubans had always migrated to the United States for political and economic reasons. Prior to Castro taking control of the Cuban government in 1959, close to 200,000 Cubans settled in the

United States. This Cuban migrant group was largely composed of three different social classes. The largest one was comprised of unskilled workers from rural areas of Cuba. As a result of their limited educational background and technical skills, this group found major difficulties getting job opportunities in Cuba and thus migrated to the United States with the hope of improving their socioeconomic conditions. The second group during this period consisted of professionals, particularly from the health care sector, who came to the United States in order to secure better employment opportunities and specialized training. For this group, although small, it was very difficult to move up professionally in Cuba as a result of the large concentration of professionals in most urban sectors of the island prior to 1959. The third group during this period consisted of a large number of workers, mainly from the tobacco industry. This group settled in the United states during the Cuban War of Independence in the last part of the 19th century.

After Castro took over Cuba, the nature and type of Cuban migration toward the United States shifted dramatically, mainly as a consequence of the profound political and economic changes that took place in Cuba after his takeover. During the 1960s, approximately 700,000 Cubans migrated to the United States. By and large, this group was composed of political refugees who fled Cuba in order to avoid living under a communist regime. This group was largely representative of middle-class families, particularly professionals and technicians. More recently, between April and June of 1980, approximately 125,000 Cubans entered the United States as part of the "Mariel" exodus. This group decided to leave Cuba when Fidel Castro opened the gates of the Peruvian embassy in Havana to those who were unhappy with the communist regime (Nielsen, Rohter & Whitmore, 1980).

In short, the wave of Cuban migration between 1959 and the present time consisted of (1) those who left Cuba in the early 1960s, and hoped for a quick return to the island, (2) those who left shortly after the Bay of Pigs invasion in order to escape political prosecution, (3) those who migrated in order to improve their socioeconomic conditions, and (4) those who were pushed out during the Mariel exodus. In general, two dynamics have played a role in this migration process. The first one relates to those who were "pushed out" and the second to those who were "pulled out" from Cuba (Amaro & Portes, 1972).

A close look at the 1990 census statistics (U.S. Bureau of the Census, 1991) permits analysis of the most relevant data pertaining to the composition of the Cuban-American population and illustrates the differences between the Cuban-American population and the two largest Hispanic-American groups of the United States, Mexican Americans and Puerto Ricans. For instance, Cuban Americans comprise 0.4% of the total U.S. population or 1,014,000 people. Twelve percent of Cuban Americans have a family income of less than $10,000 per year, compared to 28% for Puerto Ricans and 18.8% for Mexican Americans. When it comes to families earning more than $50,000 per year, 23.5% are Cuban Americans, 15.4% are Puerto Ricans, and 12.6% are Mexican Americans. In terms of unemployment rates, 5.8% of Cuban Americans are unemployed compared to 8.6% of Puerto Ricans and 9.0% of Mexican Americans, and a total United States unemployment rate of 5.5%. With respect to education, 63.5% of Cuban Americans graduate from high school, compared to 55.5% for Puerto Ricans, 44.1% for Mexican Americans, and 77.6% for the total U.S. population. A comparison of college attendance shows even more striking differences. Twenty percent of Cuban Americans attended 4 or more years of college, compared to 9.7% of Puerto Ricans and only 5.4% of Mexican Americans. With respect to occupational status, the census statistics show, as seen in Table 1, that the occupational profiles of Cuban Americans is quite similar to the occupational profile of the U.S. population. Further, the occupational profile of Cuban Americans in the managerial and professional category, as well as in the technical, sales, and administrative support category, is more favorable than that of Puerto Ricans or Mexican Americans.

In summary, the Cuban-American migration to the United States has been a diverse one. Furthermore, it has also been quite successful, particularly during the period 1960 to 1980.

THE PROCESS OF ACCULTURATION

As with any other migrant group, Cuban Americans have gone through a process of acculturation as they have adjusted and adapted to the United States. In this respect, the work of Rogler, Cortes, & Malgady (1991) related to acculturation and mental health status among Hispanics offers a unique frame of reference and is applicable to any ethnic migrant group. In this context, acculturation is the process whereby immigrants modify their behavior and attitudes toward those of the host society. This acculturation process is a fundamental part of the

Table 1. 1990 Occupational Survey

Occupation	U.S.A. %	Non-Hispanic %	Cuban %	Puerto Rican %	Mexican American %
Managerial & Professional	26.2	27.3	24.0	17.1	11.3
Technical, Sales, & Adm. Support	32.7	33.2	33.8	31.5	25.3
Service	13.6	13.0	14.8	19.7	19.5
Farming, Forestry, & Fishing	2.5	2.3	0.7	1.5	6.5
Craft, Repair, & Precision Products	10.8	10.7	11.1	11.9	12.2
Operators, Fabricators, & Laborers	14.2	13.5	15.6	18.3	25.2

This table was adapted from: U.S. Bureau of the Census, Current Population Reports, Series P-20, No. 449, 1991.

migration-influenced adaptation to a new set of values and beliefs, of which the new sociocultural environment is a manifestation. As the migrant group becomes acculturated, in this case Cuban Americans, new values and norms are acquired and thus depicted in dress codes, food selection, music, and other culturally related symbols or characteristics.

This process of acculturation shows positive as well as negative relationships, particularly from a mental health point of view. In the case of negative relationships, many migrants with low acculturation levels are uprooted from the supportive network systems they had in their native countries, without the opportunity to redevelop them in the host nation. As a result of this, they tend to become isolated and marginalized in the host society. In the case of positive relationships, increases in the level of acculturation also promote the internalization of damaging stereotypes of the new arrivals that could be present in the host country. In the presence of a weak personality, this situation can lead to self-depreciation, ethnic self-hatred, and even increases in alcohol consumption and drug abuse. Hispanic-American women, in general, have been found to increase their consumption of alcohol as they become more acculturated in this country (Markides, Krause, & Mendes De Leon, 1988).

In studying the process of acculturation of Cuban Americans,

Garcia and Lega (1979) were able to demonstrate that just as Cuban Americans were affected by the cultural characteristics of the American society, the American population was also influenced by the Cuban-American culture. Along these lines, Szapocznik, Kurtines, and Fernandez (1980) demonstrated that the general Hispanicity of Cuban Americans can be measured in accordance with adequate psychometric standards, thus permitting a bicultural approach to the understanding of the acculturation process.

When addressing issues related to the migration and acculturation of Hispanics, we must also discuss the seminal work of Rogler, Gurak, and Cooney (1987) in regard to socioeconomic levels, stress, and mental health. In this respect, they examined the interactions between life-event stressors, intrapsychic and social resources, and psychological problems of the Hispanic migrant groups in New York City. They concluded, among other things, that Hispanic migrants who enter the host society at the bottom of the socioeconomic ladder experience acculturation problems, become isolated from their supportive network systems, and tend to develop psychological problems and distress. Along the same lines, it is a well-accepted fact that the rates of all types of psychopathology in the lowest socioeconomic stratum are about 2½ times the rates of psychopathology in the highest socioeconomic categories (Dohrenwend, Dohrenwend, Gould, Link, Neugebauer, and Wunsch-Hitzig, 1980). Additionally, most migrant groups tend to enter the host nation at a lower socioeconomic level than the one they belonged to in their native countries. These facts suggest that stress tends to concentrate more at the bottom of the socioeconomic system (Portes & Bach, 1985; Borjas & Tienda, 1985). Catalano and Dooley (1977) also addressed this issue from a different perspective. They found that economic changes also affect life-event changes, thus having an impact on psychological problems. For instance, they demonstrated that unemployment rates provide the best predictor for psychological distress, particularly depression.

In discussing migration, adaptation, and acculturation, we must also focus on the issue of intergenerations. In this respect, the contributions of Rogler, Cooney, and Ortiz (1980) are extremely important and relevant. While their work focuses on Puerto Ricans, their findings are applicable to any migrant group, and to Cuban Americans in particular. They concluded that ethnic identity is influenced by the receptivity to external influences that stem from the host society and by the length of exposure to the host environment. Furthermore, they also found that the migrant's level of education and age at arrival into the host nation have a major and independent effect upon the ethnic identity of mothers, fathers, and children. Additionally, they demonstrated that the child's level of education and age at arrival to the host nation are significantly and independently related to changes in ethnic identity in their family. Arrival at a younger age restricts past social experiences in the native country, thus leading to an ethnic identity that is less established. Concomitantly, higher levels of education tend to weaken the formation of the ethnic identity since it provides for a stronger exposure to alternative values and lifestyles. This is certainly true whether the education was received in the native country or the host nation. As a result of all this, the ethnic identity of the second-generation migrants is less accentuated than the ethnic identity of the first-generation migrants. Along these lines, men tend to have weaker ethnic identities than women since they are more often employed at jobs away from home, thus increasing their opportunities to share values with the members of the host society. However, strong family cohesion might minimize the intergenerational differences between parents and their children.

In summary, during their settlement process in the United States, Cuban Americans have gone through most of the acculturation phases previously discussed. However, contrary to other Hispanic-American ethnic groups that have settled in this country, Cuban Americans have primarily used an integrational model of adaptation rather than assimilation, separation, or marginalization. We think that, among other factors, this integrational model of acculturation has been a strong causative factor in the success achieved by the Cuban Americans who settled in this nation. In using the integrational model of adaptation, Cuban Americans have been able to retain, for the most part, their Cuban heritage and cultural traditions, while at the same time engaging quite well in positive interactions with the host society. Moreover, the integrational model of acculturation has been said to be the most beneficial adaptation process for any migrant group settling in a new society, particularly from a mental health point of view (Barry & Kim, 1988).

SOCIOCULTURAL CONSIDERATIONS

Cuban Americans residing in the United States strongly display most of the sociocultural characteristics prevailing in Cuba before they departed for the United States (Queralt, 1984). This rich cultural heritage is one of the most important factors in the successful adaptation of Cuban Americans in the United States. Cuban Americans have definitely been able to maintain their sense of ethnic identity in this country.

The Cuban-American presence in the "little Havana" area of Miami is a vivid example of the profound transformation of this American neighborhood into one in which Cuban heritage and tradition are abundant. In other areas of the United States where Cuban Americans have settled such as in Union City, New Jersey, and in Washington Heights of New York City, one could also observe a microcosm of what has happened in little Havana in Miami. The preservation of the Cuban culture by Cuban Americans in the United States has definitely been a supportive environment in which ethnic identification, cultural reinforcement, and social integration can take place. Needless to say, these positive cultural factors have been of great value in maintaining a positive mental health attitude. This, in turn, will lead to mental health preservation and mental illness prevention (Ruiz, 1982a).

The existence of these Cuban-oriented communities within the United States has also permitted the development of a very strong Cuban ethnic image. The dissemination of traditional Cuban cultural characteristics such as music, clothing, literature, mass media, and cuisine have all been at the core of the Cuban network system of support in the United States. The Cuban-American process of acculturation, which is based on an integrational model, can also be an ideal model for other Hispanic-American migrant groups. A good example of this process of acculturation is the feelings of equality that Cuban-American migrants have always maintained vis-a-vis the Anglo population of this nation. Indeed, coming to the United States as political refugees is a part of the Cuban heritage. In the past, many illustrious Cuban political figures such as Jose Marti also migrated to this country during periods of political repression in Cuba.

Positive sociocultural factors, predominant among Cuban Americans in the United States, have already been alluded to in the medical literature (Rumbaut & Rumbaut, 1976). In essence, they are: (1) the presence of high levels of education, occupational skills, and motivation for success among Cuban migrants, (2) the development of good support systems within their communities and neighborhoods, and (3) the maintenance of a strong sense of Cuban identity and ethnic consciousness. Despite the difficult and traumatic experiences faced by

Cuban migrants, their strong cultural values and ethnic identity have permitted them to successfully integrate within the American society. The core concept of the Cuban family tradition is based on "love," "dignity," and "respect." These ever-present Cuban cultural values should always be kept in mind when attempting to assess the "behavior" of Cuban Americans. For instance, Cuban-American children and young adults are expected to show respect to their parents at all times, as well as to the elderly. Furthermore, Cuban Americans are taught to maintain their dignity at all costs and under all circumstances. Moreover, Cuban Americans are always encouraged to express love in every interpersonal relationship. An appropriate balance of these three relevant Cuban-American cultural characteristics will undoubtedly result in good mental health maintenance, as well as in mental illness prevention. At the same time, when these cultural values can no longer be maintained, abnormal behavior will probably develop and psychopathology could emerge.

These three pillars of the traditional Cuban-American culture are very much in opposition to the key norms of the Anglo cultural tradition, which is based primarily on economic success and independence. The mutual respect of these different cultural norms between Cuban Americans and Anglos, as well as the fostering of interchanges between both ethnic groups, has led to the highly successful integrational model of acculturation used by Cuban Americans.

Besides the Cuban cultural values of love, dignity, and respect, we must also be aware of the presence of a strong extended family network system among Cuban Americans. Contrary to Anglo families, which are rather nuclear in nature and mainly formed by parents and their offspring, Cuban-American families are composed of a large number of members such as grandparents, cousins, uncles, and aunts. Moreover, in some instances it also includes friends, neighbors, and employers. However, we must also note here that, on occasion, Cuban Americans have proceeded to assimilate with the majority culture. When this occurs, the extended family network system becomes fragmented and may disappear completely. In these cases, the extended family network system is quickly replaced by the more traditional Anglo nuclear family structure. At times, socioeconomic improvements also favor or accelerate the emergence of the nuclear family system among Cuban Americans. When these changes take place too rapidly, the end result could be behavioral abnormalities on the part of Cuban Americans, such as guilt feelings and identity conflicts. In many of these cases, the psychopathology could reach such proportions that mental health assessment and treatment are required. Unfortunately, many American/Anglo mental health practitioners are frequently unaware of the presence of this traditional extended family network system among Cuban Americans and its utilization as a tool for mental health prevention and/or treatment is not frequently taken into consideration. This extended family network system on the part of Cuban Americans living in the United States is definitely an excellent source of support and strength when Cuban Americans develop and/or confront crisis, particularly in the mental health sphere.

I would like now to discuss the most relevant religious beliefs used by the Cuban-American population living in the United States. In doing so, I will primarily focus on the religious beliefs that have a direct bearing on the mental health system of Cuban Americans. As a result of Spain's influence in Cuba during the colonization period, Cubans, for the most part, are Catholics. However, in spite of this strong Catholic influence, Cubans have also professed less traditional religious practices.

Cuban attitudes toward mental illness are largely a reflection of class. This reflection developed in Cuba much before the migration process to the United States took place. This situation is, generally, not well known in the mental health professional sector of the United States, and therefore, should be discussed thoroughly. In this context, we should look at the expression of mental health problems not as a manifestation of a disease, but rather as the result of an illness that is influenced by the native culture (Ruiz & Langrod, 1982). Two factors play a major role in this issue. One has to do with the ethnic composition of the population in Cuba. Out of an estimated 10,000,000 Cubans living on the island, 73% are white, representing the race of the Spanish colonizers, and 27% are black or mulatto, representing the slavery process originated in West Africa during the colonization period. The other has to do with the large proportion of rural population that exists in Cuba. In 1962, 42% of the Cuban labor force on the island was dedicated to agriculture, while only 18% was dedicated to industry (Navarro, 1972). Along these lines, the way in which mental illness is conceived and expressed, as well as the process of seeking and complying with mental health care, are both directly related to social classes. This situation not only applied to the Cubans in the island, but also to most Cuban Americans who settled in the United States after 1959.

In essence, there are three major types of mental health care-seeking behavior. The first type relates to the upper-class population, which was represented by a small number of people in Cuba, but is considerably larger among Cuban Americans in the United States. This group, by and large, sought mental health care among private providers. In Cuba, it was in Havana that these specialists tended to concentrate. For this group, the classical individually oriented long-term therapy or short-term hospitalization was the prevailing mode of intervention.

The second type is represented by the middle- and lower middle-class sections of the population. Although not so large in Cuba, it comprises the largest Cuban-American sector in the United States. For this group, the mental health care-seeking behavior in Cuba depended on their geographical location. If urban, particularly in Havana, their mental health care relied primarily on the many mutualistic clinics that existed in Cuba at that time. These clinics operated on a prepaid basis and offered unlimited medical services to their members. Social and recreational services were also provided, thus giving additional incentives for participation. These social and recreational services were, in a way, a small-scale imitation of the large private clubs that existed in Cuba for the exclusive benefits of the wealthy. Those who did not belong to these mutualistic clinics sought mental health care from private providers on a short-term or a crisis intervention basis. For this group, private services generally resulted in severe financial hardships. For the middle and lower middle-class Cuban Americans residing in the United States, a similar health care pattern prevails.

The third type is represented by the lower class. In Cuba, this group resided predominantly in rural areas. This large sector of the population was affected by all of the ills resulting from the socio-economic oppression that prevailed on the island at that time. For this class, access to health and mental health care was very restricted. Further, there were only four alternatives available to them: (1) the tolerance of the deviant behavior; (2) the locking up of their afflicted relatives in their homes; (3) hospitalization in the State Hospital of Havana (Mazorra), where conditions were very inhumane; and (4) the seeking of mental health care via folk healing practices.

For lower-class Cuban Americans living in the United States, the last alternative has become very popular when seeking out mental health services. In this context, folk healing practices are very much tied to various religious beliefs. The folk practices of *Santeria* and *Brujeria* were brought to Cuba by the black slaves taken to Cuba from

Africa during the colonization period. Due to the inner forces of these religious practices, they became quite widespread in Cuba, not only among the black and mulatto populations, but among a large number of whites as well. For Cuban Americans residing in the United States, these folk practices offer a unique opportunity to reinforce their Cuban heritage and tradition.

Santeria, as practiced in Cuba and in the United States, is the most evolved and influential of the Afro-Cuban religious beliefs (Sandoval, 1977). In a way, Santeria represents the search for an identification between the African gods of the slaves and the Catholic saints of their masters. In accordance to Santeria, illness is considered to be the result of either natural or supranatural forces. Brujeria has its roots in West Africa, particularly in Nigeria, Congo, and Guinea (Cabrera, 1971). At the start of the slavery process, the Brujeria practice was confined to the black slaves of Cuba in what was called the "Secret Society of Abakua," while later it spread a great deal across all socioeconomic levels and races of Cuba (Cabrera, 1970). Similarly to Santeria, Brujeria regards illness, whether physical or mental, as being caused by either natural or supranatural forces. In accordance with Santeria and Brujeria, mental symptoms can be perceived as signs of strength, and therefore are highly accepted and regarded by their followers (Ruiz & Langrod, 1976).

In the United States, Santeria is rapidly growing among Cuban Americans (Sandoval, 1977). This growth has been attributed to factors such as (1) lower class Cuban Americans have gained socioeconomic power in this country; (2) Santeria is a past-oriented religion, as well as a present-oriented system of care, and is thus easily accepted by Cuban Americans; (3) the Catholic religion has lost considerable prestige among Cuban Americans; and (4) the practice of Santeria, as well as Brujeria, permits Cuban Americans to tightly close ranks with their cultural values and traditions.

MENTAL HEALTH CONSIDERATIONS

Clinically speaking, there are two major considerations in regard to the mental health services of Cuban Americans: (1) attitudes and expectations toward mental health care and (2) treatment compliance. In many ways they are both interrelated and should be discussed together. In general, Cuban Americans expect psychiatrists and other mental health professionals to be quite knowledgeable in their field, and thus to know the causative factors of their illness as well as how to cure them. These expectations must be faced and addressed early in the treatment process. Otherwise, the patient's much-needed trust and confidence will be quickly lost. If the confidence and the trust of the patient are secured and maintained, mental health professionals will have no problems in also securing the patient's active cooperation and participation with the treatment recommended. In this regard, Cuban Americans, by and large, tend to seek acceptance and approval from the professionals who treat them, even for issues of day-to-day living. These expectations are very much culturally rooted due to the fact that professionals, particularly physicians, tend to represent authority and power because of the perceived knowledge, wisdom, and skills generally attributed to them.

Another important trait among Cuban Americans that has great relevancy in the treatment process is the role of certain key family members. On most occasions, professionals treating Cuban Americans should request the assistance of fathers, mothers, grandparents, and any other member who can exercise influence and authority within the family constellation. Failure to do this will undoubtedly lead to treatment sabotage, poor compliance, and above all, underutilization of the family network system.

Along these lines, the age of the treating professional can also play a major role in the treatment process. Cuban Americans tend to believe that older professionals have more knowledge and wisdom than younger ones. This belief is culturally vested in the power and respect that Cuban Americans deposit on their elder family members, particularly grandparents. For Cuban Americans, older people have been able to acquire knowledge and wisdom throughout the years, as well as the capacity to stay calm and serene during times of crisis. Unless young professionals are capable of proving to Cuban Americans early in the treatment process that they possess excellent clinical skills and experience, they will most likely lose them as patients.

From another context, we must also discuss the belief held by some Anglo professionals that, in general, Hispanic Americans do not believe in the efficacy of modern psychiatric treatment (Philipus, 1971; Kline, 1969). Intrinsically related to this issue is the concept of the causative factor of mental illness shared by many Cuban Americans. While in most instances the disease-biological model is the one that prevails, illness can, on occasions, be perceived as supranatural, particularly among Cuban Americans from lower social class levels or who have come from the rural areas of the island. For psychiatrists and other mental health practitioners, the respect for this belief in the supranatural is of utmost importance. Otherwise, the result will be frustration, confusion, and above all, poor treatment compliance (Ruiz & Ruiz, 1983).

This problem becomes further aggravated by the lack of distinction between illness and disease that is usually present among most medical practitioners. Disease is generally perceived by the medical profession as a malfunction of the biologic or physiologic process, while illness encompasses personal, interpersonal, and environmental reactions. Thus, illness can be shaped by psychosocial and cultural factors that relate to the perception, explanation, and assessment of the discomforts experienced by the patients. Generally speaking, illness problems resulting from disease are mainly perceived by patients as part of their entire disorder (Lipowski, 1969). Perhaps many Cuban Americans seek mental health care from indigenous healers because these folk healers often emphasize illness problems, and thus always try to provide their patients a meaningful explanation for their illness. Further, they also tend to respond with sensitivity to the personal, family, and community problems that generally surround their illness (Horton, 1967). Physicians, by and large, are mainly interested in the discovery and treatment of disease. In so doing, they tend to disregard the patient's perception of the illness, as well as their beliefs in the causative factors of the illness (Ruiz, 1977). Undoubtedly, the lack of focus on illness by the medical profession is largely responsible for the patients' noncompliance with their treatment and for their families' dissatisfaction with the professional health care system (Davis, 1968). In this regard, the interactions between practitioners and Cuban-American patients become further complicated when practitioners and patients belong to different ethnic groups, religions, and social classes. Thus, it is of paramount importance to recognize that practitioner-patient interactions could be based on different ideologies and transactions that encompass major discrepancies in therapeutic values, prognostic expectations, and treatment goals.

Among the most common psychosocial conflicts observed in treatment noncompliance are: (1) low frustration tolerance, (2) acting out, (3) denial of the sick role, (4) excessive gains from the sick role, and (5) display of aggressive behavior. In this regard, a unique challenge relates to the decision on the part of the mental health practitioners to recommend psychotherapy for Cuban-American patients. In general, Cuban Americans see physicians as proponents of the biological/ medical model and expect them to prescribe medications. When practitioners do not do this, they tend to be devalued by their patients. This situation, can be avoided, however, if practitioners are cognizant of this possibility and dedicate time to educate their patients appropriately about the benefits of psychotherapy, as well as other cognitive and behavioral approaches.

Additionally, we must also be aware of the difficulties confronted by many Cuban-American patients who cannot verbally express their feelings and emotions. In general, most mental health practitioners are trained to be passive in the therapist-patient interactions and to be observants rather than active participants in the therapeutic setting. This attitude might prove to be ineffective in the treatment process with Cuban Americans. On most occasions, it might be more effective for practitioners to be active and directive, at least in the beginning phases of the treatment.

Moreover, in day-to-day mental health clinical practice with Cuban-American patients, professionals must be aware of the cultural specific characteristics, as well as the unique somatic manifestations and adaptive behavior displayed by Cuban Americans (Ruiz, 1982b). For instance, transient paranoia is occasionally observed among Cuban Americans in connection with the political climate that is characterized by the ups and downs in relations between Cuba and the United States. By and large, these paranoid manifestations are mild and generally do not require chemotherapeutic or somatic treatment. The most effective intervention is the appropriate understanding of the deeply rooted political instability that prevails among the Cuban-American population. These paranoid trends are more commonly observed during the period following the arrival of the Cuban migrants to the United States. It also surfaces among Cuban Americans during periods of political uneasiness. Adaptational anxiety is also commonly observed among Cuban Americans during their settlement period in the United States. When present, Cuban Americans experience a sense of despair and anxiety. These clinical manifestations are generally associated with the loss of status, prestige, and financial resources suffered by Cubans when they leave the island. Conflicts relating to the exposure to new values and norms definitely reinforce this symptomatology. By and large, this type of anxiety was very often seen during the 1960s, but was also very prominent during the early 1980s following the Mariel exodus.

Commonly, adaptational anxiety reappears among Cuban Americans during periods of relocation within the United States. In these cases, it is important for the therapist not to rely too much on psychodynamic interventions, but rather to use environmental manipulations, as well as reinforcement of the Cuban cultural values and traditions. Once dignity and respect are restored in the patient, the anxiety tends to disappear rapidly. Traditional psychodynamic approaches should be kept for patients who do not respond to the environmental manipulations and the reinforcement of the cultural values.

Furthermore, the manifestation of adaptational anxiety is often expressed in terms of behavioral maladaptions which, although having similar characteristics to the more traditional anxiety disorders, are rather transient in nature. Additionally, depressive reactions secondary to diaspora are also frequently observed among Cuban Americans. Even though quite similar to situational depressions, they tend to affect Cuban Americans in relation to the political mood that prevails among them. When observed among recently arrived Cuban-American migrants, these transient depressions only require supportive measures. In this respect, the full utilization of the rich extended family network system is very much indicated (Rumbaut & Rumbaut, 1976). However, we must keep in mind that these depressive reactions might, at times, also be quite severe, particularly among older Cuban migrants. In these cases, chemotherapy and even electroconvulsive treatment are indicated. Particularly if they have lost property, loved ones, and their self-respect, suicide attempts are quite common among older Cuban-American migrants. In many instances, rapid hospitalization and somatic treatment are the appropriate treatment approaches to follow. For these older patients, group therapy approaches focusing on historic- and tradition-oriented themes are very beneficial. Furthermore, recommendation for relocation to Miami, Florida, should also be considered for those who reside in other parts of the United States.

Cuban-American migrants are definitely very sensitive to the loss of self-esteem resulting from threats to their dignity and self-respect. While these unique clinical manifestations among Cuban Americans can also be observed in other Hispanic American ethnic groups residing in this country, they are less prominent than among Cuban Americans. Moreover, it should also be mentioned here that the model of matching the treatment to the special characteristics and problems of Cuban Americans has proven to be quite successful (Szapocznik, Scopetta, & King, 1978). On the basis of this model, mutuality of patient-therapist expectations for treatment can be attained by adapting the treatment to the special characteristics of the Cuban-American patient and by focusing the treatment to their unique problems. When this method of treatment is used, issues such as preference for lineality in interpersonal relationships, present time orientation, activity orientation, and subjugation to natural/environmental conditions, all of which are quite common among Cuban Americans, can be easily resolved without any major acculturation/treatment problems. Undoubtedly, this ecological/structural therapy approach is quite effective in treating the acculturation-related dysfunctions suffered by Cuban Americans.

Also recent interest has been the response to pharmacotherapy approaches among some Hispanic–American populations. In this respect, Marcos and Cancro (1982) suggested that Hispanic Americans treated for depression require, in general, half of the dosage of tricyclic antidepressants that is customarily used with Anglo patients. Furthermore, they also demonstrated that Hispanic-American patients complain much more about the side effects of these drugs than Anglo patients. However, in another study it was advanced that Hispanic Americans treated with a wide range of psychotropic medications, including phenothiazines, antidepressants, and antiparkinsonians, required similar dosages to the Anglo population for comparable psychiatric disorders (Adams, Dworkin, & Rosenberg, 1984). So far, none of these biological findings have been specifically found among Cuban-American patients.

CONCLUSIONS AND RECOMMENDATIONS

The Cuban-American settlement in the United States, particularly during the last 30 to 35 years, has offered a unique perspective to the study of migration and acculturation. The Cuban-American pattern of adaptation/acculturation to this country, which is based on an integrational model, has proven to be very beneficial. In terms of sociocultural manifestations, Cuban Americans, for the most part, continue to adhere to their Cuban heritage and traditions. This is particularly true for first-generation Cuban-American migrants, though less so for second and third generations. From a mental health perspective, Cuban Americans have faced major stressors and challenges in their quest for adaptation and settlement in the United States. As a result of these inner and outer psychosocial conflicts/stressors, a series of psychological and emotional disturbances have emerged among some of them. In many situations, strong cultural connotations have colored these psychological manifestations. In this study, I have attempted to present an updated view of the Cuban-American population with emphasis, as previously highlighted, on their migration pattern, acculturation process, sociocultural characteristics, and mental health manifestations. In this respect, however, we need to look at the future, and thus attempt to elucidate the most appropriate pathway to follow.

I contend that research should be the number 1 priority, not only for the improved mental health treatment of Cuban Americans, but also for all ethnic minority groups residing in the United States. However, we must also attempt to define the type of research needed. In this regard, Rogler (1989) offers excellent theoretical formulations to be tried: Culturally sensitive research efforts, including ethnographic methodology, instrumentation, and conceptualization of the research paradigm, are definitely some of the best contributions made in this area. Furthermore, Rogler's formulations on what culturally sensitive research is has fostered in the field a unique perspective of the most relevant cultural connotations insofar as mental health treatment access and treatment modalities are concerned (Rogler, Malgady, Costantino, & Blumenthal, 1987). The application of research into appropriate treatment interventions has also been greatly advanced by work on the use of *cuentos* within folktale therapy in the treatment of Hispanic children and adolescents; this has already been widely recognized in the mental health field (Malgady, Rogler, & Costantino, 1990). Unfortunately, the research agenda ahead of us is a most challenging one. We must continue to pursue this research agenda. Hopefully, it will be completed in the not too distant future. Our patients need it, our community wants it. The task is ours.

REFERENCES

Adams, G.L., Dworkin, R.J., & Rosenberg, S.D. (1984). Diagnosis and pharmacotherapy issues in the care of Hispanics in the public sector. *American Journal of Psychiatry, 141*, 970–974.

Amaro, N., & Portes, A. (1972). Una sociologia del exilio: Situacion de los grupos Cubanos en los Estados Unidos [A sociology of exile: Situation of the Cuban groups in the United States]. *Aportes, 23*, 6–24.

Berry, J.W., & Kim, U. (1988). Acculturation and mental health. In P. Dasen, J.W.

Berry, & N. Sartorius (Eds.), *Health and cross-cultural psychology: Toward applications*. London: Sage.

Borjas, G.J., & Tienda, M. (1985). *Hispanics in the U.S. economy*. New York: Academic Press.

Cabrera, L. (1970). La sociedad secreta Abakua. Coleccion del Chichereku [The secret society Abakua. Collection of Chichereku]. Miami: Editorial C.R.

Cabrera, L. (1971). El monte. Coleccion del Chichereku. Miami: Editorial C.R.

Catalano, R., & Dooley, D. (1977). Economic predictors of depressed mood and stressful life-events in a metropolitan community. *Journal of Health and Social Behavior, 18*, 292–307.

Davis, M. (1968). Variations in patients' compliance with doctors advice. *American Journal of Public Health, 58*, 274–288.

Dohrenwend, B.P., Dohrenwend, B.S., Gould, M.S., Link, B., Neugebauer, R., & Wunsch-Hitzig, R. (1980). *Mental illness in the United States*. New York: Praeger.

Garcia, M., & Lega, L.I. (1979). Development of a Cuban ethnic identity questionnaire. *Hispanic Journal of Behavioral Sciences, 1*, 247–261.

Horton, R. (1967). African traditional thought and western science. *Africa, 37*, 50–60.

Kline, L.Y. (1969). Some factors in the psychiatric treatment of Spanish-Americans. *American Journal of Psychiatry, 125* 1674– 1681.

Lipowski, Z.J. (1969). Psychological aspects of disease. *Annals of Internal Medicine, 71*, 1197–1206.

Malgady, R.G., Rogler, L.H., & Costantino, G. (1990). Hero/heroine modeling for Puerto Rican adolescents: A preventive mental health intervention. *Journal of Consulting and Clinical Psychology, 58*, 469–474.

Marcos, L., & Cancro, R. (1982). Pharmacotherapy of Hispanic depressed patients: Clinical observations. *American Journal of Psychotherapy, 36*, 505–512.

Markides, K., Krause, N., & Mendes De Leon, C.F. (1988). Acculturation and alcohol consumption among Mexican-Americans: A three generational study. *American Journal of Public Health, 78*, 1178–1181.

Navarro, V. (1972). Health, health services and health planning in Cuba. *International Journal of Health Services, 2*, 397–432.

Nielson, J., Rohter, L., Whitmore, J. (1980, April 21). Cubans vote with their feet [Run on the Peruvian embassy]. *Newsweek*, p. 53.

Philipus, M.J. (1971). Successful and unsuccessful approaches to mental health services for an urban Hispano-American population. *American Journal of Public Health, 61*, 820–830.

Portes, A., & Bach, R. (1985). *Latin journey: Cuban and Mexican immigrants in the United States*. Berkeley: University of California Press.

Queralt, M. (1984). Understanding Cuban immigrants: A cultural perspective. *Social Work*, March–April, 115–121.

Rogler, L.H. (1989). The meaning of culturally sensitive research in mental health. *American Journal of Psychiatry, 146*, 296–303.

Rogler, L.H., Cooney, R.S., & Ortiz, V. (1980). Intergenerational change in ethnic identity in the Puerto Rican family. *International Migration Review, 14*, 193–214.

Rogler, L.H., Cortes, D.E., & Malgady, R.G. (1991). Acculturation and mental health status among Hispanics: Convergence and new directions for research. *American Psychologist, 46*, 585–597.

Rogler, L.H., Gurak, D.T., & Cooney, R.S. (1987). The migration experience and mental health: Some formulations relevant to Hispanics and other immigrants. In M. Gaviria & J.D. Arana (Eds.), *Health & behavior: Research agenda for Hispanics* (pp. 72–84). Chicago: The University of Illinois at Chicago.

Rogler, L.H., Malgady, R.G., Costantino, G., & Blumenthal, R. (1987). What do culturally sensitive services mean? The case of Hispanics. *American Psychologist, 42*, 565–570.

Ruiz, P. (1977). Culture and mental health: A Hispanic perspective. *Journal of Contemporary Psychotherapy, 9*, 24–27.

Ruiz, P. (1982a). The Hispanic patient: Sociocultural perspectives. In R.M. Becerra, M. Karno, & J.I. Escobar (Eds.), *Mental health and Hispanic Americans* (pp. 17–27). New York: Grune & Stratton.

Ruiz, P. (1982b). Cuban Americans. In A. Gaw (Ed.), *Cross-cultural psychiatry* (pp. 75–85). Boston: John Wright.

Ruiz, P. (1985). Cultural barriers to effective medical care among Hispanic-American patients. *Annual Review of Medicine, 36*, 63–71.

Ruiz, P., & Langrod, J. (1976). The role of folk healers in community mental health services. *Community Mental Health Journal, 12*, 392–398.

Ruiz, P., & Langrod, J. (1982). Cultural issues in the mental health of Hispanics in the United States. *The American Journal of Social Psychiatry, 2*, 35–38.

Ruiz, P., & Ruiz, P.P. (1983). Treatment compliance among Hispanics. *Journal of Operational Psychiatry, 14*, 112–114.

Rumbaut, R.D., & Rumbaut, R.G. (1976). The family in exile: Cuban expatriates in the United States. *American Journal of Psychiatry, 133*, 395–399.

Sandoval, M. (1977). Santeria: Afrocuban concepts of disease and its treatment in Miami. *Journal of Operational Psychiatry, 8*, 52–63.

Szapocznik, J., Kurtines, W.M., & Fernandez, T. (1980). Bicultural involvement in Hispanic American youth. *International Journal of Intercultural Relations, 4*, 353–365.

Szapocznik, J., Scopetta, M.A., & King, O.E. (1978). Theory and practice in matching treatment to the special characteristics and problems of Cuban immigrants. *Journal of Community Psychology, 6*, 112–122.

U.S. Bureau of the Census. (1991). Current population reports, series P-20, No. 449. Washington, DC: U.S. Government Printing Office.

AUTHOR NOTES

Correspondence concerning this chapter should be addressed to: Professor Pedro Ruiz, MD, Mental Sciences Institute, Department of Psychiatry and Behavioral Sciences, The University of Texas Health Science Center, 1300 Moursund, Houston, TX 77030.

CHAPTER 5

AN EXPLORATION OF DEPRESSION AMONG MEXICAN-ORIGIN AND ANGLO ADOLESCENTS

Robert E. Roberts, PhD

Professor of Behavioral Sciences, School of Public Health, Director, Social Psychiatry Research Group, and Associate Director, Center for Cross-Cultural Research, The University of Texas Health Center at Houston

In this paper I explore a topic much neglected by mental health researchers: the experience of depression among minority youth. More specifically, I investigate adolescent depression comparing youth from two ethnocultural groups: those of Mexican origin and non-Hispanic whites (or Anglos). The rationale for this focus emanates from the fact that there are virtually no data on depression among minority children and adolescents. An indication of the paucity of information is that three recent comprehensive reviews of the literature cite not a single study of depression among Hispanic youth and only a handful that focus on African-American youth (see Feldman & Elliott, 1990; Stiffman & Davis, 1990; Fleming & Offord, 1990). Comparative data contrasting youth from different ethnic populations are rare.

A further indication of the lack of empirical research on depression among minority youth is illustrated by the comprehensive compilation of research on Hispanics in the United States (Olmedo & Walker, 1990). This compendium contains 1,498 abstracts of articles published during the period 1980–1989, and not a single article provides data on the incidence, prevalence, or risk factors for depression among Mexican-origin adolescents.

The dearth of data on depression among minority adolescents is not surprising, given the lack of data on adolescent depression in general. There have been few community-based epidemiologic studies of adolescent depression. Perusing the studies that have been done, it is difficult to identify a coherent empirical pattern due to the great diversity in research designs, study populations, and methods of case ascertainment. For example, Fleming and Offord (1990) identified nine epidemiologic studies of clinical depression and reported that prevalence of current depression ranged from .4 to 5.7% in the five studies reporting such data. The mean prevalence of current major depression disorder (MDD) was 3.6%. There is equal diversity in studies that focus on depressive symptoms. Five school-based studies using the Beck Depression Inventory (BDI) report mean scores ranging from 6.0 to 10.3; the average was 8.6 (Baron & Perron, 1986; Gibbs, 1985; Teri, 1982; Kaplan et al., 1984; Doerfler et al., 1988). Five studies, all school-based, have used the Center for Epidemiologic Studies Depression Scale (CES-D; Schoenbach et al., 1982; Tolor & Murphy, 1985; Doerfler et al., 1988; Roberts et al., 1990; Manson et al., 1990). The latter four studies reported mean scores for the CES-D that ranged from 15.8 to 19.5, with a mean of 17.3. Using the standard CES-D caseness criterion of 16 or greater, prevalence of depressive symptoms ranges from 45 to 55%.

Given the limited number of epidemiologic studies of adolescent depression in general, it is not surprising that few studies focusing on race or ethnic status have been published. Again, even among this small subset of studies the findings are not cohesive. While some studies found no evidence of ethnic differences in adolescent depression (Kandel & Davies, 1982; Doerfler et al., 1988; Garrison et al., 1990; Manson et al., 1990), others reported that minority adolescents report greater levels of depressive symptoms (Schoenbach et al., 1982; Emslie et al., 1990), and others that minority youth have lower levels of depression (Doerfler et al., 1988). But again, it is difficult to draw any firm conclusions concerning ethnic status and risk of depression from these studies because they employ different measures of depression and they also focus on different ethnic minority adolescents (African American, Hispanic American, Native American, etc.).

Only one published study has had depression among Mexican-origin adolescents as its focus, contrasted with Anglo and African Americans. Weinberg and Emslie (1987) completed a survey of 3,294 high school students using the BDI and the Weinberg Screening Affective Scale (WSAS). The sample contained 1,825 black, 783 Anglo, and 598 Hispanic adolescents. On the BDI, 22.6% scored as mildly depressed (scores of 10–15) and 18.1% as moderately to severely depressed. Hispanic girls had the highest proportion with moderate to severe depression (31.2%); Anglo boys had the lowest (8.6%). Using the Weinberg criteria, 13.4% were depressed, with Hispanic girls most depressed (22.4%) and Anglo boys least depressed (7.9%).

A more recent study (Roberts & Sobhan, 1992) investigated differences in prevalence of depressive symptoms among adolescents from diverse ethnocultural groups. Data from a national survey of persons 12 through 17 years of age ($n = 2,200$) were analyzed, comparing symptom levels of Anglo, African, Mexican-origin, and other Hispanic Americans using a 12-item version of the Center for Epidemiologic Studies Depression Scale (CES-D). Overall, the results indicated differences in rates of depression. Girls reported more symptoms of depression than boys in every ethnic group. Among the ethnic groups,

Mexican-origin boys reported more depressive symptoms than other boys and the same was true for Mexican-origin girls, although to a lesser extent. Logistic regression of three different caseness scores (16+, 21+, 31+), adjusting for age, gender, perceived health, and occupation of the primary wage earner in the household, indicated that only Mexican-origin adolescents reported more depressive symptoms than the Anglo majority. The relative risk ranged from 1.46 to 1.83.

My purpose here is to further explore ethnic differentials in adolescent depression, contrasting non-Hispanic whites (Anglos) with Mexican Americans. The data reported are taken from one of the research initiatives (Study B) of the Center for Cross-Cultural Research. This particular study involved a school-based survey of middle school students in New Mexico.

COMPARISON OF MEXICAN AMERICAN AND NON-HISPANIC WHITE ADOLESCENTS

The data presented are taken from a series of three pilot studies conducted in Las Cruces, a community in southern New Mexico, in the 1990–1991 school year. Las Cruces has a population of approximately 100,000. With nearly 19,500 students, the district is the second largest public school system in the state. In terms of ethnic composition, the district is 41% Anglo, 56% Hispanic (virtually all Mexican origin), and 3% other. Approximately half of the students (49%) are from families with incomes below the poverty level. There are five middle schools (grades 6 through 8) with a total enrollment of more than 4,000.

Study B involved conducting surveys in the three largest middle schools (grades 6 through 8). The first was conducted in December 1990, the second in April 1991, and the third in May 1991. In the December pilot, a number of measures from the Oregon Adolescent Depression Project (OADP; Roberts et al., 1990; Hops et al., 1990) were included: the Center for Epidemiologic Studies Depression Scale, four suicide items, eight loneliness items, and five anxiety items.

The April and May pilot studies included the same OADP measures from the first pilot (CES-D, four suicide items, eight loneliness items, five anxiety items). The second pilot study included additional measures of psychopathology as well as selected measures of risk factors from the OADP battery. The second pilot added the short form (15 items) of the Weinberg Screening Affective Scale (WSAS, Weinberg and

Emslie, 1987) and the 33-item Mood and Feelings Questionnaire (MFQ) developed by researchers at Duke University (Elizabeth J. Costello, personal communication). The third pilot included the same mental health measures as the first. In both the second and third pilot, a subset of the psychosocial risk factor battery from Oregon was included: social networks (2 items), coping (17 items), mastery (3 items), self-esteem (9 items), family cohesion (5 items), subjective probability (5 items), dysfunctional attitudes (9 items), social skills (7 items), emotional reliance (10 items), and a modified Harter scale (7 items) (see Hops et al., 1990).

Completed questionnaires were obtained from 2,614 subjects. Of these, 943 (36%) were Anglo and 1,371 (52%) were Mexican American. The remainder were American Indian, black, other Hispanic groups, or those who claimed mixed ancestry. All of these individual categories were made up of small numbers of subjects.

The primary measure of depression was the CES-D, which was included in all three assessment batteries. The reliability and validity of the CES-D scale have been assessed on adult clinic populations (Craig & Van Natta, 1973; Weissman et al., 1977; Roberts et al., 1989) and on adult respondents from a number of community studies (Comstock & Helsing, 1976; Radloff, 1977; Roberts, 1980). Fewer studies have involved adolescents. However, the data that are available indicate that the CES-D exhibits similar operating characteristics with adolescents as with older populations in terms of reliability, dimensionality, and efficacy in detecting clinical depression (Wells et al., 1987; Schoenbach et al., 1982; Roberts et al., 1990; Roberts et al., 1991).

Since one of the principal objectives of Study B was to assess the operating characteristics of a range of measures with Mexican-origin adolescents, two other measures of depression were included. The WSAS (Weinberg & Emslie, 1987) is a brief instrument (12 items) developed specifically as a screen for clinical depression among children and adolescents. The MFQ, a new scale containing 33 items, was developed by Costello and her colleagues at Duke to use as a first-stage instrument with children and adolescents. Both scales are in self-report format.

Also included in the analyses are two additional measures that are correlated with depression: suicide ideation and loneliness. The suicide measure consists of four items, formatted exactly like the items in the CES-D. These items, used initially in the Oregon study, have an alpha reliability of .85. The eight loneliness items were adapted from the

UCLA loneliness measure (Russell, Peplau, & Cutrona, 1980) by the author and also included in the Oregon survey. The items exhibit good reliability (α = .78) and demonstrate good construct validity (Roberts, Lewinsohn, & Seeley, 1991).

Ethnic status was ascertained by an item that asked: What is your racial/ethnic background? The response categories were: (1) White, non-Hispanic; (2) Black or African American; (3) Hispanic (Mexican, Cuban, Puerto Rican, or other American); (4) American Indian/ Eskimo/Aleut; (5) Asian/Pacific Islander; and (6) Other. Here, the contrast of interest is white, non-Hispanic and Mexican American.

Mean age of the combined samples (schools) was 12.1 (12.1 for Anglos and 12.2 for Mexican Americans). The samples were 51.4% girls (50.3% for Anglos and 51.9% for Mexican Americans). About 84% of the Mexican American youth spoke Spanish, but only 4.2% considered themselves Spanish dominant. Nearly 80% reported they spoke mostly English or both languages equally. Questions about the educational level of parents were not very successful. More than 40% of the Anglo and 47% of the Mexican-origin youth did not report their father's education, for example. Of those who did report data for this item, 54.1% of the Anglos and 17.6% of the Mexican Americans reported their father had completed four years or more of college. Another indicator of the adolescent's social environment is household composition. One indicator frequently used is whether youth reside in one- or two-parent households. In Las Cruces, 26.4% of the Anglo and 33.5% of the Mexican-origin adolescents resided in one-parent households ($p < .001$).

The three measures of depression exhibited acceptable levels of internal consistency–reliability across subgroups. The CES-D had alphas of .86 for Anglos and .89 for Mexican Americans. Reliabilities for the MFQ were .93 for Anglos and .95 for Mexican Americans. For the WSAS, the reliabilities were .80 for Anglos and .73 for Mexican Americans. As can be seen in Table 1, the three depression scales were intercorrelated about as highly as their respective reliabilities permit. Clearly, all three are measuring a common dimension, which can be called depressive mood or depressive symptoms. There were no differences in the pattern of correlations between the two ethnic groups or between genders.

Results for the CES-D are presented in Table 2. Data are presented using mean scores and the usual "caseness" criterion of 16 or greater. For more severe impairment, scores of 21+ and 31+ have been used (Barnes

Table 1. Intercorrelation of Mental Health Measures Used in Las Cruces

Scale	CES-D	MFQ	WSAS	RULS-8	S4
CES-D	—	.71	.70	.60	.62
MFQ		—	.78	.65	.67
WSAS			—	.63	.61
RULS-8				—	.43
S4					—

Note: CES-D = Center for Epidemiologic Studies Depression Scale; MFQ = Mood and Feelings Questionnaire; WSAS = Weinberg Screening Affective Scale; RULS-8 = Roberts UCLA Loneliness Scale; S4 = Suicide items, Oregon Adolescent Depression Project.

& Prosen, 1984; Roberts et al., 1991). On the basis of our results from the Oregon study (Roberts et al., 1991), a score of 24+ proved the most efficient screen for DSM-III-R clinical depression among adolescents, so it is used as well. As can be seen, regardless of the scoring procedure used, the Mexican-origin adolescents reported significantly more depression using the CES-D, about 50% more using the criteria of 31 or greater and 24 or greater. The question of how these results compare to other studies naturally arises. The Oregon study focused on high school students who were predominantly non-Hispanic and white. In that study, the prevalences were 48% (16+), 31.4% (21+), and 12.1% (31+) for the various criterion scores. Thus, the Mexican-origin middle school adolescents are more similar to the Oregon high school sample using 16+ and 21+, but the two Anglo samples are more similar using a score of 31+.

Table 2. Scores for the CES-D

Scale scores	Anglo	Mexican American	p values
Mean	14.4	17.7	$p < .001$
%16 +	35.3	48.7	$p < .001$
%21 +	25.3	35.9	$p < .001$
%24 +	19.9	29.9	$p < .001$
%31 +	12.1	18.1	$p < .005$

Table 3. Scores for the WSAS

Scale scores	Anglo	Mexican American	*p* values
Mean	2.6	3.3	$p < .001$
%7 +	10.4	14.9	$p < .05$
%Yes on Q13	11.9	19.8	$p < .05$

Results for the WSAS are presented in Table 3. Weinberg and Emslie (1987) recommended a score of 7 or greater as indicating clinically significant depression. In terms of both mean scores and this caseness criterion, the Mexican-origin adolescents reported significantly more depression. Weinberg and Emslie also suggested that an affirmative response to Item 13 (I wish I were dead) be construed as clinically significant. Almost twice as many Mexican American youth endorsed this item as Anglo youth.

To my knowledge, the MFQ has no standard caseness criterion. Accordingly, only mean scores were examined. The mean score was 14.8 for Anglos and 19.1 for Mexican Americans ($p < .001$).

Given the high correlation between suicide ideation and depression and between loneliness and depression (see Table 1), the two groups of adolescents also were compared on these two measures. The two ethnic groups were very similar on loneliness. The mean scores were 6.9 for Anglos and 7.1 for Mexican Americans (*NS*). In comparison, the mean score on the loneliness items in the Oregon adolescent depression study was 7.1 for those high school students (Roberts, Lewinsohn, and Seeley, 1993). In contrast, there was a significant difference in suicide ideation between Anglos (1.5) and Mexican Americans (2.5, $p < .001$).

Clearly, on the basis of these comparisons using crude prevalence and mean scores, the Mexican-origin adolescents appear at substantially greater risk for depressive symptomatology.

Although we were limited by the nature of the study in the range of risk factors we could include in Las Cruces, we did attempt to assess two important constructs—socioeconomic status and acculturation (Rogler, Cortes, & Malgady, 1991). The former was measured by parental education and the latter by language use. Table 4 presents results for education of fathers. As can be seen, for those subjects who provided this information, there were no differences between Anglos and Mexican

Table 4. Prevalence of CES-D Scores Among Anglos and Mexican Americans, by Father's Education

	CES-D							
	Score above 16 (%)		Score above 21 (%)		Score above 24 (%)		Score above 31 (%)	
Highest level achieved	Anglo	Mexican American	Anglo	Mexican American	Anglo	Mexican American	Anglo	Mexican American
High school or less	38.3	41.5	26.3	31.1	22.8	26.5	14.4	14.6
Less than college	35.7	36.4	30.2	27.3	22.5	22.7	14.7	12.9
College or more	30.7	36.8	21.3	22.4	16.4	18.4	10.3	15.2

Note: $p > .05$ for all Anglo-Mexican American comparisons.

Americans in CES-D prevalence by education of father. As expected, there was an inverse relationship within each ethnic group.

Given the oft-reported relation between physical health status and depression, this association is presented in Table 5. Overall, there is a clear linear relation between prevalence of reported symptoms of depression and perceived health status. However, when the two ethnic groups are contrasted, the pattern of association is somewhat mixed. For those who reported their health as fair or poor, there was no difference between Anglos and Mexican Americans on any of the four prevalence measures. For those who reported their health as good, Mexican Americans reported significantly more depression on all measures. For those who reported their health as excellent, Mexican Americans reported more depression for 16+ and 21+ symptoms, but not the other two measures.

Table 6 presents results on language use and CES-D prevalence rates. As can be seen, those Mexican-origin adolescents who reported using English and Spanish equally and those who reported using mostly Spanish reported consistently higher rates of depressive symptoms. In fact, there is a striking linear relationship, e.g., the greater the use of English, the lower the prevalence of depression.

As one final comparison, we contrasted the two groups of adolescents on their perceptions of their overall mental health (Table 7). As can be seen, significantly fewer of the Mexican Americans perceived their mental health as excellent ($p < .001$) and more reported their mental health as fair ($p < .01$). Very few in either group perceived their mental health as poor.

To further explore the experience of depressive symptomatology among Anglo and Mexican American adolescents, the CES-D items were ranked in terms of response frequency and a Spearman rank correlation was calculated, following Roberts et al. (1990). Across the two ethnic groups, the two rank orders were found to be significantly correlated ($rs = .86, p < .01, n = 20$). Although the two rank orders were not identical, they were sufficiently alike to suggest that the saliency of the CES-D symptoms is very similar for adolescent Anglo and Mexican Americans. The greatest disparity in the rank order of symptoms between the two ethnic groups was observed for "felt sad" (Anglos, 13 and Mexican Americans, 5) and "felt people disliked me" (Anglos, 6 and Mexican Americans, 12). For all other items, the difference in ranks was 5 or less.

In fact, gender seems to play a much more important role than ethnicity in determining salience of depressive symptoms. As can be

Table 5. Prevalence of CES-D Scores Among Anglos and Mexican Americans, by Perceived Physical Health

	CES-D							
	Score above 16 (%)		Score above 21 (%)		Score above 24 (%)		Score above 31 (%)	
Perceived physical health	Anglo	Mexican American	Anglo	Mexican American	Anglo	Mexican American	Anglo	Mexican American
Fair/poor	51.3	57.7	40.7	44.5	34.5	39.9	24.7	26.4
Good	37.1	44.7**	25.7	33.8**	19.0	27.8***	11.4	16.3*
Excellent	27.2	39.6**	18.6	27.4**	15.3	20.8	9.3	11.5

*$p < .05$; **$p < .01$; ***$p < .001$.

Table 6. CES-D Scores by Language Use Among Mexican-American Adolescents

Language use	%16 +	%21 +	%24 +	%31 +
English Only[1]	36.0	25.1	19.9	11.7
Mostly English	40.1	28.9	24.3*	26.0**
Both Equally	53.2***	42.5***	35.4***	20.9***
Mostly Spanish	60.9***	51.6***	42.2***	23.4**

[1]English only = base
* $p < .05$; ** $p < .01$; *** $p < .001$.

seen in Table 8, the rank correlations are lower between genders, and lowest between Mexican-origin males and females. Table 9 summarizes differences in item salience between boys and girls in the two ethnic groups. The most discrepant item in both ethnic groups was "could not get going," with boys much more likely to endorse this item. Girls, by contrast, were more likely to endorse items on crying, eating, being sad, and being depressed.

To assess the relative contribution of ethnic status on prevalence of reported depressive symptoms, logistic regression was used to estimate the relative risk (odds ratio) of depression among Mexican-origin adolescents. As can be seen in Table 10, the crude prevalence rates suggest that the relative risk of Mexican Americans is about 1.5 times that of their Anglo counterparts. There was little variation across the four prevalence measures on the CES-D. We then calculated odds ratios, adjusting for the confounding effects of age, gender, perceived physical

Table 7. Perceived Mental Health Status

	Overall	Anglo	Mexican American
Excellent	$n = 763$	$n = 319$	$n = 340$
	29.2%	33.8%	24.8%***
Good	$n = 1347$	$n = 470$	$n = 739$
	51.5%	49.8%	53.9%
Fair	$n = 396$	$n = 122$	$n = 235$
	15.1%	12.9%	17.1%**
Poor	$n = 71$	$n = 26$	$n = 35$
	2.7%	2.8%	2.6%

* $p < .05$; ** $p < .01$; *** $p < .001$.

Table 8. Spearman Rank Correlations for CES-D

Group	Rho	*p*-values
Boys vs. girls	.7026	$p < .01$
Anglo vs. Mexican American	.8568	$p < .01$
Boys vs. boys	.8568	$p < .01$
Girls vs. girls	.8812	$p < .01$
Anglo boys vs. girls	.7579	$p < .01$
Mexican-American boys vs. girls	.6741	$p < .01$

Table 9. Gender Differences in Salience of CES-D Items

Anglo Americans	Male rank	Female rank
Q20: I could not get "going"	8	17
Q2: I did not feel like eating	14	5
Q14: I felt lonely	16	10
Q17: I had crying spells	20	14
Mexican American	**Male rank**	**Female rank**
Q20: I could not get "going"	7	18
Q17: I had crying spells	19	12
Q18: I felt sad	11	4
Q6: I felt depressed	11	5
Q11: My sleep was restless	8	14

Table 10. Odds Ratios (OR) for Depressive Symptoms (CES-D) Among Mexican-Origin and Anglo Adolescents

CES-D score	Crude OR	*p*	Adjusted OR*	*p*
16+	1.54 (1.30, 1.82)	< .001	1.08 (.85, 1.39)	.508
21+	1.54 (1.28, 1.84)	< .001	1.01 (.77, 1.32)	.945
24+	1.61 (1.32, 1.95)	< .001	1.05 (.79, 1.40)	.756
31+	1.45 (1.15, 1.84)	< .001	1.00 (.70, 1.42)	.980

*Adjusted for age, gender, perceived physical health, and father's education.

health, and father's education level. As can be seen in Table 10, adjustment eliminated the observed differential completely. After adjustment, there is no net ethnic effect in depressive symptoms. Cognizant of the findings by Kessler and Neighbors (1986), we tested for first- order interaction effects (e.g., ethnic status × father's education). None were statistically significant. In fact, the adjusted odds ratios indicated only two of the risk factors examined were significant (data not shown). Gender was a marginally significant correlate of depressive symptoms. However, perceived physical health was a strong correlate. The adjusted odds ratios were 2.28–2.75 ($p < .001$).

CONCLUSIONS

Overall, results from Study B in Las Cruces are consistent with what has been reported for adults in other studies of ethnic status and psychological distress (Roberts & Vernon, 1984; Vega et al., 1985; Roberts, 1987; Moscicki et al., 1989; Kessler & Neighbors, 1986; Kolody et al., 1986; Angel & Guarnaccia, 1989; Golding & Burnam, 1990). That is, crude prevalences are higher among girls, those with lower socioeconomic status, those who perceive their physical health as worse, and Mexican Americans. In Las Cruces, Mexican-origin adolescents are about 1½ times as likely to report depressive symptoms as are Anglo adolescents. However, as is often the case in studies of adults, adjusting for demographic and socioeconomic differences between the two ethnic groups eliminates the observed differences. The findings on ethnic status and gender among adolescents also corroborate those from other studies of this age group (Roberts et al., 1990; Roberts et al., 1991; Emslie et al., 1990; Garrison et al., 1990). The data from middle school students in Las Cruces are congruent with those from the 1985 national survey by the National Institute on Drug Abuse (Roberts & Sobhan, 1992). We found crude prevalences were higher among girls, those who perceived their health as worse, and Mexican Americans. Mexican Americans were at least 1½ times more likely to report depressive symptoms than Anglos, adjusting for the effects of age, gender, perceived health, and socioeconomic status. In the only other published study comparing Anglo-, African-, and Mexican-American adolescents on depression, Emslie et al. (1990) also found girls and Mexican Americans to be at greatest risk in terms of crude rates.

While these results are comparable to what has been reported in studies of adults and provide additional data on ethnocultural variations in depressive symptoms among adolescents, we are still left with several unresolved questions.

I should note in passing that the issue of whether the ethnic differences often reported are the product of differentials in social status or of ethnic culture is still very much unresolved. My two studies of adolescents provide mixed results, as do studies of adults. For example, Ulbrich, Warheit, and Zimmerman (1989) find mixed support for the Kessler and Neighbors outcome, depending on the measures examined. On the other hand, Somervell et al. (1989), using data from the Epidemiological Catchment Area (ECA) studies, found no evidence of interactions of race with household income.

Our findings on health status and depression are consistent with other studies of both adults (Kaplan et al., 1987; Aneshensel, Frerichs, & Huba, 1984; Turner & Noh, 1988; Wells, Golding, & Burnam, 1988) and children (Gortmaker et al., 1990; Cadman et al., 1987). Physical illness clearly is a powerful risk factor for depression, on the basis of evidence from both cross-sectional and longitudinal studies. The fact that our results are based on self-report (one item on perceived health) detracts little from our conclusions. Our research with adults (Kaplan et al., 1987) indicates that such self-report measures are strongly related to subsequent mortality experience, thus confirming their validity as measures of health status. We also have evidence that perceived health is highly correlated with other measures of physical health status across different ethnic groups (Roberts & Lee, 1980). Even so, there is also evidence that responses of Mexican Americans to questions about physical health problems differ from those of, say, Anglos or blacks (Angel & Thoits, 1987). In the absence of other measures of somatic health, we can only infer that poor physical health status is a major risk factor for adolescent depression, and that it is a risk factor in different ethnocultural contexts. What remains to be demonstrated is the risk attributable to different dimensions of physical health (acute versus chronic conditions, disability or functional limitation, duration, severity, etc.) in different ethnocultural groups, assessed prospectively.

As a survey that had as its major focus reliability and validity of selected measures with younger adolescents, the Las Cruces survey collected data on relatively few factors known or hypothesized to increase the risk for depression (see, for example, Paykel, 1982; Lewinsohn et al., 1985; Roberts, 1987; Rutter et al., 1986; Hops et al., 1990; Kovacs, 1989) among both adults and adolescents. While the questionnaires included various indicators of social status, they did not include measures of social stress, social support, coping, cognitive styles, self-esteem, peer relations, or family interaction (as examples) in all three middle schools. Beyond these types of factors, there is a set of factors believed to be salient for understanding the mental health of minority populations such as Mexican Americans. Among these are language, level of acculturation, and adherence to traditional values (Cervantes & Castro, 1985) as well as ethnic identity and socialization (Phinney and Rotherham, 1987; Alba, 1990). In the case of the findings we presented here indicating more depression among Mexican American adolescents, we are unable to explore whether this difference is due, for example, to differential exposure to stress or differential vulnerability (see, for example, Ulbrich et al., 1989). However, no study of minority adolescents to date has incorporated such a comprehensive range of putative risk factors, and the same could be said for studies of adults.

One dimension of the ethnic experience in the United States, particularly as it relates to the Mexican-origin population, is acculturation. Although acculturation has been described as a "strategic research event" by Rogler and his colleagues (Rogler, Cortes, & Malgady, 1991), our understanding of the role the acculturative process plays in the psychological adaptation (or lack thereof) of ethnic minorities remains poor. In fact, one would have to search very hard to find a body of empirical results more disparate (see Rogler, Cortes, & Malgady, 1991). The only measure included in the Las Cruces study relevant to the construct of acculturation was an item on language use. The data clearly indicate that increasing use of English greatly decreased the risk of depression among the Mexican-origin adolescents.

The results from Las Cruces are consistent with other data on this issue. As Rogler, Cortes, & Malgady (1991) have noted, studies have consistently found that exposure to, use of, and mastery of the English language appear to be the important components of acculturation, and I would argue probably the most salient variable in the perception and manifestation of psychological dysfunction. I agree with Rogler and his colleagues that what is needed now is research on how the experience of acculturation is juxtaposed, socially and psychologically, in the lives of persons of Mexican and other Hispanic origin.

The data present a somewhat mixed picture at this point. Three studies find that Mexican-origin adolescents are at greater risk of depression when crude prevalences are examined. However, in the two papers that have examined adjusted prevalences (actually, odds ratios), one (Las Cruces) finds no elevated risk and the other (NIDA) does find such risk. Clearly, more data are needed to resolve this question. Data also are needed to assess the risk for clinical depression. Essentially all studies of ethnic status and psychological disorder among adolescents have relied on nonclinical or nondiagnostic measures of dysfunction, to the exclusion of clinical disorder (for an exception, see Bird et al., 1988). Symptoms of depression are highly prevalent among adolescents in general and are the source of considerable suffering. Better understanding of their etiology and consequences is needed. However, the absence of measures of clinical depression omits the more serious forms of depressive illness. From an epidemiologic perspective, the difference in prevalence is substantial. For example, studies indicate the prevalence of clinical depression among adolescents is perhaps 3 to 4% (Fleming & Offord, 1990; Roberts et al., 1991). In the only study of clinical depression among Hispanic youth, Bird et al. (1988) report the 6-month prevalence of depression/dysthymia in Puerto Rico was 2.8%. Several alternative procedures for assessing clinical disorder that are suitable for use in community studies of adolescents are now available (American Academy of Child and Adolescent Psychiatry, 1987). As yet, no findings have been published on the prevalence of clinical depression among African- or Mexican-American adolescents or comparing rates of clinical depression between the majority and minority adolescent populations. Given the limited data on the mental health of minority adolescents, more comparative research is needed of depressive symptoms and clinical depression, of the relationship between these two manifestations of depressive phenomena, and of ethnocultural background as a possible unique risk for such dysfunction.

REFERENCES

Alba, R.D. (1990). *Ethnic identity: The transformation of white America.* New Haven: Yale University Press.

American Academy of Child and Adolescent Psychiatry. (1987). Structured diagnostic interviews for children and adolescents. *Psychiatry, 26*, 611–675.

Aneshensel, C.S., Frerichs, R.R., & Huba, G.S. (1984). Depression and physical illness: A multiwave, nonrecursive causal model. *Journal of Health and Social Behavior, 25*, 350–371.

Angel, R., & Guarnaccia, P.J. (1989). Mind, body, and culture: Somatization among Hispanics. *Social Science Medicine, 28*, 1229–1238.

Angel, R., & Thoits, P. (1987). The impact of culture on the cognitive structure of illness. *Culture, Medicine and Psychiatry, 11*, 465–494.

Barnes, G.E., & Prosen, H. (1984). Depression in Canadian general practice attenders. *Canadian Journal of Psychiatry, 29*, 2–10.

Baron, P., & Perron, L.M. (1986). Sex differences in the Beck Depression Inventory scores of adolescents. *Journal of Youth and Adolescence, 15*, 165–171.

Bird, H.R., Canino, G., Rubio-Stipec, M., Gould, M.S., Ribera, J., Sesman, M., Woodbury, M., Huertas-Goldman, S., Pagan, A., Sanchez-Lacay, A., & Moscoso, M. (1988). Estimates of the prevalence of childhood maladjustment in a community survey in Puerto Rico. The use of combined measures. *Archives of General Psychiatry, 45*, 1120–1126.

Bureau of the Census. (1980). The 1980 U.S. census of population. Alphabetical index of industries and occupations. Washington, DC: U.S. Government Printing Office.

Cadman, D., Boyle, M., Szatmari, P., & Offord, D.R. (1987). Chronic illness, disability, and mental social well-being: Findings of the Ontario child health study. *Pediatrics, 79*, 805–813.

Cervantes, R.C., & Castro, F.G. (1985). Stress, coping, and Mexican American mental health: A systematic review. *Hispanic Journal of Behavioral Sciences, 7*, 1–73.

Comstock, G.W., & Helsing, K.J. (1976). Symptoms of depression in two communities. *Psychological Medicine, 6*, 551–563.

Craig, T.J., & Van Natta, P. (1973). Validation of the community mental health assessment interview instrument among psychiatric inpatients. Working paper No. B-27a, National Institute of Mental Health, Center of Epidemiologic Studies, Rockville, MD.

Doerfler, L.A., Felner, R.A., Rowlison, R.T., Raley, P.A., & Evans, E. (1988). Depression in children and adolescents: A comparative analysis of the utility and construct validity of two assessment measures. *Journal of Consulting and Clinical Psychology, 56*, 769–772.

Emslie, G.J., Weinberg, W.A., Rush, A.J., Adams, R.M., & Rintelmann, J.W. (1990). Depressive symptoms by self-report in adolescence: Phase I of the development of a questionnaire for depression by self-report. *Journal of Child Neurology, 5*, 114–121.

Feldman, S.S., & Elliott, G.R. (1990). *At the threshold: The developing adolescent.* Cambridge, MA: Harvard University Press.

Fleming, J.E., & Offord, D.R. (1990). Epidemiology of childhood depressive disorders: A critical review. *Journal of American Academy of Child and Adolescent Psychiatry, 29*, 571–580.

Garrison, C.Z., Jackson, K.L., Marsteller, F., McKeown, R., & Addy, C. (1990). A longitudinal study of depressive symptomatology in young adolescents. *Journal of American Academy of Child and Adolescent Psychiatry, 29*, 581–585.

Gibbs, J.T. (1985). Psychosocial factors associated with depression in urban adolescent females: Implications for assessment. *Journal of Youth and Adolescence, 14*, 47–60.

Golding, J.M., & Burnam, M.A. (1990). Immigration, stress and depressive symptoms in a Mexican-American community. *Journal Nervous and Mental Disease, 178*, 161–171.

Gortmaker, S.L., Walker, D.K., Weitzman, M., & Sobol, A.M. (1990). Chronic conditions, and socioeconomic risks, and behavioral problems in children and adolescents. *Pediatrics, 11*, 267–276.

Hops, H., Lewisohn, P.M., Andrews, J.A., & Roberts, R.E. (1990). Psychological correlates of depressive symptomatology among high school students. *Journal of Clinical Child Psychology, 19*, 211–220.

Kandel, D.B., & Davies, M. (1982). Epidemiology of depressive mood in adolescents. *Archives of General Psychiatry, 39*, 1205–1212.

Kaplan, G.A., Roberts, R.E., Camacho, T.C., & Coyne, J.C. (1987). Psychosocial predictors of depression. *American Journal of Epidemiology, 125*, 206.

Kaplan, S.L., Hong, G.K., & Weinhold, C. (1984). Epidemiology of depressive symptomatology in adolescents. *Journal of American Academy of Child Psychiatry, 23*, 91–98.

Kessler, R.C., & Neighbors, H.W. (1986). A new perspective on the relationships among race, social class, and psychological distress. *Journal of Health and Social Behavior, 27*, 107–115.

Kolody, B., Vega, W., Meinhardt, K., & Bensussen, G. (1986). The correspondence of health complaints and depressive symptoms among Anglos and Mexican-Americans. *Journal of Nervous and Mental Disease, 174*, 221–228.

Kovacs, M. (1989). Affective disorders in children and adolescents. *American Psychologist, 44*, 209–215.

Lewinsohn, P.M., Hoberman, H., Teri, L., & Hautzinger, M. (1985). An integrative theory of depression. In S. Reiss & R. Bootzin (Eds.), *Theoretical issues in behavior therapy*. New York: Academic Press.

Manson, S.M., Ackerson, L.M., Dick, R.W., Baron, A.E., & Fleming, C.M. (1990). Depressive symptoms among American Indian adolescents: Psychometric characteristics of the CES-D psychological assessment. *Journal of Consulting and Clinical Psychology, 2*, 231–237.

Moscicki, E.K., Locke, B.Z., Rae, D.S., & Boyd, J.H. (1989). Depressive symptoms among Mexican Americans: The Hispanic health and nutrition examination survey. *American Journal of Epidemiology, 130*, 348–360.

Olmedo, E.L., & Walker, V.R. (1990). Hispanics in the United States: Abstracts of the psychological and behavioral literature, 1980–1989. Washington, DC: American Psychological Association.

Paykel, E. (1982). *Handbook of affective disorders*. New York: Guilford Press.

Phinney, J.S., and Rotherham, M.J. (1987). *Children's ethnic socialization: Pluralism and development*. Newbury Park, CA: Sage.

Radloff, L.S. (1977). The CES-D scale: A self-report depression scale for research in the general population. *Applied Psychological Measures, 1*, 385–401.

Roberts, R.E. (1980). Reliability of the CES-D scale in different ethnic contexts. *Psychiatric Research, 2*, 125–134.

Roberts, R.E. (1987). Epidemiological issues in measuring preventive effects. In R.F. Munoz (Ed.), *The prevention of depression: Research directions*. Washington, DC: Hemisphere.

Roberts, R.E., Andrews, J.A., Lewinsohn, P.M., & Hops, H. (1990). Assessment of depression in adolescents using the Center for Epidemiologic Studies Depression Scale. *Journal of Consulting and Clinical Psychology, 2*, 122–128.

Roberts, R.E., & Lee, E.S. (1980). The health of Mexican Americans. Evidence from the Human Population Laboratory studies. *American Journal of Public Health, 70*, 375–384.

Roberts, R.E., Lewinsohn, P.M., & Seeley, J.R. (1991). Screening for adolescent depression: A comparison of the CES-D and BDI. *Journal of the American Academy of Child and Adolescent Psychiatry, 30*, 58–66.

Roberts, R.E., Lewinsohn, P.M., & Seeley, J.R. (1993). *A brief measure of loneliness suitable for use with adolescents. Psychological Reports, 72*, 1379–1391.

Roberts, R.E., & Sobhan, M. (1992). Symptoms of depression in adolescence: A comparison of Anglo, African, and Hispanic Americans. *Journal of Youth and Adolescence, 21*, 639–651.

Roberts, R.E., & Vernon, S.W. (1984). Minority status and psychological distress reexamined: The case of Mexican Americans. In J.R. Greenley (Ed.), *Research in community and mental health*. Greenwich, CT: JAI.

Roberts, R.E., Vernon, S.W., & Rhoades, H.M. (1989). The effects of language and ethnic status on reliability and validity of the CES-D scale with psychiatric patients. *Journal of Nervous and Mental Disease, 177*, 581–592.

Rogler, L.H., Cortes, D.E., & Malgady, R.G. (1991). Acculturation and mental health status among Hispanics: Convergence and new directions for research. *American Psychologist, 46*, 585–597.

Russell, D., Peplau, A., & Cutrona, C. (1980). The revised UCLA Loneliness Scale: Concurrent and discriminant validity evidence. *Journal of Personality and Social Psychology, 39*, 471–480.

Rutter, M., Tizard, C.E., & Read, P.B. (1986). *Depression in young people*. New York: Guilford Press.

Schoenbach, V.J., Kaplan, B.H., Grimson, R.C., & Wagner, E.H. (1982). Use of a symptom scale to study the prevalence of a depressive syndrome in young adolescents. *American Journal of Epidemiology, 116*, 791–800.

Somerwell, P.D., Leaf, P.J., Weissman, M.M., Blazer, D.G., & Bruce, M.L. (1989). The prevalence of major depression among black and white adults in five United States communities. *American Journal of Epidemiology, 130*, 725–735.

Stiffman, A.R., & Davis, L.E. (1990). *Ethnic issues in adolescent mental health*. Newbury Park, CA: Sage.

Teri, L. (1982). The use of the Beck Depression Inventory with adolescents. *Journal of Abnormal Child Psychology, 10*, 277–284.

Tolor, A., & Murphy, V.M. (1985). Stress and depression in high school students. *Psychological Reports, 57*, 535–541.

Turner, R.J., & Noh, S. (1988). Physical disability and depression: A longitudinal analysis. *Journal of Health and Social Behavior, 29*, 23–37.

Ulbrich, P.A., Warheit, G.J., & Zimmerman, R.S. (1989). Race, socioeconomic status, and psychological distress: An examination of differential vulnerability. *Journal of Health and Social Behavior, 30*, 131–146.

Vega, W., Warheit, G., & Meinhardt, K. (1985). Mental health issues in the Hispanic community: The prevalence of psychological distress. In W. Vega & M. Miranda (Eds.), *Stress and Hispanic mental health: Relating research to service delivery*. Washington, DC: U.S. Government Printing Office.

Weinberg, W.A., & Emslie, G.J. (1987). Depression and suicide in adolescents. *International Pediatrics, 2*, 154–159.

Weissman, M.M., Sholmaskas, D., Pottenger, M., Prusoff, B.A., & Locke, B.Z. (1977). Assessing depressive symptoms in five psychiatric populations: A validation study. *American Journal of Epidemiology, 106*, 203–214.

Wells, K.B., Golding, J.M., & Burnam, M.A. (1988). Psychiatric disorders and limitations in physical functioning in a sample of the Los Angeles general population. *American Journal of Psychiatry, 145*, 712.

Wells, V.E., Klerman, G.L., & Deykin, E.Y. (1987). The prevalence of depressive symptoms in college students. *Social Psychiatry, 22*, 20–28.

AUTHOR NOTES

The research reported in this chapter was supported, in part, by grants MH44214 and MH44773 from the National Institute of Mental Health, by the Hogg Foundation for Mental Health, and by the Center for Cross-Cultural Research.

Appreciation is expressed to the students, teachers, and administration of Las Cruces Public Schools, particularly Dr. Bonnie L. Votaw, whose cooperation and interest made this study possible. Appreciation is also expressed to Katherine R. Higbee and Yuan-Who Chen, who assisted with analyses of the data and preparation of tables.

Correspondence concerning this chapter should be addressed to: Professor Robert E. Roberts, School of Public Health, University of Texas Health Science Center, Box 20186, Houston, TX 77225.

CHAPTER 6

MEXICAN WOMEN, MENTAL HEALTH, AND MIGRATION: THOSE WHO GO AND THOSE WHO STAY BEHIND

V. Nelly Salgado de Snyder, DSW

Research Professor, Mexican Institute of Psychiatry, Division of Epidemiology and Social Science Research, and Coordinator, Center for Psychosocial Research on Gender, San Lorenzo Huipulco-Tlalpan, Mexico

The process of international migration has two human components, both of which are equally important: those who go and those who stay behind. Most psychosocial research on international migration focuses on the immigrants and ignores their counterparts, spouses and children who stay in the community of origin but who suffer the social and psychological impact of the migration process as intensely as the immigrant.

For those who go, the process of migration involves a relocation to an unfamiliar context. People who migrate face an environment in which habits, values, and socialization practices acquired in the country of origin no longer apply. It has been proposed that migration, especially migration across international boundaries, involves a significant number of stressful experiences (Furnham & Bochner, 1986). Such experiences have been conceptualized as culture shock (O'Berg, 1960), acculturative stress, and cultural fatigue (Berry, 1988). It has been widely documented that the stressful experiences originating from the encounter of two different cultures are likely to cause confusion and uncertainty among immigrants (Furnham & Bochner, 1977). The conflicts associated with the cultural shock may persist until the immigrant becomes familiar with the mainstream and incorporates both the culture of origin and the host culture into an integral approach to life in the new country (Cohen, 1987).

Because the literature often describes the profile of the international immigrant as a young single male, immigrant women have been ignored until recently. There is now sufficient evidence that confirms women's active role in the migration process (Moretimer & Bryce-Laporte, 1981). If women do not go themselves, they play an important role in the decision-making process of their spouse's migration and as head of the household during his absence. Women, therefore, are anything but passive in the migration process.

For those who stay behind in the country of origin, the migration of family members to another country means an increasing number of new responsibilities and obligations as well as feelings of concern about the welfare of those who go to an unfamiliar context. Overall, very little is known about the psychological consequences of international migration on the dynamics and issues concerning the general welfare of wives and children of male immigrants. Women who stay face a different reality without the support of the husband, father, or son, as the case may be. Very few studies have focused on the changes that the family left behind must adapt to when the male head of household decides to cross the border in search of opportunities to improve his own and his family's life conditions (Chaney, 1980). The scattered evidence about what actually happens when adult men migrate for extended periods of time suggests that the family structure suffers considerable damage (Gordon, 1978, cited by Chaney, 1985). Women bear the burden of their own responsibilities as mothers and housewives in addition to their partners' responsibilities that include, among others, the financial survival of the domestic group.

MEXICO-U.S. MIGRATION

Migration from Mexico into the United States is a phenomenon that started in the 1880s with the construction of the railroad system in the United States and the imminent need for cheap labor. Later, with the "Bracero Program" in 1942, another large wave of Mexican immigrants arrived in the United States under farm worker contracts. Since then the migration of Mexicans to the United States has been a more or less stable phenomenon that depends on the fluctuation of both the U.S. and the Mexican economies (Arizpe, 1985).

Until recently, the available studies about Mexico-U.S. migration suggested that most of the immigrants to the United States were rural single men, young, undocumented, and with a low level of formal schooling. We know, however, that the sociodemographic profile of the immigrants to the United States has changed radically mostly because of the political and economic changes suffered in Mexico in the last decade. The changes in the demographic profile of the immigrant of the 90s are due to status variables such as higher education, urban or rural origin, and a higher proportion of women among the immigrants. In terms of numbers, De Oliveira (1984) suggested that during the mid-1970s and throughout the decade of the 1980s, the migration of Mexican women to the United States increased considerably.

In spite of the newer data regarding the demographic profile of Mexican immigrants, the lack of accurate information in terms of the number of men and women who migrate to the United States constitutes an important barrier for researchers interested in the topic. Several efforts have been made that provide approximations as to the number and sociodemographics of Mexican women who migrate to the United States.

One of such efforts is the work of Carrillo and Hernandez (1988), who conducted an analysis of the characteristics of the Mexican women who migrate to the United States using data from two independent studies conducted by the *Centro de Estudios de la Frontera Norte de México* (CEFNOMEX) and the Mexico-United States Program of University of California, San Diego. They studied 433 women residing in San Antonio, Los Angeles, Chicago, and San Diego. The results indicate that most of the immigrant women in the sample came from large Mexican cities. A very small proportion of the women had a previous migration experience (within Mexico), which suggests that women who migrate internationally have not necessarily migrated before. Of the women surveyed, two thirds reported they did not have a job in Mexico prior to their migration, and in fact their first job was in the United States. The educational level of the immigrant women was higher than the Mexican national average.

The issue of constant influx of undocumented Mexican immigrants to the United States has been a pressing one for politicians in recent years, particularly because a very large proportion of those who migrate to the United States do so without the documentation required by the U.S. government. Several researchers have suggested that although a large number of Mexican immigrants in the United States are legal workers, an even larger number of Mexicans living in the United States are probably undocumented immigrants (Estrada, 1987; Gastelum, 1991; Bustamante & Martinez, 1979). Gastelum (1991) indicated that men are overrepresented among the undocumented immigrants from Mexico because of the many risks involved in crossing the border. Undocumented male immigrants do not want their wives, daughters, or sisters to be placed in a risky situation that involves psychological and physical fatigue and often may also involve verbal and physical violence, extortion, incarceration, rape, etc. Therefore, Gastelum concluded that when women go to the United States, they are usually not alone but are accompanied by male relatives and bear proper documentation. Massey, Alarcon, Durand, and Gonzalez (1991) have reported similar findings.

Most of the studies conducted on Mexico-U.S. migration seem to consistently document that the preferred places for settling, once in the

United States, are California, Texas, New Mexico, Colorado, Arizona, and Illinois. In spite of being far from the border, Illinois is an industrial state and requires a large number of workers.

According to data collected between 1978 and 1979, California, Texas, New Mexico, Arizona, and Colorado absorb 8 out of 10 immigrants. California and Texas alone absorb 75% of the immigrants from Mexico; California absorbs 43.7%, Texas 27.4%, and Illinois 7.4% (CENIET, 1980). Similar data was reported by the Mexican National Population Council (CONAPO, 1987) through a survey conducted in 1984. The CONAPO reported that 55% of Mexican immigrants settle in California, 34.2% in Texas, 7.3% in Arizona, and the rest in various other states.

Since California receives the majority of Mexican immigrants, its demographic profile has changed considerably. One half of California's total population growth from 1970 to 1983 came from immigration, with Mexicans far and away the single largest group. Some Mexicans in California come from large cities, but most come from small villages and towns in rural Mexico. Experts have externalized that this wave of rural migration is profoundly transforming the state of California at all levels—cultural, economic, social, and demographic—and that more studies are needed to understand and respond to the needs of this population (Fletcher & Taylor, 1990).

Currently, the body of research literature addressing the social, cultural, and psychological characteristics of Mexicans living in the United States continues to grow. However, these studies seldom consider the role of women in international migration.

The purpose of this chapter is to present a review of some of the psychosocial issues and dynamics related to mental health that impact the life of Mexican women who directly or indirectly are affected by the process of international migration. Much has been written about the migration experience as a determinant of higher risk of psychopathology because of the number of negative stressors associated with that experience. However, the relationship between migration and psychopathology is mediated by other factors such as status variables, characteristics of the stressors, internal and external resources, and coping responses.

Cervantes and Castro (1985) proposed a psychosocial stress model by which it is possible to understand the process by which a mental disorder develops and manifests itself, examining the antecedents, determinants, and consequences of the behavioral patterns involved.

This model has been selected to organize the information in this chapter regarding the two groups under focus, Mexican women who go and those who stay behind. The following elements of the psychosocial stress model are included in this review: (I-II) Potential stressors, their perception and appraisal; (III) External resources (social support networks); (IV) Coping responses; and (V-VI) short- and long-term outcomes. It should be noted that the Internal Resources component of the Psychosocial Stress Model will not be addressed in a separate section, as are the other components, but integrated in the description of the other components. Finally, it is important to mention that the general sociodemographic status attributes of the population under analysis in this chapter do not vary greatly; they are adult women of low socioeconomic status who were born in Mexico, follow the Catholic faith, and have little education.

WOMEN WHO GO

The presence of women in international migration has been obscured by the fact that, until recently, most of those who dealt with immigration problems took it for granted that only young men migrated. However, as mentioned earlier, the Mexico-U.S. migration pattern in terms of gender composition has changed in the last two decades (De Oliveira, 1984). Many women who migrate north go as dependents, as part of a family unit headed by a man. However, there is an increasing number of single women who cross the U.S. border alone in search of work and opportunities for improvement.

Women today are moving from their homes in ever increasing numbers to the towns and cities of their own and other countries. In the past most women, if they went at all, journeyed with their menfolk. Today many female immigrants set out alone. Sometimes they go to establish a beachhead for those who will come afterward; in other cases they are mothers who migrate with dependent children but without men, or they are single women seeking ways to earn money and improve their life conditions.

Voluntary vs. Involuntary Migration

Women migrate for reasons similar to those given by men, that is, to improve the quality of life for them and their families through earnings in dollars. Women, however, because of the social limitations imposed by traditional gender roles, are involved in the migration process in ways that differ significantly from male migration. Women who go may do so independently (voluntary immigrants), or be forced, usually by the male head of the household (involuntary immigrants).

The voluntary immigrants tend to be more receptive to the new culture, are more willing to learn a new language, and overall have a more positive attitude toward the host country. The involuntary immigrants, on the other hand, are women who were not given the choice to go or to stay, but who had to obey an order imposed by the male authority. These women usually resent having been forced to migrate to an unfamiliar country and wish to return to their original communities. This group suffers the negative consequences of migration and acculturation in a higher degree than their voluntary counterparts (Salgado de Snyder, 1986).

In a study of 140 voluntary and involuntary Mexican immigrant women living in Los Angeles, Salgado de Snyder (1986) found that involuntary immigrants were more likely to have high scores in depressive symptomatology and feel unhappy with the decision to migrate. On the other hand, voluntary immigrants, women who took an active part in the migration process, had higher self-esteem and lower depression scores. Both groups of women reported they were generally satisfied with their life in the United States because of the opportunities to improve their education and occupation, and as a consequence, their financial status. Also important were the comforts offered by the American lifestyle (like household conveniences) that are not easily available to everyone in Mexico, such as frozen foods, dishwashers, washers, dryers, and other domestic appliances that help them considerably in carrying out their responsibilities as housewives, mothers, and working women. Another important consideration was the economic crisis in Mexico, which made life in that country extremely difficult. Overall, the women tended to see more advantages in migrating (opportunities for self-improvement) than disadvantages (missing family and friends, fearing deportation, etc.).

Potential Stressors: Their Perception and Evaluation

Immigration in and of itself is considered a very stressful experience in the lives of people. Several authors have suggested that the immigration experience can produce stressors along the continuum of transitional stages that the individual faces (Cervantes & Castro, 1985; Cohen, 1987). For instance, Salgado de Snyder (1986, 1987) reported that the women in her study expressed nostalgia and concern about the country and people left behind. Lein (1982) similarly reported the overwhelming nostalgia and sadness expressed by immigrants, especially those who had recently arrived and those who wanted to return to their country of origin.

The potential stressors encountered by Mexican immigrants are the result of the various demands for behavioral and attitudinal changes involved in the process of acculturation. The combination and chronicity of the social conditions surrounding the lives of Mexican immigrants (overcrowding, unemployment, discrimination, undocumented status, lack of health services, etc.) represent an important risk factor for the development of psychological disorders. Although many immigrants are motivated to adapt to their new environment, they may, especially at the outset, meet conditions that Seligman (1975) refers to as producing reactions of learned helplessness. The main condition he mentions is the absence of a clear connection between tried behavior and expected results. This principle can be applied to new immigrants when learning new interaction habits, role requirements, and institutional arrangements.

Women who migrate are exposed to numerous potentially stressful situations. These have been explored in several studies aimed at identifying such stressors. This literature has been of considerable help for the understanding of the psychosocial dynamics in the lives of Mexican immigrant women.

Perhaps the very first article published about the impact of migration as a major source of stress in the lives of Mexican women was the work of Melville (1978). This qualitative study, in spite of its methodological limitations, provides important information about the situations encountered by Mexican women. Melville's study was conducted in Houston, Texas, with a sample of 46 documented and undocumented immigrant women from Mexico. Melville reported that all women interviewed encountered serious problems in their immigration process. One of the sources of stress reported was loneliness caused mainly by the separation from the extended family, friends, and culturally meaningful surroundings. Loneliness was reported as most intense among those women who did not live near relatives or friends and those who had to remain at home all day to take care of their children. Feelings of helplessness were also reported by the women who did not speak English and could not communicate with others or understand such things as food labels. They also reported a sense of dependency on husbands, friends, and relatives due to limitations in language and unfamiliarity with the geographical area.

Melville reported that health concerns were the most stressful situations for immigrant women, especially medical emergencies or giving birth. In these situations women experienced frustration and anxiety by not being able to communicate with the doctors and nurses. Other sources of stress included fear of deportation among those who were undocumented and changes in their interpretation of the rights and duties associated with gender roles. Most felt that because of their lack of knowledge of the English language, they were less able to fulfill traditional female duties such as doing the laundry; shopping for and preparing food economically; and locating fresh, traditional ingredients. Among the employed women there was a feeling of inadequacy and friction with their husbands because at times the women earned more than their spouses. Overall, most women in Melville's study wished to remain in the United States. Melville further suggested that permanence could be predicted by job availability and well-being of the children. Moreover, permanent residence was desired, particularly by those who migrated as a family. Melville's study represents an important contribution to the study of Hispanic women and, although far from conclusive, it opened new doors in the investigation of psychological characteristics and their relationship to the mental health status of Mexican immigrant women.

Salgado de Snyder's study (1986, 1987), aimed at identifying some of the stressful situations Mexican women have to face when they migrate to the United States, reported findings similar to those reported by Melville. The women interviewed experience family-related stressors such as concern for the welfare of family and friends left in Mexico. They also feared for the welfare of their own children for two major reasons: their perception that U.S. culture grants too much freedom to youngsters, and not having access to a social support network that could help with child care as in their country of origin. These women also reported high levels of stress associated with situations related to their adaptation to the American lifestyle. Some of the stressful situations were not being able to communicate at all in English or speaking English with an accent. Having trouble understanding American values and culture, fear of doing something wrong when socializing with Americans, feeling discrimination because of their ethnicity, and not being able to perform the duties expected of a "good Mexican wife" were also reported as stressful situations. The situation with the highest stress rating among this group of women was not having sufficient money to pay their debts.

The development of culturally relevant instruments for the assessment of psychosocial stressors such as the Hispanic Stress Inventory (HSI; Cervantes, Padilla, & Salgado de Snyder, 1990, 1991a) have been of great importance for understanding the psychosocial context of the lives of immigrants and later generation Hispanics. The HSI was developed using a methodology that relied extensively on the responses of community members, therefore capturing the most relevant psychosocial stressors experienced by immigrants and nonimmigrant Hispanics.

In a study conducted with immigrants using the Hispanic Stress Inventory (HSI), Salgado de Snyder, Cervantes, & Padilla (1990) reported that female immigrants were significantly more concerned than their male counterparts with the issues addressed in the HSI subscale of Cultural/Family Conflict. Three specific situations were evaluated with significantly higher stress scores by females than males: "Some members in my family have become very individualistic"; "I've had serious arguments with family members"; and "I've felt that being too close to my family interferes with my own goals." These three items reflect the impact of acculturation on the immigrant who on one hand seems to negatively evaluate the family members who seek personal goals, and on the other hand perceives family ties as barriers to self-development. It is possible that during the course of early migration, females experience more stress-related family situations and evaluate these experiences as more negative than the male immigrants. The shift from the social system in Mexico, which emphasizes very structured and limited gender roles, to one that sanctions freedom, together with the self-imposed goal to succeed financially in the new country, may affect the person's self-identity and further become a potential source of personal and familial conflict (Vazquez-Nuthall, Romero-García, & de León, 1987).

External Resources: Social Support Networks

Social support and social networks have generated much discussion and a diversity of definitions that have evolved over the years. All approaches, however, have a common focus on the helping properties and processes of the social-relational system in which individuals are located. Support networks are presumed to provide resources to deal successfully with stress and its psychological consequences.

It has been proposed that when migration takes place for the first time, a social infrastructure is developed that allows the initial move to become a massive and permanent phenomenon. With time, the social networks between the "sending" and "receiving" communities grow slowly but steadily and become a source of social, economic, and moral support for those involved in international migration (Mines, 1981, 1984).

The social networks of Mexican immigrants have been studied extensively (for example, Chavez, 1988; Vega & Kolody, 1985; Vega, Kolody, Valle, & Weir, 1991). The general findings of these studies suggest that adaptation to the new country seems highly dependent on the development of a social support system in the host country. The work of Vega and associates has been of special relevance in understanding the characteristics and functions of the social network of immigrant women from Mexico. These researchers suggest that among immigrant females, the lack of adequate interpersonal coping resources such as social support may be reflected in high levels of depressive symptomatology, this problem being more prevalent among those who are socially and structurally marginal (Vega, Warheit, & Meinhardt, 1984). Vega and Kolody (1985) concluded in another report that Mexican immigrants, when compared with U.S.-born Mexican Americans and Anglos, reported the least available support from friends and relatives combined and were less satisfied with it. They also proposed the notion that availability, actual use, and satisfaction are all different components of social support. Their data challenge the belief that all social support acts as a buffer against stress and that dense networks protect people from psychopathology. Vega, Kolody, and Valle (1986) have also studied the role of confidant support as mediator of depressive symptoms among immigrant Mexican women and concluded that having a confidant available with whom to share life experiences is of great importance among low-income Mexican immigrant women. Confidant support was found to be significantly correlated with general well-being in this population; therefore, confidant support is perhaps the most important mediator for facilitating the attainment of adaptation and overall well-being among immigrant groups.

In a more recent publication, Vega, Kolody, Valle, & Weir (1991) described the characteristics of the social support networks of immigrant Mexican women. Among their relevant findings are that contact with the family of origin is the most important source of emotional support, and that the ability of family and friends to provide support varies greatly. The most relevant implication of their findings is that early access to family support is the key factor in optimizing successful personal adaptation after immigration.

Coping Responses

Coping refers to a behavioral or psychological response aimed at reducing the negative effects of stressors (Flemming, Baum, & Singer, 1984). The importance of coping responses in the study of the process of migration is of extreme relevance; however, very little information is available on specific coping responses of immigrants in general. Some of the coping-related studies with people of Mexican origin have examined nongeneralizable samples such as college students and pregnant women (Mendoza, 1981; Perez, 1983). More recent studies with immigrants follow the suggestion of Cervantes and Castro (1985) who emphasized the need to identify specific coping responses for specific stressors. Among these studies are the work of Padilla, Cervantes, Maldonado, and Garcia (1988) and Salgado de Snyder (1986). In their qualitative study, Padilla et al. (1988) identified specific coping responses for specific situations such as not speaking English, not having a job, not having sufficient money to cover basic necessities, and general worries over family issues. Most coping responses given by the immigrants included well-planned actions for overcoming a particular barrier, but when specifically asked what they had done to deal with a personally stressful event, respondents had not followed their own advice.

In her study of immigrant women, Salgado de Snyder (1986) also solicited stress-specific coping responses. Her findings showed that most stressors were dealt with by direct-action responses aimed at the solution of the problem. For instance, economic/financial stressors were dealt with by actions such as borrowing money or working overtime. Marital/family stressors were confronted by communicating with their spouses or seeking advice from others. Cultural conflict stressors were faced also with strategies, such as taking English classes and carrying a dictionary, to overcome the language problem, or maintaining close contact with their cultural group through correspondence with family and friends in Mexico.

Espin (1987) also discussed specific coping strategies of immigrant women when dealing with issues of gender roles, acculturation, language, loss, and grief associated with the migration experience. In her article she emphasized the strategies to follow when providing psychotherapy to Latina immigrant women.

Cohen (1985) elaborated on the concept of control as a central mechanism for the regulation of behavior and management of stress among Latino immigrants. "*Controlarse*" (controlling oneself) involves several emotional states such as "*resignarse*" (resigning oneself to accept a stressful event), "*no pensar*" (refers to the avoidance of confrontation with the stressor), and "*sobreponerse*" (the effort to overcome a stressful situation by confronting the problem directly). Finally, it should be noted that although Espin and Cohen's papers do not deal directly with Mexican immigrant women but with a wider population of Latino immigrants, their work was included in this review because of the scarcity of information on coping responses among immigrants in general.

Short- and Long-Term Mental Health Outcomes

The lack of data about incidence and prevalence of mental health problems among immigrants from Mexico has been widely documented (e.g., Roberts, 1987). We know little about immigrants' rates of psychiatric disorders such as depression, schizophrenia, anxiety disorders, and drug and alcohol abuse. However, several cross-sectional studies are aimed at calculating the prevalence of some of these disorders—especially depressive symptomatology—as they relate to the stressors associated with the immigration experience. Among immigrant women from Mexico, depressive symptomatology has been assessed mostly by using the Center for Epidemiological Studies Depression Scale (CES-D) (Radloff, 1977).

Pearlin, Meneghan, Lieberman, and Mullan (1981) have suggested that among the global indicators of stress, depression is the most appropriate to study, especially when other sociodemographic antecedents are being simultaneously manipulated. Pearlin et al. (1981) indicate that the study of depression is important because it "provides a clear reflecting surface for detecting problematic aspects of social and economic organizations, for observing tenacious and unwanted experiences, and for appreciating the pivotal importance of self-concept. Perhaps more than the global psychological status, it offers the researchers a chance to identify and observe crucial elements of social life, emotional life, and of their interconnection" (p. 342).

For instance, Vega, Kolody, Valle, and Hough (1986) conducted an extensive study on immigrant women from Mexico residing in San Diego County and found very high rates of depressive symptomatology (mean = 15.71) and prevalence of cases among the population studied (41.53%). Immigrant women who were single heads of household were more likely to be in a vulnerable position for caseness. Also, women with 5 or fewer years of living in the United States had higher depressive symptomatology.

Warheit, Vega, Auth, and Meinhardt (1985) reported similar findings with immigrant women from Santa Clara County. Their findings indicate a consistent relationship between immigration and increased depressive symptomatology and psychosocial dysfunction scores. More recently, Vega, Kolody, Valle, and Weir (1991) reported that family support and family income were the best predictors of low depression scores for immigrant Mexican women.

Salgado de Snyder (1986) also found elevated CES-D scores among Mexican immigrant women (grand mean = 14.5). However, it was noted that high levels of depressive symptomatology were related to whether the immigrant women maintained a sense of control over the final decision to migrate. The CES-D scores of the involuntary immigrant group were significantly higher than those of the women who migrate voluntarily. Furthermore, the majority of the involuntary immigrants reached or exceeded the CES-D customary cut-off point of 16 points or more that indicates "caseness," and one fourth of the respondents reached scores of 24 or more.

The use of alcohol among Mexican immigrants has also been studied either as outcome or as a coping response associated with their immigration experience and related stressors. Before addressing the use of alcohol among Mexican immigrant women, it is important to emphasize that many immigrants from Mexico come to the United States as adults with drinking habits already shaped by the personal and social norms of their native country. And also, once settled in the United States, most immigrants maintain close ties with Mexico and Mexicans, which reinforces the retention of cultural norms and patterns associated with alcohol consumption. Therefore, it is very difficult to assess the strength of the influence of Mexican culture on drinking practices. Changes in alcohol consumption practices have been related to the circumstances surrounding immigration (legal or illegal), the entering group's economic opportunities, and changes in beliefs concerning the beneficial or negative aspects of alcohol consumption.

Most studies with Mexican immigrant women report that this group is characterized by abstinence or very light drinking (Caetano, 1985; Gilbert & Cervantes, 1985; Holk, Warren, Smith, & Rochat, 1984; Gilbert, 1987; Cervantes, Gilbert, Salgado de Snyder, & Padilla, 1991b). This pattern among Mexican immigrant women in the U.S. is very similar to the one of Mexican women in Mexico. Caetano and Medina-Mora (1986) report that while men begin drinking more heavily within the first 5 years following migration, immigrant women maintain their pattern of abstinence and low drinking no matter how long they have been in the United States. This gender difference never disappears but begins to narrow again in the second generation and continues to do so in succeeding generations. Vega (1992) suggested that immigrant women are more likely to consume alcohol in middle age, regardless of their generation or acculturation level, if their spouses drink. He further proposed that alcohol consumption among married immigrant women may be linked to depressive symptomatology and somatic disorders; this contention has not been empirically confirmed, however.

Cervantes et al. (1991) found there was no correlation between depression and drinking levels among females; depression was not predictive of drinking levels in females as in males. Depression was found positively associated with the benefits expected from alcohol use, however.

WOMEN WHO STAY BEHIND

The Mexican women who do not migrate to the United States with their spouses, whether by choice or obligation, have the double burden of carrying their own responsibilities as housewives and mothers and taking on whatever other tasks are necessary to keep the household going. These women are left in control of their resources, and one of their major duties is to maintain the family unit until such time as their spouses return. Women left behind—especially in the rural areas of Mexico—are expected to absorb the shock of their men's departure, keep and work the land, manage the household, take care of the children, and survive with economic remittances that may not be regular and that sometimes cease altogether.

The characteristics of Mexican rural "sending" communities summarized here have been described extensively in several studies (e.g., Fonseca & Moreno, 1984; Fernandez, 1988; Trigueros & Rodriguez, 1988). These communities are patriarchal. Most men follow the tradition of having very large families; they feel that parenthood is proof of their masculinity, strength, authority, and transcendency. The male head of household is the only person in charge of providing the money necessary for the survival of the family unit. Men work very hard in agriculture, teach their sons the tradition of working the fields, and migrate to the United States when the opportunity arises. Women, on the other hand, are considered inferior and subject to the authority of their male counterparts. They are expected to be obedient, dependent, passive, and self-sacrificing to the point of accepting physical abuse. Generally speaking, men in these communities are opposed to equality for women, which is one of the reasons men migrate and women stay in Mexico (Trigueros & Rodriguez, 1988). It should be noted that in these communities, women as well as men encourage traditional gender roles by perpetuating them through teachings and socialization practices that are passed on from parents to children for many generations.

When young couples in these communities decide to marry, they usually live in separate quarters in the home of the husband's parents. When the man decides to migrate, he does so knowing that his wife and children are under the care and authority of his parents. Within the family, the role of the woman left behind is very important, as her activity is what allows the family to stay together and survive while her husband is in the United States. Regardless whether her spouse sends money or not, the woman has to solve the economic problems involved in taking care of their children and household, agricultural fields, animals, etc. Often, the woman ends up sending money to her husband in the United states until he finds a job or until such time as he decides it is time to return home (Trigueros & Rodriguez, 1988).

We were unable to locate any studies conducted in these Mexican sending communities that explored the dynamics involved in the psychosocial functioning of women left behind. However, we were able to locate a number of very interesting studies dealing with the social, economic, cultural, and demographic changes in those communities (e.g., Fonseca & Moreno, 1987; Lopez-Castro & Pardo-Galvan, 1988; Trigueros & Rodriguez, 1989; Rousse, 1990; Gonzalez de la Rocha,

1989; Mines, 1981; Lopez-Castro, 1989). Some of these reports offer ethnographic information describing family arrangements before, during, and after migration.

The lack of information on the psychological and social dynamics led us to conduct a study of the psychosocial functioning of wives left behind in rural communities in Mexico. The data presented in the following sections were mostly derived from a project conducted with 202 wives of immigrants in nine rural and semirural communities identified by previous researchers as "sending" communities in the Mexican states of Jalisco and Michoacan (Salgado de Snyder, 1991).

Reasons given for the migration of the head of the household were varied, but all reflected the motivation for improvement in life conditions and in the economic situation of the family. Most women interviewed felt that the migration of their husbands was a good decision, but the women themselves had no desire to move to the United States with their husbands. Most husbands resided in California and Texas and worked as farmers. They visited their family in Mexico an average of twice a year for periods of approximately 2 weeks.

Potential Stressors: Their Perception and Evaluation

Gonzalez de la Rocha (1989) proposed that in communities (rural or urban) where male migration is the norm, an interesting phenomenon is observed as a consequence of the prolonged absences of the men: the delegation of power by the men who go to the women who stay behind, with the purpose of allowing the continuity of the domestic unit. She further suggested that this delegation of power has become an important part of the women's resources and part of the local culture in sending communities. This "feminine empowerment", as Gonzalez de la Rocha calls it, takes place through the complete immersion of women in the economic activities of the family and the complete control of their resources, family, and household. It is important to clarify that the feminine empowerment is by cession of power from the man to the woman and not by the women's independent struggle to get it.

A somewhat opposite perspective to the one suggested by Gonzalez de la Rocha is the one of the "empowered" women left behind who in general resent being left in charge. The migration of the head of household and its consequences are stressful experiences that have a negative impact on the mental health of the women left behind. For instance, the women interviewed by Salgado de Snyder (Salgado de

Snyder & Maldonado, in press a; Salgado de Snyder, 1993) reported that the migration of their husbands was accompanied by unwanted multiple changes in their lifestyle and family dynamics. To assess the cognitive evaluation of specific stressors, an instrument was designed following the methodology used in the development of the HSI (Cervantes, Padilla, & Salgado de Snyder, 1990, 1991). The Stress Inventory for Immigrant Families (INEFAM) has a total of 20 items describing potential stressful situations that are assigned scores ranging from "not stressful at all" to "very stressful."

The potential stressors evaluated with higher scores were those related to the women's feelings of commitment to increased obligations and responsibilities that they were forced to assume as a direct consequence of their husbands' migration to the United States. The wives left behind resented that they had to face and find solutions for problems related to their children, the extended family, household maintenance, economics, agriculture, etc. by themselves. Many of the tasks imposed on them were considered almost impossible to perform correctly because they had no previous experience doing so. Such is the case with the management of household finances, farming, and care of animals.

Feelings of isolation, loneliness, and lack of support from the absent husband were also identified as highly stressful by most respondents. For many the idea of being left alone was still unbearable and unacceptable. In spite of reporting satisfactory marital happiness, the women left behind assigned high stress scores to situations that reflect the geographical, cultural, and emotional distance from their spouses. For instance, they were concerned their husbands would forget their customs and traditions. They also expressed fear of being abandoned by their spouses and fear that their spouses might start new families in the United States.

The perception of changes associated with family disintegration was also reported as stressful, such as lack of mutual help, increase in the number of problems with their children, and inability to control the increased verbal and even physical violence among their offspring.

Also, a large proportion of the women interviewed reported high stress associated with their husbands' general welfare, such as their husbands not having sufficient money to eat or to visit a physician in case of illness. They were also concerned about their husbands' housing arrangements, such as not knowing who their men lived with. Associated with this issue was their concern about "bad influences" from friends in the United States and fear of their husbands' use of alcohol or drugs.

External Resources: Social Support Networks

Salgado de Snyder and Maldonado reported that the social support network of women left behind was formed principally by their children, members of the extended family, and very close female friends. Only a very small number of women reported fictitious kin (for example, *comadres* or *compadres*), neighbors, priests, or teachers as members of their support network. The density of their network was formed by an average of six people. Very few women reported not having any social support network.

Financial and emotional were the two types of support most important to these women. Emotional support was received from almost everyone in their network, but it was perceived as significantly more effective when the source of support was their children. Children also provided economic support that was also perceived as very effective. The economic support provided by the migrant husband was considered significantly more effective than that provided from other sources. In fact, emotional support from children and economic support from the husband were both found to be associated with lower scores in stress and depressive symptomatology.

Coping Responses

The work of Salgado de Snyder and Maldonado (1992) is the only published report on coping responses of Mexican rural women married to immigrants. Women were asked their specific coping responses when dealing with specific problem areas such as conflict with self, spouse, children, extended family, friends, and financial difficulties. The coping responses of the women interviewed ranged from total passivity to engaging in physical violence, depending on the source of stress.

Personal problems such as feeling lonely and isolated were responded to with avoidance and internalization of emotions such as "not thinking about it" or crying and enduring suffering. Problems with their offspring were dealt with in a direct way, mostly by using physical punishment and trying to establish verbal communication. Conflict with their spouses was in most cases faced directly through verbal communication and externalization of emotions, not necessarily aimed at the solution of the specific problem, through behaviors such as refusing to do things for him like cooking, washing and ironing his clothes, etc. The conflicts arising with the extended family were mostly dealt with using avoidance, negation, and externalization of emotion such as doing nothing about it, denying the existence of problems, or engaging in a verbal or physical fight with the other party. Finally, economic conflicts were solved through direct action such as borrowing money, working overtime, limiting their expenses, etc.

Women who used coping strategies aimed at the direct solution of the problem had lower anxiety and depressive symptomatology scores and higher levels of self-esteem than the women who faced troubles by externalizing their emotion (getting angry, fighting, etc.). It should be noted, however, that the women who responded to conflict using mostly passive responses (such as negation, avoidance, or internalized emotion) did not differ significantly from the active problem solvers in terms of the mental health indicators explored.

The results may be explained by the fact that the women interviewed were from rural communities where the role of women is extremely traditional. In these communities, characteristics such as passivity, submission, self-denial, and suffering are not only expected from women but positively acknowledged and praised by the local society. Melgoza-Enriquez and Diaz-Guerrero (1993) proposed that Mexicans in general have a very enduring quality that the authors call "emotional fiber," by which they mean the potential to put up with and to resist the negative impact of life crises. From this perspective, it can be argued that the high scores in depressive symptomatology and anxiety as well as the passivity in their responses could be considered elements of internal strength of an ethnocultural nature.

Mental Health Outcomes

Depressive symptomatology was the outcome variable assessed among women left behind by Salgado de Snyder and Maldonado. Among the women interviewed the scores in the CES-D were high, with a mean group score of 23.2. Depressive symptomatology scores were found significantly negatively correlated with self-esteem. Furthermore, self-esteem was the single variable with the highest predictive power for depressive symptomatology. The depression symptoms reported more frequently were emotional states characterized by negative affect such as feeling depressed, sad, and lonely. They also expressed inability to experience positive affect, such as not feeling optimistic, not enjoying life, and not feeling happy. It has been documented that clinical depression episodes are characterized by a lack of positive affect and the presence of negative affect. However, in this group of women, the possibility of most of them suffering clinical depression is excluded, since all women were productive members of their communities and functioned adequately and accordingly to the expected gender roles. The findings of the study, thus, must be interpreted within the sociocultural context surrounding the lives of these women. Such high depressive symptomatology scores and lack of positive affect may be a reflection of the women's ability to perform and feel according to the social expectations (suffering, enduring, crying, etc.) in their communities. This interpretation does not mean that the women of the study do not suffer from psychological conflicts, but that their expression of depressive symptomatology is different. A detailed account of the results with the CES-D can be found elsewhere (Salgado de Snyder & Maldonado, in press b).

CONCLUSION

This chapter reviewed some aspects of the mental health literature on Mexican women involved—directly or indirectly—in international migration. Despite the fact that the body of literature on immigrant women has increased considerably in the last decade, our knowledge of this population's mental health is still limited. Hopefully, the research reported in this chapter will facilitate a greater understanding of the mental health dynamics of those Mexican women affected by international migration and will serve as a catalyst for the identification of relevant problems and areas for further research in this field.

REFERENCES

Arizpe, L. (1985). *Campesinado y migración* [Farming and migration]. Mexico: Secretaría de Educación Pública.

Berry, J. W. (1988). Acculturation and adaptation: A conceptual overview. In J. W. Berry & R. C. Annis (Eds.), *Ethnic psychology: Research and practice with immigrants, refugees, native peoples, ethnic groups and sojourners* (pp. 41–52). Amsterdam: Swets & Zeitlinger.

Bustamante, J., & Martinez, G. G. (1979). Undocumented migration from Mexico: Beyond borders but within systems. *Journal of International Affairs, 33*, 265–268.

Caetano, R. (1985, September). *Drinking patterns and alcohol problems in a national sample of U.S. Hispanics*. Paper presented at the conference Epidemiology of Alcohol Use and Abuse Among U.S. Ethnic Minorities, Bethesda, MD.

Caetano, R., & Medina-Mora, M. E. (1986). *Immigration, acculturation and alcohol use: A comparison between people of Mexican descent in Mexico and the U.S.* (Working Paper No. C-46). Berkeley, CA: Alcohol Research Group.

Carrillo, J. H., & Hernandez, A. (1988). La migración femenina hacia la frontera norte y los Estados Unidos [Feminine migration to the northern border and the United States]. In G. Lopez-Castro (Ed.), *Migración en el Occidente de Mexico* (pp. 85–112). Zamora, Michoacán, México: El Colegio de Michoacán.

CENIET (Centro Internacional de Estudios sobre el Trabajo) (1980). *Encuesta Nacional de Emigración a la Frontera Norte del pais y a los Estados Unidos* [*National survey on emigration to the north of Mexico and the United States*]. Mexico City: Author.

Cervantes, R. C., & Castro, F. G. (1985). Stress, coping and Mexican American mental health: A systematic review. *Hispanic Journal of Behavioral Sciences, 7*, 1–73.

Cervantes, R. C., Gilbert, M. J., Salgado de Snyder, V. N., & Padilla, A. M. (1991b). Psychosocial and cognitive correlates of alcohol use in younger adult immigrant and U.S. born Hispanics. *International Journal of the Addictions, 25*, 687–708.

Cervantes, R. C., Padilla, A. M., & Salgado de Snyder, V. N. (1990). Reliability and validity of the Hispanic Stress Inventory. *Hispanic Journal of Behavioral Sciences, 12*, 76–82.

Cervantes, R. C., Padilla, A. M., & Salgado de Snyder, V. N. (1991a). The Hispanic Stress Inventory: A culturally relevant approach to psychosocial assessment. *Psychological Assessment, 3*, 438–447.

Chaney, E. M. (1980). *Women in international migration: Issues in development and planning* (Document AID/OTR-147-80-46). Washington, DC: Office of Women in Development/USAID.

Chaney, E. M. (1985). Women who go and women who stay behind. *Migration Today, 10*, 7–13.

Cohen, R. E. (1987). Stressors: Migration and acculturation to American society. In M. Gaviria & J. Arana (Eds.), *Health and Behavior: Research Agenda for Hispanics* (Monograph No. 1, pp. 59–71). Chicago: Simon Bolivar Hispanic American Psychiatric Research and Training Program, University of Illinois.

Cohen, R. E. (1985). *Controlarse* and the problems of life among Latino immigrants. In W. A. Vega, & M. R. Miranda (Eds.), *Stress and Hispanic mental health: Relating research to service delivery* (pp. 202–218). Rockville, MD: ADAMHA.

CONAPO [Consejo Mexicano de Población] (1987). *Encuesta en la frontera norte a trabajadores indocumentados devueltos por las autoridades de los Estados Unidos de America. Resultados Estadisticos* [Survey in the border with undocumented workers returned by U.S. authorities: Statistical results]. Mexico: Author.

De Oliveira, O. (1984). Migración femenina, organización familiar y mercados laborales en México [Female migration, family organization and labor markets in Mexico]. *Comercio Exterior, 34*, 676–687.

Espin, O. (1987). Psychological impact of migration on Latinas: Implications for psychotherapeutic practice. *Psychology of Women Quarterly, 11*, 489–504.

Estrada, L. (1987, November). *Mexico-U.S. migration: Demographic characteristics of immigrants.* Paper presented at the First Binational Conference on Migration and Mental Health: Psychosocial Aspects, Guadalajara, Mexico.

Fernandez, C. (1988). Migración hacia los Estados Unidos: Caso Santa Inés Michoacán [Migration to the United States: The case of Santa Ines, Michoacan]. In G. Lopez-Castro & S. Pardo-Galvan (Eds.), *Migracion en el Occidente de Mexico* (pp. 113–124). Zamora, Michoacán, Mexico: El Colegio de Michoacán.

Flemming, R., Baum, A., & Singer, J. E. (1984). Toward an integrative approach to the study of stress. *Journal of Personality and Social Psychology, 46*, 939–949.

Fletcher, P. L., & Taylor, E. J. (1990, Winter/Spring). A village apart. *California Tomorrow*, pp. 9–17.

Fonseca, O., & Moreno, L. (1984). *Jaripo, Pueblo de Migrantes.* [Jaripo: A town of migrants]. Jiquilpan, Michoacán, Mexico: Centro de Estudios de la Revolución Mexicana "Lázaro Cárdenas".

Furnham, A., & Bochner, S. (1986). *Culture Shock.* New York: Methuen.

Gastelum, M. A. (1991). *Migración de trabajadores Mexicanos indocumentados a los Estados Unidos* [Migration of Mexican undocumented workers to the United States]. México, D. F.: Unversidad Nacional Autónoma de México.

Gilbert, M. J. (1987). Alcohol consumption patterns in immigrant and later generation Mexican American women. *Hispanic Journal of Behavioral Sciences, 9*, 299–314.

Gilbert, J. M., & Cervantes, R. C. (1985). Patterns and practices of alcohol use among Mexican Americans: A comprehensive review. *Mexican Americans and Alcohol* (Research Monograph No. 11). Los Angeles: Spanish-Speaking Mental Health Research Center, UCLA.

Gonzalez de la Rocha, M. (1989, October), *El poder de la ausencia: Mujeres y migración en una comunidad de los Altos de Jalisco* [*The power of absence: Women and migration in a community of Los Altos de Jalisco*]. Paper presented at the XI Colloqium of Las Realidades Regionales de la Crisis Nacional, Zamora, Michoacán, México.

Holck, S. E., Warren, C., Smith, J., & Rochat, R. (1984). Alcohol consumption among Mexican American and Anglo women: Results of a survey along the U.S.-Mexico border. *Journal of Studies on Alcohol, 45*, 149–153.

Lein, H. B. (1982). *The psychological aspects of the first stages of the acculturation process among Spanish speaking immigrants to the United States*. Unpublished doctoral dissertation, United States International University, San Diego, CA.

Lopez-Castro, G. (1989). *La casa dividida* [The divided house]. Zamora, Michoacán, Mexico: El Colegio de Michoacán.

Lopez-Castro, G., & Pardo-Galvan, S. (Eds.) (1988). *Migración en el occidente de México [Migration in Western Mexico]*. Zamora, Michoacán, Mexico: El Colegio de Michoacán.

Massey, D., Alarcon, R., Durand, J., & Gonzalez, H. (1991). *Los ausentes: El proceso social de la migración internacional en el occidente de México*. [The absents: The social process of international migration in western Mexico]. Mexico City: Alianza Editorial.

Melgoza-Enriquez, E., & Diaz-Guerrero, R. (in press). Fuerza personal: Medida breve de fibra emocional [Personal strength: A brief measurement of emotional fiber]. *Revista Mexicana de Psicología Social y Personalidad.*

Melville, M. (1978). Mexican women adapt to migration. *International Migration Review, 12*, 225–235.

Mendoza, P. (1981). Stress and coping behavior of Anglo and Mexican American university students. In T. H. Escobedo (Ed.), *Education and Chicanos: Issues and research* (Monograph No. 8) (pp. 89–111). Los Angeles: Spanish Speaking Mental Health Research Center, University of California at Los Angeles.

Mines, R. (1981). *Developing a community tradition of migration: A field study in rural Zacatecas, Mexico and California settlement areas* (Monograph No. 3). La Jolla, CA: Program on Mexico-U.S., University of California at San Diego.

Mines, R. (1984). Network migration and Mexican rural development: A case study. In R. C. Jones (Ed.), *Patterns of undocumented migration: Mexico and the United States* (pp. 136–155). Totowa, NJ: Rowman & Allanheld.

Mortimer, D. M., & Bryce-Laporte, R. S. (Eds.). (1981). *Female immigrants to the United States: Caribbean, Latin American, and African experiences* (RIESS Occasional Paper No. 2). Washington, DC: Smithsonian Institution.

O'Berg, K. (1960). Cultural shock: Adjustment to a new environment. *Practical Anthropologist, 7*, 177–182.

Padilla, A. M., Cervantes, R. C., Maldonado, M., & Garcia, R. E. (1988). Coping responses to psychosocial stressors among Mexican and Central American immigrants. *Journal of Community Psychology, 16*, 418–427.

Pearlin, L. I., Meneghan, E. G., Lieberman, M. A., & Mullan, J. T. (1981). The stress process. *Journal of Health and Social Behavior, 19*, 77–85.

Perez, R. (1983). Effects of stress, social support and style in the adjustment to pregnancy among Hispanic women. *Hispanic Journal of Behavioral Sciences, 5*, 141–161.

Radloff, L. (1977). The CES-D scale: A self-report depression scale for research in the general population. *Applied Psychological Measurement, 1*, 385–401.

Roberts, R. (1987). An epidemiological perspective on the mental health of people of Mexican origin. In R. Rodriguez & M. T. Coleman (Eds.), *Mental health issues of the Mexican American origin population in Texas* (pp. 55–70). Austin, TX: Hogg Foundation for Mental Health.

Rousse, R. (1989). *Mexican migration to the United States: Family relations in the development of a transnational migrant circuit*. Unpublished doctoral dissertation, Stanford University.

Salgado de Snyder, V. N. (1986). *Mexican immigrant women: The relationship of ethnic loyalty, self-esteem, social support, and satisfaction to acculturative stress and depressive symptomatology*. Unpublished doctoral dissertation, University of California at Los Angeles.

Salgado de Snyder, V. N. (1987). Factors associated with acculturative stress and depressive symptomatology among Mexican immigrant women. *Psychology of Women Quarterly, 11*, 475–488.

Salgado de Snyder, V. N. (1991). *Estres psicosocial y salud mental en esposas de migrantes a los Estados Unidos* [Psychosocial stress and mental health among wives of immigrants to the United States] (Internal Research Report No. 91-4230). México: División de Investigaciones Epidemiológicas y Sociales, Instituto Mexicano de Psiquiatría.

Salgado de Snyder, V. N. (1993). Family life across the border: Mexican wives left behind. *Hispanic Journal of Behavioral Sciences, 15*, 391–401.

Salgado de Snyder, V. N., Cervantes, R. C., & Padilla, A. M. (1990). Gender and ethnic differences in psychosocial stress and generalized distress among Hispanics. *Sex Roles, 22*, 441–453.

Salgado de Snyder, V. N., & Maldonado, M. (1992). Respuestas de enfrentamiento e indicadores de salud mental en esposas de migrantes a los Estados Unidos [Coping responses and mental health indicators among wives of immigrants to the United States]. *Salud Mental, 15*, 28–35.

Salgado de Snyder, V. N., & Maldonado, M. (in press a). Caracteristicas del funcionamiento psicosocial de esposas de migrantes mexicanos a los Estados Unidos [Characteristics of psychosocial health functioning among wives of immigrants to the United States]. *Revista Latinoamericana de Psicología*.

Salgado de Snyder, V. N., & Maldonado, M. (in press b). Características psicométricas de la Escala de Depresión del Centro de Estudios Epidemiológicos (CES-D) en una muestra de mujeres adultas de áreas rurales [Psychometric characteristics of the CES-D in a sample of adult rural women]. *Salud Pública de México*.

Trigueros, P., & Rodriguez Piña, J. (1988). Migración y vida familiar en Michoacán: Un estudio de caso. [Migration and family life in Michoacan: A case study]. In G. Lopez-Castro (Ed.), *Migración en el Occidente de Mexico* (pp. 201–232). Zamora, Michoacán, Mexico: El Colegio de Michoacán.

Vazquez-Nuthall, E., Romero-Garcia, I., & de Leon, B. (1987). Sex roles and perceptions of masculinity and femininity of Hispanic women: A review of the literature. *Psychology of Women Quarterly, 11*, 409–426.

Vega, W. A. (1992, October). *Immigration and drug use: Toward a model for increasing knowledge.* Paper presented at the Conference Bridging the Borders: US/Mexico Perspectives on Hispanic Immigration and Drug Use. Los Angeles.

Vega, W. A., & Kolody, B. (1985). The meaning of social support and the mediation of stress across cultures. In W. Vega & M. Miranda (Eds.), *Stress and Hispanic Mental Health* (pp. 48–75). Rockville, MD: ADAMHA.

Vega, W. A., Kolody, B., & Valle, R. (1986). The relationship of marital status, confidant support, and depression among Mexican immigrant women. *Journal of Marriage and the Family, 48*, 597–605.

Vega, W. A., Kolody, B., & Valle, R. (1987). Migration and mental health: An empirical test of depression risk factors among Mexican women. *International Migration Review, 21*, 512–530.

Vega, W. A., Kolody, B., Valle, R., & Hough, R. (1986). Depressive symptoms and their correlates among immigrant Mexican women in the United States. *Social Science Medicine, 22*, 645–652.

Vega, W. A., Kolody, B., Valle, R., & Weir, J. (1991). Social networks, social support, and their relationship to depression among immigrant Mexican women. *Human Organization, 50*, 154–162.

Warheit, G., Vega, W. A., Auth, J., & Meinhardt, K. (1985). In W. A. Vega & M. R. Miranda (Eds.), *Stress and Hispanic mental health. Relating research to service delivery* (pp. 76–109). Rockville, MD: ADAMHA.

AUTHOR NOTES

Correspondence concerning this chapter should be addressed to: V. Nelly Salgado de Snyder, Mexican Institute of Psychiatry, Calzada Mexico-Xochimilco 101, San Lorenzo Huipulco-Tlalpan, Mexico, D.F.; Telephone (011525) 655-28-11; FAX (011525) 655-04-11.

THEME II:

CULTURAL ISSUES IN MENTAL HEALTH EVALUATION AND TREATMENT OF HISPANICS

CHAPTER 7

THE PSYCHIATRIC EXAMINATION OF HISPANICS: ACROSS THE LANGUAGE BARRIER

Luis R. Marcos, MD, MScD, Commissioner, New York City Department of Mental Health, Mental Retardation and Alcoholism Services and Professor of Psychiatry, New York University School of Medicine

> And the whole earth was of one language, and of one speech. And it came to pass as they journeyed from the east, that they found a plain in the land of Shinar; and they dwelt there. . . . And they said Come, let us build a city and a tower, whose top may reach unto heaven; and let us make us a name, lest we be scattered abroad upon the face of the whole earth. And the Lord came down to see the city and the tower, which the children of men builded. And the Lord said, . . . Come let us go down, and there confound their language, that they may not understand one another's speech. So the Lord scattered them abroad from there upon the face of all the earth: and they ceased building the city. Therefore is the name of it called Babel, because the Lord did there confound the language of all the earth; and from there did the Lord scatter them abroad upon the face of the earth (Genesis 11:1–9, KJV).

According to the 1990 U.S. census, the population of Hispanic origin excluding Puerto Rico, was 21.4 million, or 8.6% of the total population. Other than English, the most common language spoken at home is Spanish, which is used by more than 14.5 million people. Of this group, a large proportion do not speak English well or do not speak it at all (U.S. Bureau of the Census, 1980). Today, the number of limited-English and non-English-speaking Hispanic persons in the United States is higher due to the immigrants admitted since 1990 and to the thousands of additional undocumented aliens who continuously enter and take residence in the United States (U.S. Immigration and Naturalization Service, 1989; U.S. Bureau of the Census, 1991).

Although it is axiomatic that good verbal communication between physician and patient is essential to proper psychiatric care, the number of psychiatrists who can communicate in the Spanish language so frequently spoken in the United States is limited (American Psychiatric Biographical Directory, 1989). When a patient who is not fluent in English requires a psychiatric examination and no bilingual clinician is available, the usual practice is to conduct the evaluation in English and to use an interpreter only if the person is unable to communicate at all. In this paper I will summarize the findings of a wide selection of clinical and research reports on the problems associated with employing English to assess the psychopathology of Hispanic patients who have a limited command of the language. I will not address here the issues involved in the use of interpreters (Marcos, 1979a; Putsch, 1985).

A review of the literature on the evaluation of global psychopathology reveals disagreement as to whether the evaluation of limited-English-speaking Hispanic psychiatric patients in English raises or lowers clinician ratings of these patients' severity of illness. Some studies show that primarily Spanish-speaking psychiatric patients are assessed as presenting higher levels of pathology when the interview is conducted in Spanish than when it is conducted in English (Del Castillo, 1970; Gonzalez, 1978; Ruiz, 1975; Price & Cuellar, 1981). On the other hand, there are reports indicating that English-speaking clinicians infer greater psychopathology during English language interviews than do Spanish-speaking clinicians during Spanish language interviews of the same patients (Marcos, Alpert, Urcuyo, & Kesselman, 1973; Marcos, Urcuyo, Kesselman & Alpert, 1973).

Although it is difficult to compare these studies given their different populations and research designs, it is possible that the diverse findings may simply represent different snapshots of interactions among language, culture, clinical judgment, bias, and psychopathology (Vazquez, 1982; Malgady, Rogler, & Costantino, 1987; Rogler, Malgady, & Rodriguez, 1989; Abad & Boyce, 1979; Lopez, 1988). At a more specific level of analysis, however, the literature suggests that several areas of the psychiatric examination appear to be influenced by the language barrier. These are: the patient's general attitude toward the examiner and toward the interview situation, motor activity, speech and stream of talk, affect and emotional tone, and sense of self. Each of these are examined in more detail below.

GENERAL ATTITUDE

Patients struggling with a language barrier often behave in a self-effacing manner that clinicians may interpret as guarded behavior or uncooperativeness (Fitzpatrick & Gould, 1970; Kline, 1969; Simmons, 1961). These patients sometimes speak in ways that may create the impression of slow or reluctant participation in the interview. For example, in a comparative analysis of the speech of primarily Spanish-speaking schizophrenic patients who were interviewed in both English and Spanish, a striking tendency was found for patients to answer

English questions with just a word, a silent pause, or a short sentence such as "I don't know," "I don't think so," or "yes sir," all easily interpreted by clinicians as a reluctance to communicate (Marcos, Urcuyo, Kesselman, & Alpert, 1973). Also, some Hispanic immigrants whose English is limited can have a negative predisposition toward the English language. This attitude can permeate their general predisposition toward the non-Hispanic clinician and the interview situation (Marcos, 1988; Buxbaum, 1949; Marcos, & Trujillo, 1981; Edgerton & Karno, 1971; Rogler, Cooney, & Ortiz, 1980; Marcos, 1982).

Because the language barrier also interferes with the patient's ability to understand the clinician's verbalizations, particularly vocal cues such as intonation, pauses, and emotional tone, the flow of the interview tends to be stilted and to lose emotional connectedness (Solomon & Ali, 1975). In turn, the demands placed upon the clinician to decide which of the patient's verbal cues are relevant and which are a mere consequence of his or her linguistic deficit can cause frustration and uncertainty in the interviewer about the accuracy of the examination (Kline, 1969; Marcos & Urcuyo, 1979). Another factor that may affect the interview situation is that some bilinguals, when communicating in a secondary or nondominant language, tend to feel less intelligent, less friendly, and less self-confident than they might feel if they were speaking their primary language (Segalowitz, 1976).

MOTOR ACTIVITY

Clinicians generally view the quality and quantity of patients' body movements as a reflection of their affect (e.g., motor retardation and depression; enhanced physical tension and anxiety). In one study, Spanish-speaking schizophrenic patients, with a clear deficit in the English language, were rated by clinicians as more tense when interviewed in English than when the interview language was Spanish (Marcos, Alpert, Urcuyo, & Kesselman, 1973). A subsequent comparative analysis of their body movements showed that there was increased motor activity during the English interviews, but that the additional movements may have been associated with the more demanding task of verbalizing in the English language and not necessarily with psychopathology (Grand, Marcos, & Freedman, 1977). Other experimental studies have confirmed that individuals produce more nonverbal activity, particularly hand movements, when communicating in a secondary language they do not know well. This finding may reflect either an increase in the cognitive work involved in verbalization or the patients' extra effort to reach the interviewer and establish contact (Marcos, 1979b). Clinicians evaluating patients' motor activity in the face of a language barrier, therefore, confront the difficult task of separating verbalization-related movements from those reflecting tension or anxiety (Freedman, Blass, & Rifkin et al., 1972).

SPEECH AND STREAM TALK

There is clinical and experimental evidence indicating that the speech of bilinguals in general, and primarily Spanish-speaking patients in particular, is affected in important ways when they speak in a nondominant language (Fishman, Cooper, & Ma, 1971; Marcos, 1976a; Lambert, 1956; Tanaka, Oyama, & Osgood, 1963). For example, some patients verbalize Spanish words during their English interviews (Marcos, Urcuyo, Kesselman, & Alpert, 1973). This "language mixing," or primary language intrusion, which occurs more often in answers to emotionally charged questions or in situations of higher stress (Javier & Alpert, 1986; Javier & Marcos, 1989), makes a patient's flow of thought sound less logical and more confused. Further, patients struggling with a language barrier produce both longer silent pauses and more speech disturbances, such as incomplete sentences, self-corrections, repetitions, stuttering, and incoherent sounds (Marcos, Urcuyo, Kesselman, & Alpert, 1973). While these long pauses and speech disturbances have been considered to be indicators of depression and anxiety, respectively, in the monolingual patient, they can also be a consequence of the efforts of non-English-speaking patients to communicate in a nondominant language (Mahl, 1959; Pope, 1965; Alpert, Frosch, & Fisher, 1967).

AFFECT

Many studies suggest that speaking in a nondominant language diminishes the emotional involvement of the patient and may produce the impression of emotional withdrawal or affective detachment (Buxbaum, 1949; Marcos, 1976b; Stengel, 1939; Kraft, 1955). It has been postulated that this effect is due to secondary language words having less vivid associations, evoking weaker references, carrying less emotional charge, and being less meaningful and emotionally stimulating than primary-language words (Marcos, 1976b, Javier, 1989; Gonzalez-Reigosa, 1976). If so, it may explain why limited English-speaking Hispanic schizophrenic patients often display more intense emotions when they are interviewed in the Spanish language (Del Castillo, 1970; Gonzalez, 1978; Ruiz, 1975).

There is also evidence that when speaking in a nondominant language, some patients focus their attention on the cognitive task of verbalization and appear to concentrate primarily on the manner in which they say things and less on the content of what they are saying (Stengel, 1939; Kraft, 1955; Javier, 1989; Gonzalez-Reigosa, 1976; Sollee, 1970). These patients may, for example, speak about emotionally charged issues without displaying the appropriate intensity or emotion. As a result, certain experiences can remain vague and unreal for both the patient and the interviewing clinician (Buxbaum, 1949; Marcos, 1976; Stengel, 1939; Kraft, 1955). Conversely, some clinical reports suggest that some patients may be able to reveal experiences in their secondary language that were left untold in the primary language because of their high emotional content (Marcos & Alpert, 1976; Pitta, Marcos, & Alpert, 1978).

SENSE OF SELF

Individuals communicating in a secondary language, as opposed to their mother tongue, not only have to deal with a different set of words but, in some cases, may perceive and describe themselves differently and experience a different sense of identity (Marcos, Eisma, & Guimon, 1977; Velikovsky, 1934). In fact, there are times when Hispanic bilingual patients give different responses to the same questions in their primary and nondominant languages (Ervin, 1964; Findling, 1969; Marcos, 1972). Indeed some bilingual patients report hallucinations only in their second language and deny hallucinations in their primary language (Hemphill, 1971), or they may describe different hallucinations, such as threatening voices in their nondominant language and "good" voices in their primary language (Frank, Rendon, & Siomopoulous, 1980; Lukianowicz, 1962).

A classic and still controversial explanation of this phenomenon is the language-relativity hypothesis, which postulates that language is not merely a vehicle of communication, but is a reality through which people perceive and organize their worlds (Sapir, 1929; Fishman, 1960). Alternatively, these findings may be associated with the bilingual person's capacity to acquire, maintain, and use two separate language codes, each with its own lexical, syntactic, phonetic, and ideational component (Greenson, 1950). Compelling evidence for this language independence can be found in clinical and psycholinguistic studies (Ervin, 1964; Findling, 1969; Marcos, 1972). In addition, following cerebrovascular accidents, bilingual individuals often exhibit differential impairment of their two languages (Critchley, 1974; Marx, 1966; Paradis, 1977).

CONCLUSION

The psychiatric examination of limited-English-speaking Hispanic patients places tremendous demands on clinicians who must face the difficult task of deciding which of the patient's verbal and nonverbal cues are relevant for the assessment of psychopathology and which are "noise" or mere consequences of the language deficit. Ideally, clinicians should be able to communicate in each patient's primary language. As achievement of this state is unlikely at the very least, it is essential that clinicians performing these evaluations be sensitive to the linguistic and attitudinal effects of the language barrier that can substantially influence the patient's general attitude, motor activity, speech, affect, and sense of self, as well as the clinician's perception and interpretation of these. Potential misevaluation of the patient's responses may be minimized if the clinician is careful to anticipate these possible distorting effects. Beyond these educational efforts, one can envision having trained interpreters readily available to intervene in situations where the patient's low proficiency in the English language could substantially interfere with the accuracy of the examination.

REFERENCES

Abad, V., Boyce, E. (1979). Issues in psychiatric evaluations of Puerto Ricans: A socio-cultural perspective. *Journal of Operational Psychiatry, 10*, 28–39.

Alpert, M., Frosch, W.A., & Fisher, S.H. (1967). Teaching the perception of expressive aspects of vocal communication. *American Journal of Psychiatry, 124*, 202–211.

American Psychiatric Association Biographical Directory 1989. Washington, DC: American Psychiatric Association.

Buxbaum, E. (1949). The role of the second language in the formation of the ego and superego. *Psychoanalytic Quarterly, 18*, 279–289.

Critchley, M. (1974). Aphasia in polyglots and bilinguals. *Brain and Language, 1*, 15–27.

Del Castillo, J. (1970). The influence of language upon symptomatology in foreign-born patients. *American Journal of Psychiatry, 127*, 242–244.

Edgerton, R.B., & Karno, M. (1971). Mexican-American bilingualism and the perception of mental illness. *Archives of General Psychiatry, 24*, 286–290.

Ervin, S.M. (1964). Language and T.A.T. content in bilinguals. *Journal of Abnormal Social Psychology, 68*, 500–507.

Findling, J. (1969). Bilingual need affiliation and future orientation in extragroup and intragroup domains. *Modern Language Journal, 53*, 227–231.

Fishman, J.A. (1960). A systematization of the Whorfian hypothesis. *Behavioral Science, 4*, 323–339.

Fishman, J., Cooper, R.L., & Ma, R. (1971). *Bilingualism in the Barrio*. Bloomington, Indiana: Indiana University Publications.

Fitzpatrick, J.P., & Gould, R.E. (1970). Mental illness among Puerto Ricans in New York: Cultural conditions or intercultural misunderstanding. *American Journal of Orthopsychiatry, 40*, 238–239.

Frank, S.M., Rendon, M.I., & Siomopoulous, G. (1980). Language in hallucinations of adolescent schizophrenics. In R.W. Rieber (Ed.), *Applied psycholinguistics and mental health* (pp. 115–126). New York: Plenum Press.

Freedman, N., Blass, T., Rifkin, A., & Grant, S. (1972). Body movements and the verbal encoding of aggressive affect. *Journal of Personality and Social Psychology, 79*, 239–258.

Gonzalez, J.R. (1978). Language factors affecting treatment of bilingual schizophrenics. *Psychiatric Annals, 8*, 68–70.

Gonzalez-Reigosa, R. (1976). The anxiety arousing effect of taboo words in bilinguals. In C.D. Spielberger & R. Diaz-Guerrero (Eds.), *Cross-Cultural Anxiety*, Volume I (pp. 89–106). Washington, DC: Hemisphere.

Grand, S., Marcos, L.R., Freedman, N., & Barroso, F. (1977). Relations of psychopathology and bilingualism to kinetic aspects of interview behavior in schizophrenics. *Journal of Abnormal Psychology, 86*, 492–500.

Greenson, R.R. (1950). The mother tongue and the mother. *International Journal of Psychoanalysis, 31*, 18–23.

Hemphill, R.E. (1971). Auditory hallucinations in polyglots. *South African Medical Journal, 45*, 1391–1394.

Javier, R.A. (1989). Linguistic consideration in the treatment of bilinguals. *Journal of Psychoanalytic Psychology, 6*, 87–96.

Javier, R.A., & Alpert, M. (1986). The effect of stress in the linguistic generalization of coordinate bilinguals. *Journal of Psycholinguistic Research*, 419–435.

Javier, R.A., & Marcos, L.R. (1989). The role of stress on the language independence and code switching phenomena. *Journal of Psycholinguistic Research, 18*, 449–472.

Kline, L.Y. (1969). Some factors in the psychiatric treatment of Spanish Americans. *American Journal of Psychiatry, 125*, 1674–1681.

Kraft, E.E. (1955). The choice of language in polyglot psychoanalysis. *Psychoanalytic Quarterly, 24*, 343–357.

Lambert, W.E. (1956). Developmental aspects of second language acquisition: Associational fluency, stimulus provocativeness and word order influence. *Journal of Social Psychology, 43*, 83–89.

Lopez, S.R. (1988). The empirical basis of ethnocultural and linguistic bias in mental health evaluations of Hispanics. *American Psychologist, 43*, 1095–1097.

Lukianowicz, N. (1962). Auditory hallucinations in polyglot subjects. *Psychiatria et Neurologia, 143*, 274–294.

Mahl, G.F. (1959). Measuring the patient's anxiety during interviews from expressive aspects of his speech. *Transcripts of the New York Academy of Science, 21*, 249–257.

Malgady, R.G., Rogler, L.H., & Costantino, G. (1987). Ethnocultural and linguistic bias in mental health evaluation of Hispanics. *American Psychologist, 42*, 228–234.

Marcos, L.R. (1972). Lying: A particular defense met in psychoanalytic therapy. *American Journal of Psychoanalysis, 32*, 195–202.

Marcos, L.R. (1976a). The linguistic dimensions of the bilingual patient. *American Journal of Psychoanalysis, 36*, 347–354.

Marcos, L.R. (1976b). Bilinguals in psychotherapy: Language as an emotional barrier. *American Journal of Psychotherapy, 30*, 552–560.

Marcos, L.R. (1979a). Effects of interpreters on the evaluation of psychotherapy in non-English speaking patients. *American Journal of Psychiatry, 136*, 171–174.

Marcos, L.R. (1979b). Nonverbal behavior and thought processing. *Archives of General Psychiatry, 36*, 940–943.

Marcos, L.R. (1982). Adults' recollection of their language deprivation as immigrant children. *American Journal of Psychiatry, 139*, 607–610.

Marcos, L.R. (1988). Understanding ethnicity in psychotherapy with Hispanic patients. *American Journal of Psychoanalysis, 48*, 35–42.

Marcos, L.R., & Alpert, M. (1976). Strategies and risks in the psychotherapy with bilingual patients: The phenomenon of language independence. *American Journal of Psychiatry, 133*, 1275–1278.

Marcos, L.R., Alpert, M., Urcuyo, L., & Kesselman, M. (1973). The effect of interview language on the evaluation of psychotherapy in Spanish-American schizophrenic patients. *American Journal of Psychiatry, 130*, 549–553.

Marcos, L.R., Eisma, J.E., & Guimon, J. (1977). Bilingualism and sense of self. *American Journal of Psychoanalysis, 37*, 285–290.

Marcos, L.R., & Trujillo, M. (1981). Culture, language and communicative behavior: The psychiatric examination of Spanish-Americans. In R. Duran (Ed.), *Latino language and communication behavior* (pp. 187–194). Trenton, NJ: Ablex Publications.

Marcos, L.R., & Urcuyo, L. (1979). Dynamic psychotherapy with the bilingual patient. *American Journal of Psychotherapy, 33*, 331–338.

Marcos, L.R., Urcuyo, L., Kesselman, M., & Alpert, M. (1973). The language barrier in evaluating Spanish-American patients. *Archives of General Psychiatry, 29*, 655–659.

Marx, O.M. (1966). Aphasia studies and language theory in the 19th century. *Bulletin of History of Medicine, 40*, 328–339.

Paradis, M. (1977). Bilingualism and aphasia. In H. Whitaker & H.A. Whitaker (Eds.), *Studies in neurolinguistics* (pp. 65–121). New York: Academic Press.

Pitta, P., Marcos, L.R., & Alpert, M. (1978). Language switching as a treatment strategy with bilingual patients. *American Journal of Psychoanalysis, 38*, 255–258.

Pope, B. (1965). Anxiety and depression in speech. *Journal of Consulting and Clinical Psychology, 4*, 188–192.

Price, C., & Cuellar, I. (1981) Effects of language and related variables on the expression of psychotherapy in Mexican American psychiatric patients. *Hispanic Journal of Behavioral Sciences, 3*, 145–160.

Putsch, R.W. (1985). Cross-cultural communication: The special case of interpreters in health care. *Journal of the American Medical Association, 254*, 3344–3348.

Rogler, L.H., Cooney, R.S., & Ortiz, V. (1980). Intergenerational change in ethnic identity in the Puerto Rican family. *International Migration Review, 13*, 193–213.

Rogler, L.H., Malgady, R.G., & Rodriguez, O. (1989). *Hispanics and mental health: A framework for research*. Malabar, FL: Krieger.

Ruiz, E.J. (1975). Influence of bilingualism on communication in groups. *International Journal of Group Psychotherapy, 25*, 391–395.

Sapir, E. (1929). The status of linguistics as a science. *Language, 5*, 207–214.

Segalowitz, N. (1976). Communicative incompetence and the non-fluent bilingual. *Canadian Journal of Behavioral Science, 8*, 122–131.

Simmons, O. (1961). The mutual image and expectations of Anglo-Americans and Mexican Americans. *Daedalus, 90*, 286–299.

Sollee, N.D. (1970). A study of perceptual defense involving bilinguals. *Philippine Journal of Psychology, 3*, 3–17.

Solomon, D., & Ali, F.A. (1975). Influence of verbal content and intonation on meaning attributions of first and second language speakers. *Journal of Social Psychology, 95*, 3–9.

Stengel, E. (1939). On learning a new language. *International Journal of Psychoanalysis, 20,* 471–479.

Tanaka, Y., Oyama, R., & Osgood, C.E. (1963). A cross-cultural and cross-concept study of the generality of semantic spaces. *Journal of Verbal Learning and Verbal Behavior, 2,* 392–405.

U.S. Department of Commerce, Bureau of the Census. (1980). General social and economic characteristics, Table 99. *Nativity and Language 1980.* Washington, DC: Author.

U.S. Department of Commerce, Bureau of the Census. (1991). *The Hispanic population in the United States: March 1991.* Series P-20, No. 455. Washington, DC: Author.

U.S. Department of Immigration and Naturalization Service. (1989). Immigrants admitted and refugee arrivals, Table 9. *Statistical Yearbook.* Washington, DC: Author.

Vazquez, C.A. (1982). Research on the psychiatric evaluation of the bilingual patient: A methodological critique. *Hispanic Journal of Behavioral Sciences, 4,* 75–80.

Velikovsky, I. (1934). Can a newly acquired language become the speech of the unconscious? *Psychoanalytic Review,* (*21*) 329–335.

AUTHOR NOTES

Correspondence concerning this chapter should be addressed to: Dr. Luis R. Marcos, MD, MScD, Commissioner, New York City Department of Mental Health, Mental Retardation, and Alcoholism Services, 125 Worth Street, Room 410, New York, NY 10013.

CHAPTER 8

THE INTERPLAY OF ADVANCES AMONG THEORY, RESEARCH, AND APPLICATION IN FAMILY INTERVENTIONS FOR HISPANIC BEHAVIOR-PROBLEM YOUTH

Jose Szapocnik, PhD,
Professor of Psychiatry,

William Kurtines, PhD,
Professor of Psychiatry, and

Daniel A. Santisteban, PhD,
Assistant Professor of Psychiatry

Spanish Family Guidance Center,
Center for Family Studies,
Department of Psychiatry,
University of Miami School of Medicine

Progress in an applied science is fostered through the continuous interplay among theory, research, and application. Treatment is presumably the application of a set of theoretically derived scientific principles. In the ideal case, treatment research is the process by which these scientific principles are tested through their application to real clinical problems. This chapter illustrates how the interplay among theory, research and practice has resulted in important breakthroughs in the treatment of clinical problems among Hispanic youths and their families. This issue is discussed in the context of an ongoing program of intervention research that targets for intervention Hispanic behavior problem youth.

In our work, the interplay of theory, research, and application takes place at several levels. The theoretical orientation of our research program is systemic and draws on both the structural (Minuchin, 1974) and strategic (Haley, 1976; Madanes, 1981) traditions in systems theory. With respect to application, our work has developed along two lines. The first has involved the investigation of the cultural characteristics of our Hispanic population (primarily Cuban American but increasingly Nicaraguan, Colombian, Puerto Rican, Peruvian and Salvadoran), the role that cultural factors may play in the process of treatment, and the role cultural factors may play in determining differential outcomes.

The second has involved the application of systems theory to what has emerged as a remarkably recalcitrant clinical problem, namely behavior problems and drug abuse among children and adolescents. In summary, the research program described in this article is a direct outgrowth of our efforts to develop and investigate novel, theoretically based, and culturally appropriate interventions that can be used in the prevention and treatment of behavior problems and drug abuse among Hispanic youth and families.

In this article we describe five major challenges that had to be tackled in order to make progress either in the treatment of Hispanic adolescent drug abuse and problem behavior or in its investigation. We reframed these challenges into research questions and chose to pursue answers within the framework of a rigorous program of systematic research. In translating these challenges into research questions, methodological issues had to be resolved, resulting in some of our most important breakthroughs in theoretical understanding. Likewise, advances in our theoretical understanding have resulted in progress in overcoming obstacles to resolving clinical problems as well as in some of our most important methodological advances (Szapocznik & Kurtines, 1989, 1993; Szapocznik, Perez-Vidal, Hervis, Brickman, & Kurtines, 1990; Szapocznik, Kurtines, Perez-Vidal, Hervis, & Foote, 1990). We thus argue that progress in the field is facilitated by the interplay of theory, research, and application. Research must be both a final step in the completion of each stage of knowledge development and a solid foundation from which to pursue new theoretical and applied breakthroughs.

IDENTIFICATION/DEVELOPMENT OF CULTURALLY SPECIFIC INTERVENTIONS

The 1970s witnessed a tremendous increase in the number of Hispanic adolescents involved with drugs. In response to this problem, our work began in 1972 as a small storefront location funded by the Office of Economic Opportunity, Department of Health, Education, & Welfare. The program was established to provide services to the local Hispanic community. The program of research that emerged from these activities was thus rooted in a very real and pressing problem.

The first challenge encountered by our clinical program (from 1972 to 1978) was to identify and develop culturally appropriate and acceptable treatment intervention for Cuban youths with problem behaviors. In order to define the Cuban culture and to develop a better understanding of how it resembled and differed from the mainstream culture, a comprehensive study on value orientations was designed based on the pioneer work on world views by Kluckhohn and Strodtbeck (1961).

The major study on value orientation (Szapocznik, Scopetta, Aranalde, & Kurtines, 1978) that ensued determined that a family-oriented approach in which therapists take an active, directive, present-oriented leadership role matched the expectations of the population. This finding was the first indicator that structural family therapy was particularly well suited for this population (Szapocznik, Scopetta, King, & Hervis, 1978). Structural family therapy (SFT) had been developed a decade earlier by a team of primarily Hispanic therapists (Salvador Minuchin, Braulio Montalvo, and Jay Haley) working with inner-city African-American and Hispanic families in Philadelphia.

A second indicator was that in working with Hispanic families with children and adolescents, the stress of acculturation may cause disruptions within the family that require direct intervention (Szapocznik & Kurtines, 1980; Szapocznik, Scopetta, Kurtines, & Aranalde, 1978; Szapocznik, Kurtines, & Fernandez, 1980). More specifically, normal family processes may combine with acculturation processes to exaggerate intergenerational differences and exacerbate intrafamilial conflicts (Szapocznik, Santisteban, Rio, Perez-Vidal, Kurtines, & Hervis, 1984). A prototypical example can sometimes be found in the case of Hispanic immigrants who find themselves in a bicultural context. In this case, the adolescent's normal striving for independence combines with the adolescent's powerful acculturation to the American cultural value of individualism. The parent's normal tendency to preserve family integrity, on the other hand, combines with the parent's tenacious adherence to the Hispanic cultural value on strong family cohesion and parental control. The combination of the intergenerational and cultural differences add together to produce an exacerbated and intensified intrafamilial conflict in which parents and adolescents feel alienated from each other as depicted in Figure 1.

Structural family therapy is particularly well suited to address this type of situation because it is possible to separate content from process. At the content level, the cultural and intergenerational conflicts and issues can be the focus of attention and make the therapy particularly attuned to the Hispanic family. At the process level, SFT seeks to modify the breakdown in communication resulting from these intensified cultural and intergenerational conflicts. More specifically, in treating Hispanic families, the content of therapy may be issues of culture differences, differences in rates of acculturation, parental adjustments to changes in their youngster, etc. Work at the process level promotes more adaptive communication between family members, thus dissolving barriers to discussion of topics such as those outlined above. In this fashion therapy can be tailored to the specific and unique cultural and intergenerational conflicts of our Hispanic families.

In order to investigate the effectiveness of a family-oriented intervention with Hispanic families, a series of pilot research studies (Scopetta, Szapocznik, King, Ladner, Alegre, & Tillman, 1977) was conducted comparing individual, conjoint family, and family ecological

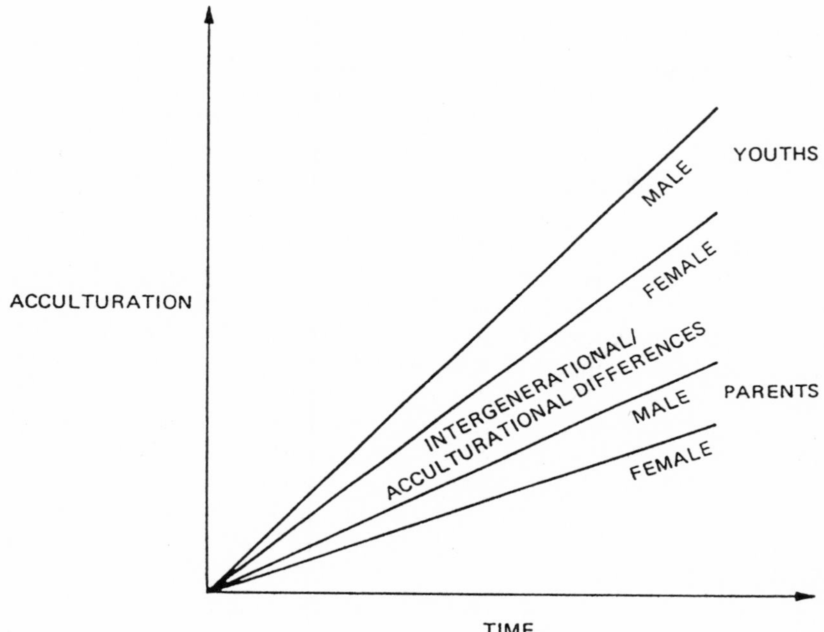

Figure 1. The development of intergenerational/acculturation differences in nuclear families as a function of time. Reproduced from Szapocznik, J., Scopetta, M.A., Kurtines, W., & Aranalde, M.A. (1978). Theory and measurement of acculturation. *Interamerican Journal of Psychology*, *12*, 113–130.

interventions. These pilot studies provided evidence for the efficacy of family therapy in a conjoint mode. In particular, SFT was found to be compatible with the issues and problems of our Hispanic population. As a result of the experience of these pilot studies, the effectiveness of this modality with behavior-problem youths was enhanced by modifying and/or adapting certain components such as making the modality strategic and time limited. To distinguish the particular structural family therapy approach that emerged from this phase of our work, we termed it *brief strategic family therapy* (BSFT).

In the application of BSFT to recent immigrant families, we came to realize how profoundly the process of immigration and acculturation could affect the family as a unit as well as each of its individual members. It became evident that for a subset of families, these clinical/

cultural issues required an intervention designed specifically for this constellation of problems. As a result of this experience, the next step was the development of an intervention that was specifically designed to address the constellation of immigration/acculturation stressors that this population was facing and the clinical problems this constellation of stressors was producing. From these efforts to have a very specialized and focused intervention emerged bicultural effectiveness training (BET). BET is an intervention model specifically designed to ameliorate the acculturation-related stresses confronted by two-generation immigrant families. While BET is based on SFT concepts, it is delivered as a psychoeducational modality. BET is based on a strategy that provides families and family members with skills for effectively coping with the acculturation stress and conflict that confront families living at the interface of manifestly conflicting cultural values and behavioral expectations. BET teaches families to feel enriched rather than stressed by the unique opportunities provided them in their daily transcultural existence. In its application, BET is a package of 12 lessons described in more detail in Szapocznik, Santisteban, Kurtines, Perez-Vidal, and Hervis (1984).

A major research study funded by the National Institute of Mental Health (Grant # MH31226) was conducted to investigate the relative effectiveness of BET in comparison to SFT (Szapocznik et al., 1986). An experimental design was achieved by randomly assigning 41 Cuban-American families with behavior-problem adolescents to either the BET or SFT conditions. Client families were administered a comprehensive battery of tests at the time of intake (pretesting), and at the time of termination (posttesting). Instruments were selected so that outcome could be examined from several perspectives, including the areas of adolescent symptomatology, the family's functioning, and the family's level of acculturation.

The data were analyzed using a mixed design analysis of variance. The results (Szapocznik et al., 1986) indicated that BET was as effective as SFT in bringing about improvement in adolescent and family functioning. These findings suggested that BET could accomplish the goals of family therapy while focusing on the cultural content that made therapy attractive to Hispanic families.

Subsequently, we combined BSFT and BET into a package we called Family Effectiveness Training (FET; Szapocznik, Santisteban, Rio, Perez-Vidal, & Kurtines, 1986). A major research study funded by the National Institute on Drug Abuse (Grant # 1E0702694) was conducted to investigate the effectiveness of Family Effectiveness Training, a prevention/intervention modality for Hispanic families with children ages 6 to 11 presenting with emotional and behavioral problems (Szapocznik, Santisteban, Rio, Perez-Vidal, Santisteban, and Kurtines, 1989). An experimental design was achieved by randomly assigning 79 Hispanic American families and their preadolescents to the FET or minimum contact control conditions. Considerable work went into the designing of not only the experimental condition (FET), but also a control condition that would minimize the amount of therapeutic interactions while keeping the family safe and under professional supervision. Client families were extensively tested at the time of intake (pretesting), termination (posttesting), and at two follow-up assessments. Instruments were selected such that outcome could be examined from the perspectives of both the child's behavior and of the family's functioning.

The data were analyzed using a mixed design analysis of variance. The results of this study (Szapocznik et al., 1989) indicated that families in the FET condition showed significantly greater improvement than did control families on independent measures of structural family functioning, problem behaviors as reported by parents, and on a self-administered measure of child self-concept. Thus the intervention was able to successfully improve functioning in both the areas of child and family functioning. Furthermore, the results of the follow-up assessments indicated that the impact of the FET intervention was generally maintained at the time of follow-up.

MEASUREMENT OF STRUCTURAL FAMILY CHANGE

The second challenge was to develop a measure that was theoretically appropriate and clinically relevant for assessing structural family change. In attempting to test the effects of interventions that were based on structural family systems theory, we required a theoretically and clinically relevant measure of family functioning.

To launch this work, we borrowed from the work of Minuchin and his colleagues with the Wiltwick Family Tasks (Minuchin, Rosman, & Baker, 1978). The tasks were useful as standard stimuli, but the scoring of these tasks presented problems of standardization and reliability. For this reason, we reorganized the scoring procedure into broad, theoretically and clinically important dimensions of structural family functioning; standardized the administration procedure; developed a detailed manual with anchors and examples to enhance reliability and replicability of the scoring procedure; and obtained validational evidence for the usefulness and nonobtrusiveness of the procedure for use in family therapy outcome studies (Szapocznik, Rio, Hervis, Mitrani, Kurtines, & Faraci, 1991).

The Structural Family Systems Ratings (SFSR), developed in response to this research need, defines family structure as the family's repetitive patterns of interactions. The SFSR defines family structure in terms of five interrelated dimensions:

1. *Structure* is the basic and most important dimension and is a measure of leadership, subsystem organization, and communication flow.
2. *Resonance* is a measure of the sensitivity of family members toward one another. It focuses on boundaries and emotional distance between family members.
3. *Developmental stage* assesses the extent to which each family member's roles and tasks correspond with the developmental stage of the family and its members.
4. *Identified patienthood* assesses the extent to which the family demonstrates that the primary family problem is the fault of one member who exhibits the symptom.
5. *Conflict resolution* is a measure of the family's ability to express, confront, and negotiate differences of opinion, disagreements, and conflicts.

The psychometric properties of the SFSR have been investigated with more than 500 Hispanic families in treatment. Content and construct validity were both explored (Szapocznik, Rio, Hervis, Kurtines, Faraci, & Mitrani, 1990). Content validity was built into the SFSR by developing the scales to tap structural concepts. Construct validity was extensively examined, revealing that the SFSR measures improvements resulting from SFT and that it discriminates between interventions that are and are not expected to bring about structural family change. Further data addressing the factor structure of the scales and interrater reliabilities are available elsewhere (Szapocznik, Rio, Hervis, Mitrani, Kurtines, & Faraci, 1991).

The SFSR represents one of the most important measurement advances of our program of research (Kazdin, 1993). The SFSR is a theoretically meaningful measure of structural family functioning that has become an essential tool for answering some of the critical questions posed by subsequent steps in our program of research. We have continued to refine the SFSR, including extending its use to nonresearch clinical settings (cf., Szapocznik & Kurtines, 1989).

The applied nature of our program of clinical research using the SFSR with today's families and problems has led us to the next step in assessing family functioning: investigating the measurement of functioning of nontraditional family constellations such as single-parent families. Our current work involves an investigation of the role that traditional concepts such as triangulation play in these types of families and how the measurement of these concepts may need to be revised.

ONE-PERSON FAMILY THERAPY

A national survey sponsored by the National Institute on Drug Abuse (NIDA) revealed that family therapy was widely viewed as a treatment of choice for behavior-problem, drug-abusing adolescents (Coleman, 1976). Unfortunately, the vast majority of counselors who worked with this population reported they were not able to bring whole families into treatment. Thus, the third challenge was to develop a procedure that would achieve the goals of family therapy (changes in maladaptive family interactions) without having to have the whole family present.

In order to meet this challenge, it was necessary to question some basic theoretical assumptions of conventional family systems practice. Structural family systems theory postulates that drug abuse in adolescents is a symptom of maladaptive interactional patterns in the family. That is, the family may unwittingly support or encourage the symptomatic behavior, or alternatively, the family may be incapable of behaving in ways that would eliminate the undesirable behavior. Theoretically, it follows that in order to eliminate problem behaviors, a change to more adaptive family interactions is required. Finally, a basic assumption of conventional family systems theory has been that in order to bring about changes in family interactions, it is necessary to work directly with the conjoint family. Moreover, family intervention strategies are typically designed for work with the conjoint family.

In an effort to meet the requirements of a modality that would change family functioning while working only with one person, we developed One-Person Family Therapy (Szapocznik, Kurtines, Perez-

Vidal, Hervis, & Foote, 1990; Szapocznik & Kurtines, 1989). The one-person modality differs from conjoint family therapies in that it attempts to achieve the goals of family therapy (i.e., the reduction or elimination of problem behaviors in the youth and the development of more adaptive family functioning) while working primarily with only one family member.

What made One-Person Family Therapy possible was the novel application of the principle of complementarity (Minuchin and Fishman, 1981). This basic systems principle establishes the nature of the interdependency of the behaviors of the members of a system by postulating that a change in the behavior of one family member will require corresponding changes in the behavior of other family members. What is novel about the one person modality is the deliberate and strategic use of this principle in directing the identified patient in therapy to change her/his behavior in ways that will require an adjustment in the behavior of other family members toward the identified patient. One-Person Family Therapy is thus unique as an approach to family therapy in that it strategically attempts to bring about therapeutic changes in both the behavior-problem, drug-abusing adolescent and the adolescent's family while working primarily with the adolescent.

Having developed a clinical modality based on the assumption that by working strategically with one person it was possible to change family functioning, we designed a rigorous investigation to test these assertions. Such a study was now possible because of the availability of the SFSR to test for changes in family structure. A major research project funded by NIDA (Grant # DA0322) from 1979 to 1982 was conducted comparing the conjoint and one person modalities of BSFT (Szapocznik, Kurtines, Foote, Perez-Vidal, & Hervis, 1983; 1986). An experimental design was achieved by randomly assigning 72 Hispanic-American families with drug-abusing adolescents to the conjoint or one-person modalities. Both conditions were designed to use exactly the same theoretical framework (BSFT) so that only one variable (conjoint or one person) would differ between the conditions. Considerable work was done in developing a treatment manual and modality guidelines for both the one person (cf., Szapocznik, Hervis, Kurtines, & Spencer, 1984; Szapocznik, Kurtines, Perez-Vidal, Hervis, & Foote, 1990) and the conjoint (cf., Szapocznik and Kurtines, 1989) conditions in order to ensure standardization and replicability of the study. Client families were extensively tested at the time of intake (pretesting), termination (posttesting), and a 6-month follow-up. Instruments were selected such that outcome could be examined from several perspectives, with special emphasis on measures of the adolescent behavior problem and the family's structural dynamics, the latter as measured by the SFSR.

The data were analyzed using a mixed design analysis of variance. The results (Szapocznik et al., 1983; 1986) indicated that One-Person Family Therapy was not only as effective as the conjoint modality in bringing about significant improvement in behavior problems and drug abuse in the youths, but also that it was as effective as conjoint in bringing about and maintaining significant improvements in family functioning. The results of this project thus demonstrated that it is possible to change family interactions even when the whole family is not present at most sessions, resulting in an important advance in our theoretical understanding of family treatment. As became evident in our later research, one person interventions that do not specifically target family change are not likely to bring about desirable changes in family interactions (Szapocznik, Rio et al., 1989). Hence it is possible to change maladaptive family interactions while working primarily with one person, but apparently in order to accomplish these changes it may be necessary to strategically target family interactions as part of the therapeutic process. It is noteworthy that testing of this family theoretical/clinical advance would not have been possible without the availability of a theoretically based, psychometrically sound measure of structural family functioning.

ENGAGING HARD-TO-REACH FAMILIES

Although our work has established that it is possible to conduct family therapy through one person, getting that one person into treatment has continued to be a problem. For example, in the previous study only 250 client/families of approximately 650 initial contacts (who met intake criteria on the basis of a phone screen) came for intake. Of this number, only 145 completed the intake procedure and only 72 completed treatment. Clearly, a very large proportion of client families who seek treatment are never engaged into therapy.

The fourth major challenge was to develop a procedure to more effectively engage drug abusers and their families in treatment. The approach that we developed, Strategic Structural Systems Engagement (Szapocznik, Perez-Vidal, et al., 1990; Szapocznik & Kurtines, 1989) is based on the premise that resistance to change within the family results from two systems properties. First, the family is a self-regulatory system. That is, the family system will attempt to maintain structural equilibrium or the status quo, which in the case of drug-abusing/problem behavior youth can certainly be accomplished by staying out of therapy. Second, while the presenting symptom may be drug abuse, the initial obstacle to change is resistance to coming into treatment. When resistance to coming into treatment is defined as the symptom to be targeted by the intervention, from a structural systems perspective we redefine resistance as a symptom that is maintained by the family's current pattern of interaction. Therefore, we have argued (Szapocznik, Perez-Vidal, et al., 1990) that the same systemic and structural principles that apply to the understanding of family functioning and treatment also apply to the understanding and treatment of the family's resistance to engagement.

Our work on Structural Systems Engagement was made possible by the advances in the theoretical understanding that came out of our earlier research on One-Person Family Therapy. In this work, we developed a more profound understanding of the power of the principle of complementarity as a mechanism for bringing about change in family interactions through one person. In developing our specialized engagement procedures, we drew from One-Person Family Therapy techniques designed to bring about changes in family interactions through one person. Typically, initial contacts requesting treatment for problem-behavior and drug-abusing youths are made by a parent. However, in the vast majority of these families either a parent is unwilling to become involved in therapy on a conjoint basis, or more frequently the problem youth refuses to come into treatment.

Having defined resistance to treatment as an undesirable problem or symptom to be overcome, from a strategic structural perspective we postulate that this symptom of resistance to engagement into treatment is maintained or encouraged by the family's patterns of interactions. Thus, within our framework the solution to overcoming the undesirable "symptom" of resistance is to restructure the family's patterns of interaction that permit the symptom of resistance to continue to exist. It is here that One-Person Family Therapy techniques become useful since in fact the person making the contact requesting help becomes our "one person" through whom we can potentially work to restructure the family's pattern of interaction that is maintaining the symptom of resistance. Having accomplished this first phase of the therapeutic process in which resistance has been overcome and the family, including the "offending" drug-abusing youth, have now agreed to participate in therapy, it becomes possible to shift the focus of the intervention toward the removal of the presenting symptoms of problem behavior and drug abuse.

Our clinical work suggests that the patterns of interactions that maladaptively permitted the presenting symptom to exist may be the same maladaptive patterns of interactions that keep the family from coming into treatment. Hence, in these so called "hard to reach" families, in order to have the opportunity to intervene, the therapist must begin the intervention with the first phone call. That is, in Structural Systems Engagement, therapy does not begin with the first office session; rather it is extended forward to the initial contact.

In order to test the effectiveness of Structural Systems Engagement in engaging and bringing to therapy completion families with drug abusing youths, an experimental study was conducted (Szapocznik, Perez-Vidal, Brickman, Foote, Santisteban, Hervis & Kurtines, 1988) funded by NIDA (Grant # DA2059) from 1983 to 1986. An experimental design was achieved by randomly assigning 108 Hispanic families with behavior problem adolescents (who were suspected of, or were observed using drugs) to one of two conditions: structural systems engagement and engagement as usual. In the control condition, engagement as usual, the clients were approached in a way that resembled as closely as possible the kind of engagement that usually takes place in outpatient centers. In order to define this engagement as usual condition, we conducted a survey of a representative sample of local outpatient treatment centers using role-playing techniques. In these role plays, a staff member went through a standard protocol on the phone in which the staff member played a mother or father wanting treatment for an adolescent suspected of using drugs who refused to come into treatment at the parents' request. The results of this survey were used to define the parameters for the engagement as usual condition. In the experimental condition, client families were engaged using techniques developed specifically for use with families that resist therapy. Considerable work was done in developing a manual for the experimental condition (Szapocznik & Kurtines, 1989; Szapocznik, Kurtines, et al., 1990) and in describing modality guidelines for both conditions in order to ensure the standardization and replicability of the study.

Treatment integrity guidelines and checklists were developed for both conditions, and six levels of engagement effort were identified. In order to monitor for treatment integrity, all contacts were logged and all sessions were reviewed and rated by an independent clinical research supervisor who was blind to condition. Treatment integrity analyses revealed that interventions in both conditions adhered to guidelines and that the two modalities were clearly distinguishable by the level of engagement effort applied.

Measurement

The theoretical advances in understanding the nature of resistance to entering treatment, and the concomitant advances in developing strategies for overcoming this type of resistance, required a reconceptualization of our approach to treatment outcome measures. Because the problem this study addressed was that of getting the family into therapy, we had to move beyond the analysis of outcome measures pre to post. For this study we had to turn our attention to engagement and maintenance through treatment completion as indices of intervention effectiveness.

In most treatment outcome studies, treatment outcome is assessed for those subjects who survive the intervention or control conditions. Since so many studies suggest there are no differential treatment effects among completers, differential retention/attrition rates may be a critically important measure that distinguishes among different types of interventions (Kazdin, 1986). Acknowledgment of the fact that treatment outcome only assesses efficacy on highly selected samples of treatment survivors highlights the enormous importance that attrition and retention have as complementary measures of efficacy. It follows that interventions should be assessed first in terms of their ability to engage and retain subjects/clients. Only after equivalence on these measures has been investigated can proper conclusions be drawn concerning the significance of more conventional measures of outcome efficacy applied to treatment survivors.

Results

There were two basic findings from the study (Szapocznik et al., 1988). The first had to do with the effectiveness of the Structural Systems Engagement intervention. As Figure 2 shows, the effects of the experimental condition were dramatic. More than 57% of the families in the engagement as usual condition failed to be engaged into treat-

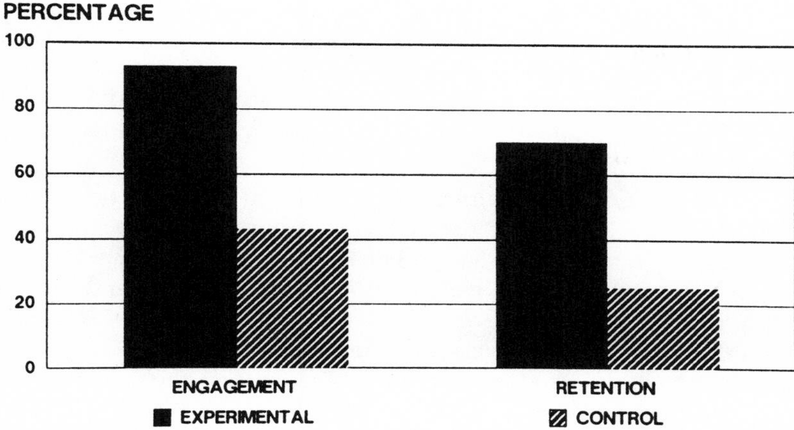

Figure 2. Differential engagement and retention rates across the experimental and control conditions.

ment. In contrast, only 7.15% (4 families) in the structural systems engagement condition were lost to treatment. The differences in the retention rates were also dramatic. In the engagement as usual condition, dropouts represented 41% of the cases that were engaged, whereas dropouts in the structural systems engagement condition represented 17% of the engaged cases. Thus, of all of the cases that were initially assigned, 25% in the engagement as usual condition and 77% in the structural systems engagement condition were successfully terminated. For families that completed treatment in both conditions, there were highly significant improvements in the problematic adolescent's functioning, and these improvements were not significantly different across the engagement conditions. The critical distinction between the conditions was in their differential rates of engagement and retention.

A second major finding of the project (Szapocznik et al., 1988) was the identification of a number of types of resistant families and the development of intervention strategies for engaging these families (Szapocznik & Kurtines, 1989). Four general types of resistant families were identified in the population under study. These four types are listed below in the order of frequency of occurrence.

One type of resistant family was characterized by a very powerful identified patient. In these families, the Structural Systems Engagement intervention required joining the powerful identified patient in order to bring the family into treatment. Particularly in these cases, meeting the identified patient on his or her own "turf" was frequently needed.

In the second type of family, mother and son tended to be strongly allied, while the father was disengaged or distant. In this type of family, the therapist worked with the mother to encourage and coach her to behave in ways that would bring the father closer to her, and thus be willing to attend treatment.

A third type of family was characterized by an ambivalent mother. Although she had called for help for a problem youth, she was also likely to protect the identified patient and be ambivalent about having her husband involved in the therapy process. In these cases, the therapist typically circumvented the mother and went directly to the father (with mother's permission) and placed the father in a more central role in bringing the family into treatment.

In the fourth type, one or more members of the family were concerned that some family secret would be revealed in therapy. In these cases, the therapist would work to establish a treatment contract, accepted by all parties involved, that would restrict the problems to be addressed in therapy.

A second study designed to replicate these findings and to further explore the mechanisms by which the intervention efficacy is achieved is currently being completed. Preliminary results (Santisteban, Szapocznik, Perez-Vidal, Kurtines, Murray, & LaPerriere, 1993) replicate the original findings and support the notion that specialized interventions can dramatically increase the rates of engagement of "hard to reach" families. A second clinically significant preliminary finding is that the cultural background of the client family can contribute significantly to the differential efficacy of the intervention. More specifically, our sample of non-Cuban Hispanics (composed primarily of Nicaraguan families but including also Colombian, Puerto Rican, Peruvian, and Mexican families) were engaged into treatment at significantly higher rates than were our Cuban families. A systematic case-by-case structural analysis is currently under way to shed light on the mechanism by which culture and the engagement procedures "interact" to produce differential treatment effects.

STRUCTURAL FAMILY AND INDIVIDUAL CHILD PSYCHODYNAMIC THERAPIES

Our previous research concentrated on the development, refinement, and testing of structural family theory and strategies. However, the question of the relative effectiveness of a structural family systems approach, when compared to other widely used theoretical orientations, became our fifth challenge. A major study was conducted under funding from the National Institute of Mental Health (Grant # DA34821) from 1981 to 1986 to investigate the relative effectiveness of structural family therapy, individual psychodynamic child therapy, and a recreational activity control group.

In this study we were initially interested in testing the efficacy of structural family therapy with problem children and adolescents since the literature reflected a rapid increase in the use of structural family therapy during the 1970s. Our aim in testing the efficacy of SFT was to conduct the therapy itself in a fashion that reflected as closely as possible the way in which this therapy may have been typically conducted in the field. For this reason, we chose to model the implementation of this therapy after the work of Minuchin and his colleagues (Minuchin, 1974; Minuchin and Fishman, 1981) and used their books as reference manuals.

In order to test the relative efficacy of SFT, adequate comparison and control conditions needed to be identified. The ideal comparison condition would be a widely used therapy representing a distinctly different theoretical orientation. On the basis of extensive contact (including an informal survey) with local child and adolescent therapists, we found that when asked about their clinical/theoretical orientation to working with children with emotional and/or behavioral problems, most defined themselves as "psychodynamically oriented." However, there was greater consensus in applying a psychodynamic intervention to children than to adolescents. Hence, the most theoretically interesting comparison condition for testing the efficacy of SFT was the most commonly and widely used treatment approach for children, the psychodynamic approach.

In addition to a comparison of treatment effectiveness, a particular focus of this study was to investigate the putative mechanisms for change postulated by each of the two theoretical/clinical approaches. Both theoretical approaches, structural family and child psychodynamic, assume underlying etiologies to symptoms. Both treatment modalities aim at the elimination or reduction of symptoms. However, they postulate different processes as being primarily responsible for symptom resolution. The child psychodynamic approach postulates that child psychodynamic functioning is the intervening variable that needs to be modified in order to eliminate the symptom. Structural family therapy, on the other hand, postulates that family interactions represent the intervening variable that needs to be modified in order to eliminate the symptom. Because of these important differential theoretical predictions, one aim of this study was to explore the impact of each theoretical modality (structural family and child psychodynamic) on theoretically sensitive measures of functioning and change (family structure and child psychodynamic functioning, respectively). This study thus sought to address two complementary research aims: an investigation of efficacy and an exploratory articulation of mechanisms that may account for effectiveness.

A final problem remained to be resolved in this study: controlling for attention placebo effects. For this purpose we called upon the experience of others (Strupp & Hadley, 1979; McCardle & Murray, 1974) in designing an intervention that was comprised of the kinds of activities that might be carried out by these children "naturally," that is, when not engaged in therapy. Hence, we designed an attention placebo control condition comprised of recreational activities led by a recreational worker who had no training in psychotherapy.

The basic design used in the study was a mixed experimental design. The between-groups factor was intervention condition with three levels (family structural, child psychodynamic, and control). The within-groups variable was time, using a repeated measures approach with three assessment points (pretherapy, posttherapy, and one-year follow-up). An experimental design was achieved by randomly assigning 69 6-to 12-year-old Hispanic boys to the three intervention conditions (Szapocznik, Rio, et al., 1989).

Treatment integrity guidelines and checklists were developed for both conditions. In order to monitor for treatment integrity, all sessions were videotaped and randomly selected sessions were rated on the checklist. Interjudge reliability on treatment integrity ratings yielded a Kappa of .89. Treatment integrity analyses revealed that therapists adhered to guidelines and conducted interventions in a fashion consistent with their respective modes of interventions. (In the child psychodynamic condition, 78% of interventions were rated as child psychodynamic. In the structural family condition, 61% of interventions were rated as structural family.) Analyses also revealed that the two modalities were applied in a clearly distinguishable fashion.

Results

Attrition data were analyzed using chi squares and outcome data were analyzed using a mixed design analysis of variance. The results of the analyses revealed several important findings, the first three of which involved treatment outcome and relative effectiveness of the conditions. The fourth finding concerned the articulation of mechanisms that may account for the specific effects of differential treatments.

First, with respect to efficacy, the control condition was significantly less effective in retaining cases than the two treatment conditions with more than two thirds of dropouts occurring in the control condition. These attrition results support our earlier recognition that dropout rates are important outcome measures that may distinguish the effectiveness of different intervention/control conditions. Indeed, these results (Szapocznik, Rio et al., 1989) were consistent with our earlier findings in suggesting that the mechanism of specificity (treatment) versus nonspecificity (control conditions) may have made an important contribution to differential retention rates. A second finding was that the two treatment conditions, structural family therapy and psychodynamic child therapy, were both apparently equivalent in reducing behavior and emotional problems based on parent reports and self-reports.

A third finding involves the greater effectiveness of family therapy over child therapy in protecting family integrity in the long term. In this study, psychodynamic therapy was found to be efficacious in bringing about symptom reduction and improved child psychodynamic functioning, but it was also found to result in undesirable deterioration of family functioning. The findings provided support for the SFT assumption that treating the whole family is important because it improves the symptoms and protects the family, whereas treating only the child may result in deteriorated family functioning.

The fourth important finding revealed that there is a complex relationship between specific mechanisms (family interaction vs. child psychodynamic functioning) and related outcome variables. On the one hand, an examination of the relationship between the putative etiologic factors postulated by the two theoretical/clinical approaches supports some of the underlying assumptions of psychodynamic theory, and on the other does not support some of the underlying assumptions of family therapy, that is, that changes in family functioning are necessary for symptom reduction. Hence, there was considerable value in extending the investigation beyond a simple horserace to a study of postulated underlying mechanisms.

Measurement

This study compared SFT with individual child psychodynamic therapy. In testing intervention modalities derived from different theoretical orientations, it is desirable to investigate theoretically relevant mechanisms of change in both conditions. In order to test theoretically based mechanisms of change, however, we had to address the issue of the unavailability of a measure of psychodynamic functioning with psychometric properties suitable for use in research settings.

In response to this research need, we developed the Psychodynamic Child Rating System (Szapocznik, Rio, Murray, Richardson, Alonso, & Kurtines, in press), a theoretically based measure of child psychodynamic functioning specifically designed for use in treatment outcome research. This instrument was designed for use in evaluating the impact of therapies on the psychodynamic functioning of latency-age children. Eight scales were constructed: Intellectual Functioning, Ego Functioning, Self-Concept, Aggression Control, Emotional Adjustment, Family Relations, Peer Relations, and Psychosexual Adjustment. Ratings on these scales are based on the administration of a standardized psychological test battery and standardized interviews with children and with their parents. The ratings are summed to obtain a Total Psychodynamic Functioning score. Two factorially derived scores are also derived from the individual scales: Interpersonal Functioning and Intrapersonal Functioning. The Interpersonal factor represents the child in relation to his social world, including the social self. The Intrapersonal factor represents internal cognitive-affective developmental processes. A detailed report of its psychometric characteristics can be found in Szapocznik, Rio, Murray, Richardson, Alonso, & Kurtines (in press) and the manual for scoring is available from the senior author.

The Psychodynamic Child Rating System is another important measurement advance to come out of our program of research. This instrument is a theoretically meaningful psychodynamic measure that appears to be useful in evaluating outcome for psychodynamic and other forms of child therapy. This measure can be included in research that requires an assessment of psychodynamic changes in children as a result of psychotherapy. The Psychodynamic Child Rating System, or a comparable measure, allows for an investigation of the impact of any therapy on a child's psychodynamic functioning.

CONCLUSION

Throughout the entire course of our work we have sought to integrate theory, application, and research. Our work began in the 1970s in an effort to address an issue of growing concern: promoting culturally competent therapists and therapies to address behavior problems and drug abuse among our community's Hispanic youth. Since then, structural systems theory has provided the foundation from which our breakthroughs in assessment, engagement, and treatment were developed. Our program of research, in turn, provided a solid foundation from which to pursue new advances in the field. For example, the SFSR enabled us to evaluate the effectiveness of structural family therapy in a way that is immensely relevant to structural family theory and therapy. After all, structuralists are by definition interested in structural change. Our refinement of structural family theory strategies and goals in the form of BSFT, in turn, enabled us to understand how to modify these strategies to achieve the same goals without having the entire family in therapy, thus making One-Person Family Therapy possible. Our success in bringing about change in family interactions by working primarily through one person became the foundation of our breakthrough in engaging hard-to-reach families into treatment. Our finding, that changes in family functioning may not be necessary for achieving reduction in symptomatology, has challenged our most basic postulate regarding the relationship between family interaction and symptom change. While it appears that family therapy "works," our findings raise more questions than they answer about the mechanisms through which family therapy brings about change.

Our efforts have also had significant methodological implications. In response to the challenge of having theoretically appropriate measures (Kazdin, 1986), we have achieved some of our most important breakthroughs in the area of measurement (Kazdin, 1993). Thus, we found it necessary to develop measures that would assess changes in family interactional functioning and child psychodynamic functioning that met a number of stringent criteria: that they be constructed consistent with the theoretical underpinnings of the theory of pathology and behavior change under investigation; that they be clinically relevant and found acceptable by clinicians in each of the theoretical areas under investigation, in an attempt to ensure that the findings based on these measures are relevant and acceptable within the field of practice; and that these measures meet acceptable psychometric standards.

RECOMMENDATION FOR FUTURE RESEARCH

Much remains to be done in the continued development of empirically tested advances in clinical application. In this section we limit ourselves to some of the more obvious recommendations that have emerged from our research.

Among these, perhaps one of the most important recommendations involves the use of rigorous research strategies in developing and investigating culturally specific interventions, i.e., interventions developed from an emic perspective. Although our work serves as a model for emic (within cultural group) research, some of the concepts, methods, and strategies developed with our Hispanic samples would appear to have a certain universality. The extent to which these concepts, methods, and strategies may be generalizable to non-Hispanic populations must be determined via appropriate research.

Along similar lines, much work remains to be done in investigating more rigorously the unique characteristics of Mexican American, Puerto Rican, Nicaraguan, Salvadoran, Colombian, and other Hispanics as a way of complementing the work that has focused on these groups' shared characteristics.

With regard to methodological recommendations, the role of attrition as an important outcome variable needs to be investigated further. In two of the studies reported here (Szapocznik, Perez-Vidal, et al., 1988; Szapocznik, Rio, et al., 1989), control conditions had significantly greater dropout rates than intervention conditions. In our results as well as in those of Elkin and her colleagues (Elkin, Parloff, Hadley, & Autrey, 1985), the mechanisms of specificity versus nonspecificity may have been an important contributor to differential dropout rates. Because so many studies appear to suggest that completers in treatment as well as in control conditions seem to have similar improvement in measures of adjustment, differential retention/attrition rates may be the ultimate evidence that certain interventions (specific factors) are more efficacious than control interventions (nonspecific factors).

A final recommendation is for further investigation of the process by which change occurs. While most psychotherapy studies have been primarily concerned with tests of efficacy, more attention must be paid to the investigation of underlying mechanisms of change on the one hand and to issues of safety or undesirable side effects on the other. Further research in both of these areas is recommended. With regard to the latter, it has been the concern of family therapists that nonfamily interventions may help the individual but hurt the family. As our research reveals, this is a testable hypothesis that warrants further investigation and should be of particular importance given the strong family orientation found among a number of Hispanic groups.

REFERENCES

Coleman, A.F. (1976). How to enlist the family as an ally. *American Journal of Drug and Alcohol Abuse, 3*, 167–173.

Elkin, I., Parloff, M.B., Hadley, S.W., & Autry, J.H. (1985). NIMH treatment of depression collaborative research program. *Archives of General Psychiatry, 42*, 305–316.

Haley, J. (1976). *Problem-solving therapy*. San Francisco: Jossey-Bass.

Hervis, O.E., Szapocznik, J., Behar-Mitrani, V., Rio, A.T., & Kurtines, W. M. (1991). *Structural Family Systems Ratings: A revised manual.* Unpublished manuscript, Spanish Family Guidance Center, University of Miami.

Kazdin, A.E. (1986). Comparative outcome studies of psychotherapy: Methodological issues and strategies. *Journal of Consulting and Clinical Psychology, 54*, 95–105.

Kazdin, A.E. (1993). Adolescent mental health: Prevention and treatment programs. *American Psychologist, 48*, 127–141.

Kluckhohn, F.R., & Strodtbeck, F.L. (1961). *Variations in value orientations.* Evanston, IL: Row, Peterson.

Madanes, C. (1981). *Strategic family therapy*. San Francisco: Jossey-Bass.

McCardle, J., & Murray, E.J. (1974). Nonspecific factors in weekend encounter groups. *Journal of Consulting and Clinical Psychology, 42*, 337–345.

Minuchin, S. (1974). *Families and family therapy*. Cambridge: Harvard University Press.

Minuchin, S., & Fishman, H.C. (1981). *Family therapy techniques*. Cambridge: Harvard University Press.

Minuchin, S., Rosman, B.L., & Baker, L. (1978). *Psychosomatic families: Anorexia nervosa in context.* Cambridge: Harvard University Press.

Santisteban, D.A., Szapocznik, J., Perez-Vidal, A., Kurtines, W.M., Murray, E.J., & LaPerriere, A. (1993). *Efficacy of interventions for engaging youth/families into treatment and the factors that contribute to differential effectiveness.* Manuscript submitted for publication.

Scopetta, M.A., Szapocznik, J., King, O.E., Ladner, R., Alegre, C., & Tillman, M.S. (1977). *Final Report: The Spanish drug rehabilitation research project* (NIDA Grant # HB1 DA01696). Miami: University of Miami, Spanish Family Guidance Center.

Strupp, H.H., & Hadley, S.W. (1979). Specific vs. nonspecific factors in psychotherapy: A controlled study of outcome. *Archives of General Psychiatry, 36,* 1125–1136

Szapocznik, J., Hervis, O., Kurtines, W.M., & Spencer, F. (1984). One person family therapy. In B. Lubin and W.A. O'Connor (Eds.), *Ecological approaches to clinical and community psychology* (pp. 335–355). New York: John Wiley & Sons.

Szapocznik, J., and Kurtines, W. (1989). *Breakthroughs in family treatment.* New York: Springer.

Szapocznik, J., and Kurtines, W.M. (1993). Family psychology and cultural diversity: Opportunities for theory, research and application. *American Psychologist, 48,* 400–407.

Szapocznik, J., Kurtines, W., & Fernandez, T. (1980). Biculturalism and adjustment among Hispanic youths. *International Journal of Intercultural Relations, 4,* 353–375.

Szapocznik, J., Kurtines, W., Foote, F., Perez-Vidal, A., & Hervis, O. (1983). Conjoint versus one person family therapy: Some evidence for the effectiveness of conducting family therapy through one person. *Journal of Consulting and Clinical Psychology, 51,* 889–899.

Szapocznik,, J., Kurtines, W. M., Foote, F., Perez-Vidal, A., & Hervis, O. (1986). Conjoint versus one person family therapy: Further evidence for the effectiveness of conducting family therapy through one person. *Journal of Consulting and Clinical Psychology, 54,* 395–397.

Szapocznik, J., Kurtines, W., Perez-Vidal, A., Hervis, O., & Foote, F. (1990). One person family therapy. In R.A. Wells & V.A. Gianetti (Eds.), *Handbook of Brief Psychotherapies* (pp. 493–510). New York: Plenum.

Szapocznik, J., Perez-Vidal, A., Brickman, A., Foote, F.H., Santisteban, D., Hervis, O., & Kurtines, W.H. (1988). Engaging adolescent drug abusers and their families into treatment: A Strategic Structural Systems approach. *Journal of Consulting and Clinical Psychology,* pp. 552–557.

Szapocznik, J., Perez-Vidal, A., Hervis, O., Brickman, A.L., & Kurtines, W. (1990). Innovations in family therapy: Overcoming resistance to treatment. In R.A. Wells & V.A. Gianetti (Eds.), *Handbook of Brief Psychotherapy* (pp. 93–114). New York: Plenum.

Szapocznik, J., Rio, A.T., Hervis, O.E., Mitrani, V.B., Kurtines, W.M., & Faraci, A.M. (1991). Assessing change in family functioning as a result of treatment: The structural family system rating scale (SFSR). *Journal of Marital and Family Therapy*, *17*, 295–310.

Szapocznik, J., Rio, A., Murray, E., Cohen, R., Scopetta, M., Rivas-Vasquez, A., Hervis, O., Posada, V., & Kurtines, W. (1989). Structural family versus psychodynamic child therapy for problematic Hispanic boys. *Journal of Consulting and Clinical Psychology*, *57*, 571–578.

Szapocznik, J., Rio, A., Murray, E.J., Richardson, R., Alonso, M., & Kurtines, W.M. (in press). Assessing change in child psychodynamic functioning in treatment outcome studies: The Psychodynamic Child Ratings. *Interamerican Journal of Psychology*.

Szapocznik, J., Santisteban, D., Kurtines, W.M., Perez-Vidal, A., & Hervis, O. (1984). Bicultural Effectiveness Training (BET): A treatment intervention for enhancing intercultural adjustment. *Hispanic Journal of Behavioral Sciences*, *6*, 317–344.

Szapocznik, J., Santisteban, D., Rio, A., Perez-Vidal, A., & Kurtines, W.M. (1986). Family Effectiveness Training for Hispanic families: Strategic structural systems intervention for the prevention of drug abuse. In H.P. Lefley & P.B. Pedersen (Eds.), *Cross Cultural Training for Mental Health Professionals*, Springfield, IL: Charles C. Thomas.

Szapocznik, J., Santisteban, D., Rio, A., Perez-Vidal, A., Kurtines, W., & Hervis, O. (1986). Bicultural effectiveness training (BET): An intervention modality for families experiencing intergenerational/intercultural conflict. *Hispanic Journal of Behavioral Sciences*, *8*, 303–330.

Szapocznik, J., Santisteban, D., Rio, A., Perez-Vidal, A., Santisteban, D. A., and Kurtines, W. (1989). Family effectiveness training: An intervention to prevent problem behaviors in Hispanic adolescents. *Hispanic Journal of Behavioral Sciences*, *11*, 4–27.

Szapocznik, J., Scopetta, M.A., Aranalde, M.A., & Kurtines, W. (1978). Cuban value structure: Clinical implications. *Journal of Consulting and Clinical Psychology*, *46*, 961–970.

Szapocznik, J., Scopetta, M.A., King, O., & Hervis, O. (1978). Theory and practice in matching treatment to the special characteristics and problems of Cuban immigrants. *Journal of Community Psychology*, *6*, 112–122.

Szapocznik, J., Scopetta, M.A., Kurtines, W., & Aranalde, M.A. (1978). Theory and measurement of acculturation. *Interamerican Journal of Psychology*, *12*, 113–130.

AUTHOR NOTES

This work was funded in part by a National Institute on Drug Abuse grant (#DA5334) and a Center for Substance Abuse Prevention grant (#2350).

This chapter is a revised version of the following article: Szapocznik, J., Kurtines, W.M., Santisteban, D.A., & Rio, A.T. (1990). Interplay of advances between theory, research, and application in treatment interventions aimed at behavior problem children and adolescents. *Journal of Consulting and Clinical Psychology*, *58*, 696–703. Copyright 1990 by the American Psychological Association. Adapted by permission.

Correspondence concerning this chapter should be addressed to: Jose Szapocznik, PhD, Department of Psychiatry, University of Miami, 1425 N.W. 10th Avenue, Suite 302, Miami, FL 33136; telephone (305)-326-0024.

CHAPTER 9

CULTURALLY SENSITIVE TREATMENT MODALITIES FOR PUERTO RICAN CHILDREN, ADOLESCENTS, AND ADULTS

Giuseppe Costantino, PhD,
Clinical Director, Sunset Park Mental Health Center, Lutheran Medical Center, Brooklyn, New York and Senior Research Associate, Hispanic Research Center, Fordham University, and

Carmen Rivera, PhD,
Senior Psychologist, Sunset Park Mental Health Center, Lutheran Medical Center, Brooklyn, New York

Kaplan (1963), expanding on the Worfian hypothesis, affirms that language and culture affect not only the logic in use but also the state of knowledge, the stage of inquiry, and the special condition of the particular problem we are investigating. Levine (1984) defines a culture as a group of individuals who share the same language and heritage and intellectual, moral, and ethical standards. Language and culture, therefore, become the two most important variables in psychotherapy, whether psychodynamically or cognitive oriented (Costantino, Malgady, & Rogler, 1986; Padilla & Ruiz, 1973; Rogler, Malgady, Costantino, & Blumenthal, 1990; Rogler, Malgady, & Rodriguez, 1991; Sue & Sue, 1977; Szapocznik, Scopetta, & King, 1978).

Traditional therapy modalities that are historically based on the psychological, social, and cultural needs of nonminority middle-class clients have dominated the field of mental health service delivery. However, in the late 1950s and during the 1960s, the large state psychiatric hospitals began the mass deinstitutionalization of inpatient psychiatric clients, who drifted into the poor neighborhoods of the big cities. This mass exodus of psychiatric patients promoted the development of community mental health centers in the poor, inner-city communities where the discharged psychiatric clients lived and marked the birth of community psychology. This, in turn, planted the seed for the creation of new nontraditional therapy modalities to treat poor, culturally diverse mental health clients.

The 1970s witnessed early research on Hispanic mental health services and the following decade ushered in the development of culturally sensitive therapy modalities for Hispanics. According to Rogler and associates (1987, 1991), culturally sensitive treatment for Hispanics can be organized into three different approaches. The first endeavors to render traditional treatment more accessible to Hispanics by increasing the congruence between professional mental health values and indigenous Hispanic values: hiring bilingual/bicultural clinical and clerical staff and coordinating referrals with community-based agencies and churches, among other things. This approach has been shown to increase use of mental health services among Hispanics (Acosta & Cristo, 1980; Costantino & Stiles, 1984; Scott & Delgado, 1979; Trevino, Bruhn, & Bunce, 1979). The second approach to cultural sensitivity involves the selection of a therapy modality to fit the perceived cultural characteristics of Hispanics. It generally uses traditional therapy modalities for acculturated Hispanic clients and selects available modalities, such as crisis intervention, pharmacotherapy, and family-oriented therapy, for less acculturated Hispanic clients (Ruiz, 1981).

The third approach to cultural sensitivity involves some modification of traditional therapy modalities to fit the Hispanic client's cultural values. The third approach can be subdivided into two subapproaches. One is illustrated by Szapocznik and colleagues (1978, 1980, 1991) at the Spanish Family Guidance Center at the University of Miami. On the basis of their perceptions that Cubans are primarily family oriented, they have modified traditional family therapy to treat the mental health problems of Cuban clients. This subapproach emphasizes the concept of *isomorphism* in that the client's value system matches that of the traditional therapy system. The second subapproach, developed by the Hispanic Research Center at Fordham University in New York City (Costantino, Rogler, & Malgady, 1980; Costantino, Malgady, & Rogler, 1982; Rogler et al., 1987), starts with the client's cultural value system and uses it as a vehicle for therapeutic intervention. An illustration of this is the use of *cuento* or folktale therapy for children and their mothers.

The use of folktales or storytelling is rapidly gaining strong and growing acceptance as a culturally sensitive therapy modality. Several cognitive psychologists, such as Bruner (1986), Mair (1988), and in particular Howard (1991), affirmed that the development of human identity occurs as a result of life-story construction. They likened psychopathology to an incoherent story with a wrong ending and psychotherapy as a process of retelling coherent stories with right endings. Howard (1991) described the technique of storytelling as the most adept process in understanding culturally diverse individuals and in conducting cross-cultural psychotherapy. He emphasized:

> If one considers *thinking a storytelling* and if one sees cross-cultural differences as rooted in certain groups entertaining different stories and roles within stories, then one might see some examples of psychotherapy as interesting cross-cultural experiences in story repair. (p. 194)

THE FUNCTION OF FOLKTALES

For millennia, storytelling—perhaps the oldest form of literature—was the sole method of educating the young. For untold centuries, societal rules and customs, standards of morality, and the achievements of heroes were divulged across generations in folktales as narrated by professional storytellers, parents, or elders. For this reason, folktales have come to be perceived as a repository of the cultural heritage of a given ethnic or racial group and as a vehicle for the transmission of societal values and cultural traditions from one generation to the next. From an anthropological viewpoint, Arbuthnot (1965) wrote:

> Folktales have been the *comment of society*. They not only expressed but codified and reinforced the way people thought, felt, believed and behaved. Folktales taught children and reminded their elders of what was proper and moral. They put the stamp of approval upon certain values held by the group and thus cemented it together with a common code of behavior. They taught kindness, modesty, truthfulness, courage in adversity, and they made virtue seem worthwhile because it was invariably rewarded and evil just as invariably punished. This idea of folktales as the carriers of the moral code helps explain the ethical significance and emotional satisfaction they still hold for us today. (p. 255)

In addition to the importance of folktales as a means of transmitting a cultural heritage, folktales have the ability to transmit abstract concepts in an easily understandable way. The language of folktales is a poetic language that effectively communicates complex messages. Often through metaphorical representation, they concretize abstract concepts such as obedience toward parents and authorities. For example, conflict between parents and children, sibling rivalry, and parental and filial love are represented in the "Parable of the Prodigal Son" found in the Bible.

It appears that the metaphorical language of folktales has an intrinsic expressive ability to transform words into poetic forms, and the expressed forms represent imaginal models that have pedagogical and therapeutic values. Goethe often wrote that the fairytales his mother told him during childhood had been one of the most important factors contributing to his poetic imagination and his motivation to become a great poet (Bettelheim, 1977).

Folktales have also been one of the most instrumental means of keeping intact the identity of an ethnic group under foreign domination or in adverse social conditions. Black slaves in the United States found solace from inhuman hardship by chanting folk tunes from their motherland. Biron (1948) stated that oral literature and folk songs have been "one of the most important factors in the survival of French culture in Canada." Speaking of Latin America, Faro (1939) stated, "that which most truly expresses the spirit of our country is folklore."

Latin American people have been acknowledged for the richness and importance of their traditions of folktales (Madrid, 1953). Among them, Puerto Ricans occupy a special place, judging by the results of efforts to collect their folktales. More than 70 years ago, J. Alden Mason (1921), a scholar interested in Puerto Rican culture, undertook the prodigious task of collecting the folktales of the island. He concluded that the collection ". . . is by far the most abundant and most important Spanish folktale material collected in Spanish America. Its importance for American-Spanish folklore studies is inestimable" (p. 143).

Yesterday's Puerto Rican culture was suffused with the traditions of folktales that were told from one person to another and handed down from one generation to the next. As they were told and retold, the folktales underwent change, with additions and subtractions being made, modifications and alterations being introduced, the stories sometimes bent in one direction or another. Whatever the changes, however, the folktales retained their fidelity to Puerto Rican culture. As parents and grandparents, neighbors and friends recounted the folktales to the children, the children learned the traditions of their Puerto Rican culture while vicariously or symbolically enjoying the plots of the stories.

Today, the modernization of Puerto Rico, in particular, the growth of the mass media through radio, television, audio and video recorders, newspapers, and magazines, has probably attenuated the once pervasive importance of folktales in transmitting culture from one generation to the next. Nevertheless, the intrinsic interest that folktales retain for children, the tales' retention of indigenous cultural elements, and their easy malleability make them, from our viewpoint, well worth considering as a means of relieving the psychological distress of Puerto Rican children living in a different society, New York City.

Storytelling in Psychology

Puerto Ricans in the United States live between two cultures, and the healthy development of their children depends on a balanced integration of values, beliefs, and behaviors of both the Hispanic and the Anglo cultures. Taking both cultures into consideration, the present study uses not only original stories taken from Puerto Rican culture, but also adapted stories that reflect the dominant Anglo culture. Folktales have survived for centuries only because they have constantly changed by incorporating new elements while maintaining the content of the tale. Furthermore, it is the folktales' ability to incorporate new elements from the dominant culture that makes it a contemporary instrument to effect change and, at the same time, retain the basic cultural values of the ethnic group.

History has presented us with examples of the survival of ethnic minorities through the lengthy process of adapting their cultural heritage within the dominant culture. For example, an important factor in the struggle of black slaves to survive psychically and culturally in the dominant Spanish culture of colonial Cuba was their ability to integrate their ancient African rituals with the Christian religion of the Spaniards, thus creating a new synthesis, *santeria* (Amos, 1959).

The cultural survival of the Puerto Rican group within the dominant American society rests on their ability to bridge the gap between the Hispanic heritage and the prevailing Anglo values. However, transcultural adaptation is a lengthy process but it can be shortened through appropriate culturally sensitive therapy interventions. For example, Toldson and Pasteur (1976) conducted a psychotherapy program using black folklore to foster more adaptive personality functioning among black adolescents and young adults. The authors reported that they were able to develop more adaptive interpersonal relationships among black adolescents, foster more responsible behavior, and help troubled teenagers gain insight into their problems.

Perhaps the most compelling evidence that the telling of folktales promotes personality development comes from studies of achievement motivation. During the past three decades, the research literature on achievement motivation, which began with the work of McClelland, Atkinson, Clark, and Lowell (1953), has accumulated ample evidence showing that fairytales tend to influence growth in children and that the achievement motive can be enhanced through storytelling. McClelland and Friedman (1952) studied cross-cultural relationships between childrearing patterns in eight North American Indian cultures and the strength of the achievement motive as reflected in folktales dealing with the coyote as the main character. Their findings revealed a striking correlation between achievement motivation as expressed in folktales and achievement as exhibited in the culture at large, concluding that:

> . . . a general emphasis on achievement in the culture influences both child training and the kind of stories which are told in the culture—particularly since the stories may often be used to educate the young (p. 240).

Similarly, in a study of the relationship between independence training in children and achievement motivation in ancient cultures, Friedman (1950) reported that early emphasis on independence training was related to the degree of achievement motivation presented in the mythology of the cultures studied. Furthermore, Wright (1954) conducted cross-cultural research on the socialization of aggression and reported a significant correlation between the aggressive content of the folktales and the aggression exhibited in the culture.

Additional evidence of how folktales are used to foster education and personality development in certain cultures comes from an anthropological field study conducted in Alaska (Rooth, 1976). Rooth (1976) reported that before the implementation of a public school system to educate youngsters in Alaska, the native Alaskan Indians had an informal school for their children. He reported an anecdote from an informant who attended the informal school as a youngster: "We got an old man who told us stories and we were listening to his stories just like school. He told us about life and his experiences and what was good and what was bad and his stories were told in order that we should learn from him" (p. 24). Another informant in the Alaskan field study reported: "And (they) tell us the stories and we pick it up and then, after we get old, we have to try to tell the stories to (our) young people. Our father, our mother, our grandmother, that's the way they always teach us way back. No school. They just teach us what no good (in) the stories. We have to learn to listen to stories all the time" (p. 35). Thus, in this field study, folktales were told by parents or other authority figures to foster good social judgment and reality testing, moral judgment, work motivation, and interpersonal relationships with parents and the elderly.

Despite the ostensible psychological value of folktales, there have been surprisingly few attempts to use folktales as a systematic therapy modality. Nevertheless, some eminent clinicians are beginning to use folktales to ameliorate emotional problems in children. Bettelheim (1977) wrote:

> . . . fairy stories represent in imaginative form what the process of healthy human development consists of, and how the tales make such development attractive for the child to engage in. This growth process begins with resistance against the parents and fear of growing up, and

> ends when the youth has truly found himself, achieves psychological independence and moral maturity . . . and is able to relate positively to . . . the other sex. (p. 12)

Bettelheim has used fairytales to treat severe psychological dysfunctions in children and adolescents and reported that this technique makes a positive psychological contribution to the child's personality growth. Furthermore, Gardner (1971) indicated that his innovative "mutual storytelling" modality effected positive therapeutic change in both neurotic and borderline children. This technique uses stories created by the children themselves during the therapy session, which are then retold by the therapist during the same session with changes to reflect more adaptive personalities of the characters. In a similar study, Jilek-All (1976) described the use of the mutual fairytale technique in order to gain the trust of Canadian Indian patients and to understand their symptoms within their cultural context. Irwon (1977) also supported the effectiveness of drama therapy based on children's stories in dealing with psychic integration, reenactment of past traumatic experiences, transformation from passivity to activity, and inculcation of mastery in children. Still another study in the Soviet Union (Polcz, 1966) exposed children to fairytale puppets, highlighting the advantages of using both fantasy and realism for the therapist's understanding of the underlying dynamics of behavioral change.

The clinical utility of folktales as a therapeutic modality also is buttressed by two psychiatric case studies. In one, Klosinski (1978) reported the successful treatment of a 12-year-old anorexic girl by the use of painting and fairytale therapy, which brought about the amelioration of obsessional symptoms that had afflicted the girl since the age of 4. In another study, Weimer (1978) reported a case of a 22-year-old woman with depression and psychotic symptomatology who was treated successfully by using fairytales. The fairytale of Rapunzel was used allegorically to give the patient insight into her excessively dependent relationship upon her mother and to point out the role of this symbiosis in the patient's illness.

Notwithstanding the growing clinical interest in folktales as a therapy modality, carefully controlled evaluation of treatment outcomes is scarce. Saltz and Johnson (1973, 1976), in their preliminary evaluation of a 4-year follow-up study, indicated that thematic fantasy play (TFP) may be a promising therapeutic modality for culturally disadvantaged children. The children were from the lower socioeconomic class, and included Southern and Northern whites, blacks, and Chicanos. The treatment involved verbal role dramatization in a group setting where the children dramatized traditional fairy tales such as The Three Billy Goats and Cinderella. The results indicated that:

> TFP was found to be significantly associated with a higher incidence of spontaneous socio-dramatic play, superior performance on Borke's (1972) Interpersonal Perception Test, and better story memory and storytelling skill on specially constructed tasks. The effects of fantasy play on intelligence were more borderline. (p. 15)

Amato, Emans, and Ziegler (1973), studying the effectiveness of drama and storytelling in a group of primary school subjects, found that neither modality appeared to have any effect on children's interest and reading achievement. However, there were indications that storytelling may have more influence than creative dramatics on self-image and empathy. Westone and Friedlander (1974) explored the effect of live, televised, and audio story narration on primary school children and found that their listening comprehension significantly improved the most when exposed to videotaped presentation, next when exposed to live presentation, and the least when exposed to audio presentation. These data suggest that the storytelling technique may be a promising modality to foster cognitive skills.

FOLKTALE THERAPY WITH CHILDREN

In our first study of cultural intervention with children, Costantino, Malgady, and Rogler (1986) developed a storytelling modality using Puerto Rican *cuentos* (folktales) organized within the framework of modeling therapy. Because folktales convey a message or moral to be emulated by others, the characters were posed as therapeutic role models of adaptive emotional and behavioral functioning within Puerto Rican and American cultures. The presentation of indigenous Puerto Rican folktale characters serves first, to motivate children's attention to the models; second, to portray beliefs, values, and behaviors with which children can easily identify; and third, to reinforce children's imitation of the role models in a therapeutic setting, thereby facilitating social learning of the target behaviors.

As we have discussed earlier, other studies have used storytelling of fairytales and fantasy play to treat dysfunctional nonminority (Bettelheim, 1977; Gardner, 1971) and minority children (Freyberg, 1973; Smilansky, 1968), and quantitative evaluations have suggested favorable treatment outcomes. Thus, the *cuento* study was designed to evaluate treatment outcomes of cultural intervention compared to a standard therapy and no therapy. Two versions of *cuento* therapy were developed, one based on original Puerto Rican folktales, and the other based on those original folktales adapted to reflect the life experience of Puerto Rican children in the United States to bridge Puerto Rican and American cultures. This variation on cultural intervention provided for a test of the two approaches guiding the third method of cultural sensitivity.

Methods

Treatments were conducted in group sessions with 210 Puerto Rican child-mother dyads, boys and girls (grades kindergarten to 3; mean age = 7.45) and their mothers. The children were screened for behavior problems in school and at home (by teacher and parental ratings) and were classified in the secondary prevention stage for risk of mental disorder. The children's families were of low socioeconomic status. The father was absent from 68% of the households; most parents were unemployed (mothers, 88%; fathers in household, 39%) and had not completed high school (mean education = 8.5 years).

A panel of Puerto Rican psychologists and parents selected 40 *cuentos* from Puerto Rican folklore on the basis of thematic content expressing cultural values. Development of a therapy modality from these original *cuentos* was consistent with the approach of isomorphic reproduction of culture in treatment. A second modality was developed by adapting these *cuentos* to bridge Puerto Rican and American cultures and to redirect the thematic content of each story to be more adaptive. The cuentos were rewritten to reflect settings common in urban life (e.g., a rural plantation was changed to an inner-city playground; mango trees were changed to apple trees). While the ethnic identity of the main character remained Puerto Rican, secondary characters were presented as multiethnic (i.e., Hispanic, black, and white) to more naturally reflect inner-city social interactions. Original themes were altered to stress social judgment, control of anxiety and aggressive impulses, delay of gratification, and compliance with parental authority. For example, in an original *cuento*, a poor boy who steals capriciously from a farmer is punished and he learns from his mother why stealing is wrong.

In these cultural intervention sessions, therapists and mothers of the children read one *cuento* bilingually as the children followed the narration. To balance sex-role modeling, the protagonist of one *cuento* was a boy and in the other was a girl. Therapists then conducted group discussion of the character's feelings and behavior and the moral of the story. Once the target behaviors of the session were understood, the opportunity for imitative behavior was provided as the mother-child dyad dramatized the story and resolved the basic conflict. Videotapes of the role-playing exercise were reviewed by the groups, and the therapist led discussions of members' personal experiences with similar conflict, and which solutions were adaptive and maladaptive in terms of reducing family conflicts. A second no-treatment control group participated in traditional play/activity therapy sessions conducted by a therapist and a school teacher.

Children were randomly assigned by sex and grade level to treatment groups and 20 weekly 90-minute sessions were led by male and female Puerto Rican therapists. Sessions were held in two public schools within the Hispanic community. Attendance at the sessions generally was above 80%.

Treatment Outcomes

Children were pretested and posttested individually with a battery of measures by bilingual Puerto Rican examiners blinded to treatment group assignments. Tests were administered in the child's preferred language or bilingually. A second follow-up posttest administration was conducted one year later on 178 (85%) of the children (Costantino, Malgady, & Rogler, 1986).

The screening criteria for inclusion in the study and the targets of the therapy intervention were anxiety symptoms, conduct problems (aggressiveness, disruptiveness, inability to delay gratification), poor social judgment, and low self-esteem. Results indicated that, relative to a play therapy and nonintervention control groups, children participating in the *cuento* groups evidenced significantly reduced anxiety symptoms and more adaptive social judgment. These effects were more enhanced for the adapted *cuento* group. Moreover, the effects persisted on the follow-up assessment one year later.

Cuento Therapy Session Format

The typical session took place in a school classroom from 3 p.m. to 4:30 p.m. Chairs for the participants were assembled in a circle. Five mothers came to the room with their children and each mother-child dyad sat next to each other. The session was led by a group leader and co-leader. Both leaders welcomed the participants. While the group leader took note of attendance, the co-leader distributed both Spanish and English versions of the *cuentos* to the mothers and their children. Two *cuentos* were read in each therapy session, generally by the mothers in turn, while the children followed the narration by listening or reading silently from the *cuento* booklet. In order to balance the role modeling of the *cuento* characters in each session, one *cuento* had a female person or animal as the principal character, while the other *cuento* had a male person or animal as the principal character.

Sample Cuento and Analysis

"The Donkey Who Wanted to be a Thief"

Once there was a donkey who owned a small field of vegetables. One day, as he was tilling the earth with his shovel; that is, loosening the earth, his shovel hit a hard object. When the donkey took the hard object out of the ground, he discovered that it was an old, rusty pistol, a pistol like the ones the pirates once used.

The donkey said, "I wish I would have found a pot of gold. What am I going to do with this pistol?" The donkey thought and thought. Suddenly he said, "I know! I'll be a robber, a thief."

He took the pistol and went looking for his first victim. Soon Alfred the dog passed by the road. The donkey cried, "Stick 'em up, Alfred. You're finished. Your money or your life!"

Alfred the dog responded, "What in heavens' name is wrong with you? We've known each other for years." The donkey only said, "Stop talking and give me what I want!"

The dog growled, "I'll give you what you want, you dumb donkey." And he bit the donkey on his rear end and on one of his ears. The donkey jumped and ran away.

He went looking for another victim near a yard where there were many animals. He hid behind some bushes and, soon, Penny the hen passed by.

The donkey shouted, "Stick 'em up! I want every last cent you have." Penny the hen was scared and began to yell, "Help me! Help me! This thief is trying to hurt me!" A turkey, a pig, a goose, and a rooster all ran after the donkey, attacking him. The donkey ran and ran, very far away from the yard.

Then he passed by Miss Kitty the cat's house and, as he was about to hold her up, the police dog came, grabbed the donkey, and put him in jail.

A small mouse that had made his house in the jail looked at the donkey from the little hole he lived in. The donkey began to speak to the mouse. He said, "Boy, I really deserve all the trouble I've gotten into. Do you know why this has happened to me? It's happened because I got lazy and didn't want to work in my field anymore. I wanted to have an easy life. All I've gotten are bruises, cuts, and bumps. And now nobody likes me. Oh! What a fool I've been!"

The mouse, who was a very good friend of the police dog, told him what the donkey had said. The police dog asked the donkey, "Do you promise never to do this again?" The donkey answered, "Yes, I promise," And the police dog let him go.

From that day on the donkey worked very hard in his field and lived happily ever after.

1. *Moral or Basic Meanings*
   Stealing does not pay. In fact, sooner or later those who steal will end up in jail. On the other hand, good, honest, hard work is rewarding.
2. *Achievement Motivation/Productive-work Behavior*
   At the very beginning, the donkey shows some productive work behavior. In fact, he was working his garden planting vegetables. However, he is not so strongly motivated to work hard because, as soon as he finds a gun, he decides to start robbing instead of working. (In his case, the circumstances make a thief out of the donkey.)
3. *Moral Judgment*
   The donkey shows very poor moral judgment. In fact, he decides to rob others instead of working. Furthermore, he shows very few guilt feelings. However, he has the capacity of learning; that is, once he is arrested mugging others, he decides he will not steal again. (The donkey learns not to steal because he is afraid of punishment.)
4. *Object Relations*
   When the donkey worked very hard, in an honest way, he had several friends. However, when he becomes a thief, his friends become his enemies. He even steals from them. However, when the donkey is in jail and shows some guilt feelings and feels sorry for the wrong he has done, the mouse feels sorry for the donkey and helps the donkey get out of jail.
5. *Aggression*
   In mugging and stealing from others, the donkey shows aggressive

behavior. He does violence against others and causes damage. The other animals also show aggression, but only to defend themselves.

6. *Anxiety-Depression*
   Penny the hen and Kitty the cat don't fight back. They feel very scared when the donkey stages a stick up.

HERO/HEROINE THERAPY WITH ADOLESCENTS

Interviews with the older (third-grade) children participating in the *cuento* therapy study, combined with small-sample pilot studies on adolescents, revealed their tendency to view the folktales as juvenile and the characters as cartoonlike (Costantino, Malgady, & Rogler, 1988). In conjunction with the anxiety outcomes specific to the younger children in the *cuento* study, these findings inspired the development of a similar approach to the introduction of cultural sensitivity into modeling therapy. Following the promising treatment outcomes emerging from the evaluation of the *cuento* therapy study, the program of research on culturally sensitive psychotherapy was extended to an adolescent Puerto Rican population, basing the cuento therapy modality on "heroic" adult role models instead of folkloric heros.

Adolescence is considered a critical period in the psychosocial development of most youngsters, and the literature suggests that Puerto Rican adolescents may be at increased risk of mental disorder. It appears that the identity crisis of Puerto Rican adolescents is compounded by strong intercultural and intergenerational conflicts (Lewis, 1966). Consequently, Puerto Rican adolescents would appear to be suitable candidates for modeling therapy that fulfills their need for adaptive adult role models in a culturally sensitive way.

In our second study, Malgady, Rogler, and Costantino (1990) developed a *cuento* (storytelling) therapy using biographical stories of prominent Puerto Ricans to bridge the identity, bicultural, and intergenerational conflicts confronted by Puerto Rican adolescents. This modality sought to enhance the relevance of therapy for adolescents by exposing them to successful adult role models in their own culture, thus fostering ethnic pride and identity as a Puerto Rican, and to model achievement-oriented behavior and adaptive coping with stress common to life in the Puerto Rican community. The content of the biographies embodied themes of cultural conflict (e.g., expression of cultural pride juxtaposed with experiences of discrimination) and group discussion and imitative role playing drawn upon experiences in Puerto Rico and the United States. Therefore, hero/heroine modeling therapy endeavors to bridge cross-cultural conflict much in the manner of the adaption of folktales in the previous study.

Methods

This culturally sensitive therapy was conducted in group sessions with 40 male and 50 female Puerto Rican adolescents in grades 8 and 9 (mean age = 13.67), who were screened for behavior problems by teacher rating and classified as presenting secondary risk status. All households were of low socioeconomic status; 64% were receiving welfare benefits and 71% were headed by a female. The major differences from the children participating in the *cuento* therapy study were that these adolescents all were U.S.-born and English-dominant and their mothers did not participate in treatment. Attempts were made for mother participation, but adolescents felt very much inhibited by their mothers' presence in the sessions. Children were randomly assigned to either the hero/heroine intervention group (n = 70, with 9 dropouts) or an attention control group (n = 40, with 11 dropouts). The intervention group participated in 18 weekly 90-minute therapy sessions and the attention control group participated in 8 monthly discussion sessions, each led by male and female Puerto Rican therapists in a public school within the Hispanic community. Attendance at the sessions averaged 68% in the intervention and 84% in the control group.

Four practical professionals selected and compiled biographies of nine male and nine female "heroic" role models, sampling diverse periods of Puerto Rican history. The role models were chosen on the basis of their significant achievements (in politics, sports, arts, and education) and adaptive coping to overcome adversities such as poverty and prejudice. A different male or female biography was presented in each session. Intervention sessions were conducted in three phases. First, group members read the biography and the therapists (group leader and his/her cotherapist) led a discussion of the source of stress and behavior reflecting ethnic pride, positive self concept, and adaptive coping strengths. Second, in order to promote identification with the model, the therapists led group discussion through structured questioning comparing group members' experiences to the model's biography. Therapists verbally reinforced group members' self-reported behavior that was consistent with the model and explored alternatives to maladaptive behavior. Third, group members dramatized an open-ended skit related to the biography with direction to resolve the conflict posed. Peer reinforcement of adaptive resolutions was encouraged and also verbally reinforced by the therapists.

Thus, the hero/heroine modeling therapy promoted adolescents' identification with the heroic role models through ethnic and cultural congruence and also by comparison of stressful experiences. Group discussion and imitative role playing then were used to reinforce appropriate target behaviors.

Treatment Outcomes

Adolescents were pretested and posttested individually in their preferred language or bilingually with a battery of measures by bilingual Puerto Rican examiners blinded to treatment group assignments (see Malgady, Rogler, & Costantino, 1990). The main findings were decreased anxiety symptoms and increased ethnic identity and self-esteem relative to adolescents participating in an attention-control group. However, unlike the results of the *cuento* intervention with young children, the hero/heroine treatment outcomes were moderated by adolescents' sex and family structure. Negative treatment outcomes were evident among adolescent girls from intact households, who felt less ethnic pride and lower self-esteem than boys and girls in single-parent households. Our hypothesis about this finding was that girls may have transferred idealized images of role models to their parents, while boys did not. Similarly, the role models fulfilled their purpose to boys and girls from single-parent families.

Sample Biography and Analysis

Roberto Clemente

Roberto Clemente was born in 1934 in the town of Carolina in Puerto Rico. He began playing baseball when he was 8 years old. He wanted to buy his own baseball equipment, but his father told him that there was no money for that kind of expense. Roberto wanted this equipment so badly that when his father said "no," he felt that he was never going to be able to practice. Then he thought of how he could get his equipment by himself. He was very good with his hands and his imagination. He looked around him and decided to make the equipment with materials he had at hand. He made a bat by carving it out of a piece of wood from a guava tree. He made his glove by putting beans inside a coffee sack. His ball was made out of a tight knot of rags. By using his imagination and the simple materials around him, he got his basic sports equipment: a bat, a glove, and a ball.

When he was 18 years old, he was signed as a rookie player for the Santurce team of the Winter League in Puerto Rico. This was a great honor because most of the players on this team were young men brought from the United States to Puerto Rico. Roberto played so well that soon the U.S. major leagues began to show an interest in him. Finally, Roberto accepted an offer from the Brooklyn Dodgers. Later he joined the Pittsburg Pirates, and with Roberto on the team, the Pirates went from last place in the National League to the top.

Roberto was one of the first black players in baseball at that time. The major league teams in the United States usually rejected black players even though many of them were excellent. Jackie Robinson was the first major league baseball player in the United States. When Roberto signed with the Brooklyn Dodgers, there were only five other black men on the team. His life in the United States was not easy. He had to learn to speak English and he had to fight against racism. Many times when the team was playing baseball in the South, Roberto could not stay at the same hotel as the other players on his team because of the color of his skin. He couldn't even eat at the same restaurants as the other players. The sports commentators would make fun of his Spanish accent and ridicule him whenever he was hurt during a baseball game.

Roberto believed in hard work and in every human being's personal worth and dignity. He took immense pride in being a black Puerto Rican and always held his head high. He did not waste time in fighting with people to assert his work; instead he showed it by working so hard that he was voted baseball's highest honor, the Most Valued Player of the Year.

One day, he was in a baseball game and he batted a home run. An adult and a boy ran to catch it together. The adult got the ball and the boy was left with empty hands. The next inning, Roberto went to bat again and when he had a break, he took a ball and walked to the bleachers. He told the boy: "Take this ball because I saw how sad you were before. I'm giving this to you so you can always remember that for everything you lose in life, there is another door that opens up for you." The boy grew up to become a man and always remembered Roberto's lesson. After many years, Roberto went to a store get some supplies. To his surprise, the store owner was the little boy he had met many years back. Roberto did not recognize him, but the owner remembered him perfectly. He expressed all his gratitude for the good example that

Roberto had set for him. When Roberto tried to pay, the store owner refused to accept any money.

Roberto's love for his parents was deep and constant. The night Roberto played with the Pittsburg Pirates and they became the champions of the World Series, the reporters swarmed around him asking him to make a statement for the television audience. Roberto answered: "I want to dedicate this triumph to all the mothers in Puerto Rico. I ask that those who are watching this program be close to their parents, ask them for their blessing, and embrace them. I would now like to say something in Spanish to my mother and father in Puerto Rico. On this, the proudest moment of my life, 'Bendición, Mama y Papa.'"

In Puerto Rico Roberto was and still is considered a national hero for his achievements in the game of baseball and for his concern for the people of Latin America. He dreamed one day of building sports camps for poor children so they would have the chance to develop their abilities in sports. He also hoped that such camps would keep the children busy enough to prevent them from becoming delinquents. He gave money and his time to many charities.

In 1972, when Roberto was still a young man, he was deeply moved by news of an earthquake that destroyed many parts of Nicaragua in Central America. Roberto began to raise money for the earthquake victims so that he could buy food and medicine for them. To make sure that these supplies would reach the people that most needed them, Roberto decided to deliver the supplies himself. He chartered a plan one New Year's Eve, but only a few minutes after the plane had taken off, it crashed into the sea. His body was never found. Today the name of Roberto Clemente is a respected one.

Main Points of Story

1. He was a black Puerto Rican who was never ashamed of his humble origins, his country, the language he spoke, or the color of his skin.
2. He created his own opportunities. When he didn't have any money to buy baseball equipment, he made his own.
3. To make his way, he had to fight against racism. He also had to learn to speak English.
4. He loved his parents deeply and felt deeply for other people. He wanted to build sports camps for poor children and lost his life bringing supplies to the earthquake victims of Nicaragua.
5. He never let his tremendous success as a baseball player give him a swelled head. Even when his team won the World Series, he remembered his parents.

Discussion

Roberto said: "Remember that for everything you lose in life, there is another door that opens up for you." What do you think he meant by this?

When Roberto became a champion in the World Series, why did he dedicate his triumph to his mother and ask everyone to be close to their parents?

Roberto did not waste time in fighting with people to assert his worth.

What does this mean?

Relate Main Points of Story to Subjects' Lives

1. Have you ever played baseball? What does it take to be a good player?
2. Have you ever solved a problem by inventing something like Roberto did when he made his own bat, glove, and ball?
3. How would you feel if you went to a restaurant and they refused to serve you because you were Puerto Rican?
4. What are some ways you feel you can use to assert your worth?
5. Do you get along with your parents? With your teachers? With your classmates?
6. Do you think sports is a good way to keep kids out of trouble?

Role Playing

Ask one student to pretend to be a Puerto Rican who is speaking English with a heavy accent. Enlist another student to imitate a Chinese person speaking English. Find out if anyone can imitate an Italian accent, a British accent, a Southern accent, or a Brooklyn accent. Guide students in a discussion of the different ways people talk and explain that what seems funny to one person may not seem funny to another (the Puerto Ricans may laugh at the Chinese accent, but the Chinese may think the Puerto Rican accent is even funnier).

Discuss why people have accents. Should you laugh at them?

The members of the group pretend to be seniors who are planning their class trip to Washington, D.C. Some of the students are white and others are black. The students discover that Washington, D.C. is segregated. The white students will have to stay at a hotel just for whites. The black students will have to stay at a much more inferior hotel just for blacks across the other end of the city. The students discuss what they will do.

Should they cancel the senior trip? How do the white students feel about staying at a separate hotel? How do the black students feel? What can they do?

STORYTELLING THROUGH PICTURES

Earlier studies of high-risk Puerto Rican children (Costantino, Malgady, & Rogler, 1986) and adolescents (Malgady, Rogler, & Costantino, 1990a) have demonstrated positive treatment outcomes using small-group modeling interventions, changing the culturally sensitive modality according to age cohort. A study with 5- to 8-year-old children used Puerto Rican folktales, whereas 12- to 15-year-old adolescents used biographies of heroic role models taken from Puerto Rican history. The characters in both these modalities were presented to the children and adolescents as peer role models exhibiting adaptive attitudes, values, and behaviors reflective of the designated targets of therapeutic intervention, such as acting out, anxiety symptoms, and low self-esteem. The participants engaged in therapeutic role playing and imitation of the models' appropriate behavior was reinforced. Thus, the modality was presented in an age-appropriate format with which the children or adolescents could readily identify and imitate, the goal being to improve personality functioning and psychosocial adjustment. Treatment outcomes of the cultural interventions were evaluated relative to nonintervention control and traditional play therapy groups with the children and relative to a school-based dropout prevention group with the adolescents. The results were that the culturally sensitive interventions reduced anxiety symptomatology and increased self-esteem, social judgment, and ethnic identity.

This study took into consideration several new therapeutic variables in this program of culturally sensitive treatment outcome research. First, whereas in previous studies inclusion criteria were based on teacher ratings of school behavior, in the present study research participants were screened for DSM-III-R symptomatology using a standardized structured clinical interview. Second, the present study included older children and young adolescents 9 to 13 years old, an age range not addressed in previous studies. Third, in contrast to previous studies that presented written and verbal modeling stimuli, this study presented pictures, which we thought would be more effective in communicating with a more psychologically disturbed and educationally disadvantaged group. Fourth, this study included diverse Hispanic groups, whereas previous studies focused exclusively on Puerto Ricans.

Methods

The participants in the study were recruited from a public school in Brooklyn, New York. The school is located in a low socioeconomic community of 102,000 residents, mostly Hispanics (more than 60%), largely of Puerto Rican descent. In recent years, however, there has been rapid population growth due to immigration from the Dominican Republic and Central and South America. The school has a population of approximately 1,400 students, 95% Hispanic.

More than 500 students in grades 4 through 6 whose self-reported ethnicity was Hispanic were contacted for participation. Student and parental consent was obtained from 363 respondents, who were subsequently screened for DSM-III-R symptomatology using a structured clinical interview (*Child Assessment Schedule*; CAS). Interviewers were two graduate PhD psychology students who were trained to administer the CAS. None of the students satisfied the diagnostic criteria of the selected DSM-III-R disorders assessed by the CAS. The three most prevalent categories of symptomatology, however, were associated with anxiety, conduct, and phobic disorders. Students presenting symptoms that were primarily in categories other than these were excluded. The three symptom categories were highly comorbid; most (n = 276) students presented at least three symptoms in at least two of the three categories. Among those screened, the 30 most symptomatic males and females in each of the three primary symptom categories (n = 90) were selected for the study. The number of the symptoms presented per category ranged from 5 to 11 on any one of these disorders and at least three on a second disorder. The most prevalent subdiagnostic symptoms were in the conduct category, followed by anxiety, and then phobic symptoms. The most common pattern of comorbidity was conduct/phobic symptomatology, followed by conduct/anxiety and phobic/anxiety. Approximately 60% of the participants were of Puerto Rican descent (n = 55), 25% were Dominican (n = 22), and 15% were San Salvadoran, Nicaraguan, Peruvian or Colombian (n = 13). All were bilingual, according to teacher and parental report.

Procedures

Participants were stratified by sex and grade level and then randomly assigned to either the experimental intervention or an attention-control group (n = 45 per treatment group). The experimental and attention-control groups were further subdivided randomly into six subgroups of seven to eight participants each. Members of each group participated in eight weekly 90-minute sessions. Sessions were videotaped to monitor the fidelity of treatments and to facilitate discussion among group therapy members. Sessions were conducted by six Hispanic graduate psychology trainees (PhD and PsyD students) in a private room in the participating school. All therapists had completed at least three years of graduate study and were trained with videotape feedback by the first author. Three therapists conducted experimental sessions, while the remaining three conducted the control sessions; each therapist administered two subgroups. Both groups were pretested before the first session and posttested after the eighth session with a battery of outcome measures. To promote attendance, participants in both groups were given token rewards, such as T-shirts and school supplies, each time they attended two consecutive sessions.

Treatment Modalities

The experimental intervention consisted of a storytelling modality based on pictorial stimuli depicting Hispanic cultural elements (e.g., traditional foods, games, sex roles) and Hispanic families and neighborhoods (e.g., stores or *bodegas*), in urban settings. These stimuli were eight pictures from the Tell-Me-A-Story (TEMAS) thematic apperception test (Costantino, 1988) portraying multiracial Hispanic characters interacting in a variety of urban, familial, and school settings. The TEMAS pictures were developed by a professional artist who attempted to capture elements of Hispanic culture as described by a panel of cultural experts (Costantino, Malgady, & Rogler, 1988). Research on TEMAS indicates that Hispanic children and adolescents readily identify the characters and families in the pictures as Hispanic and the settings as similar to their own neighborhoods, and that they tell substantially longer stories about TEMAS pictures than about stimuli with less cultural emphasis, such as Thematic Apperception Test (TAT) cards (Costantino et al., 1988).

The TEMAS pictures have been empirically shown to "pull" designated themes among Hispanic children and adolescents. The pictures chosen were particularly likely to evoke storytelling related to anxious, depressed, and fearful feelings and to disruptive/cooperative, aggressive/nonaggressive, and achieving/failing behaviors. Some TEMAS pictures are designated for both sexes, while others are pairs of parallel sex-specific pictures. In the therapy sessions, a single picture (one boy, one girl) was presented.

Therapy sessions were conducted in three phases. The goal of the first phase, which averaged about 30 minutes, was for the group members to develop a composite story in response to the preselected TEMAS picture. The participants told stories about the pictures, either spontaneously or when necessary with prompting, identifying the characters, setting, sequence of events, and resolution of the plot. After the third session, as rapport was established, little prompting by the therapist was required. The therapist attempted to capture those thematic elements in the individual narratives that provided the most adaptive solution in order to synthesize the most therapeutic composite story.

In the second phase of the sessions, which averaged about 40 minutes, group members were motivated to share their personal experiences as related to the composite story. The therapist stressed that members should share their true experiences and should be respectful of others' self-disclosures. Personal experiences, feelings, and significant life events were readily projected into the participants' storytelling, requiring very little prompting on the part of the therapist. The therapist then compared the behaviors, attitudes, and feelings expressed in the personal events disclosure with the corresponding elements of the composite story constructed in the first phase. The therapist verbally reinforced themes in the participants' personal narratives that were adaptive or consistent with the composite story. Maladaptive themes were referred to the group to discuss alternative, more adaptive resolutions of personal conflict. In this process, participants were encouraged to express their own value judgments about their peers' experiences. The most common reactions expressed were judgments of good or bad behavior, verbal reinforcement, disapproval, socially supportive encouragement, and empathy. Thus, this phase engaged the participants in verbalizing personal conflicts in their lives and how they coped, seeking to symbolically reinforce and internalize adaptive resolutions of stressful situations. In the third phase, which averaged about 20 minutes, the participants dramatized the composite story by performing the roles of the characters in the original picture and of characters who had been constructed in the group interaction. Verbally supportive reinforcement of imitative target behaviors (e.g., confronting one's fears, proper behavior, adaptive coping with stress) was given by the therapist and by peers during the dramatization. The psychodrama was videotaped and played back to the group for critical review and reinforcement of desired behavior. Thus, the goal of this phase was to provide reinforcement through personal dramatization of adaptive symbolic narrative models.

The attention-control group engaged in discussion sessions with emphasis on psychoeducational content. Four different children's videos were shown in alternate weeks: *The Adventures of Tom Sawyer*, *Pinocchio*, *The Black Stallion*, and *Star Wars*. A video was shown during the first session, and participants were told to pay close attention because the following week they would be discussing and drawing pictures about what they saw. The video sessions were conducted by a schoolteacher and a teaching assistant, whose main task was to promote participants' attention to the video while managing their behavior and minimizing disruptions.

The sessions following a video presentation were conducted by a school teacher and a therapist. The therapists conducting these sessions were not involved in conducting the TEMAS therapy sessions. The participants were first asked to recall the content of the movie. Much like the discussion of TEMAS pictures, the participants related the characters, setting, events, and story ending. The teacher and therapist facilitated the recollection of the movie content, when necessary, by prompting as in the therapy condition. The participants were then asked to share with the group the themes and characters in the video they liked best and then to draw them. Finally, the participants dramatized the theme or the actions of their favorite characters in the movie. Repeating the procedures in the experimental group, the skits were videotaped and played back to the participants. The emphasis of the attention-control group was to show symbolic models, such as Pinocchio or Tom Sawyer, thus fostering cognitive functioning without direct therapeutic impact. Drawing and dramatization were activities resembling play therapy. Otherwise, the TEMAS therapy and the attention-control sessions were structured to be as similar as possible.

Treatment Outcomes

Following the same procedures as the *cuento* and hero/heroine intervention studies, participants in the storytelling study were pretested and posttested with a battery of outcome measures. Results indicated there were no treatment group differences in depressive symptoms (as measured by the CES-D), but the storytelling intervention significantly reduced participants' anxiety and phobic symptoms and improved their behavioral conduct in school (as rated by teachers).

Underlying these findings runs a common thread: the abiding interest of youngsters in participating actively in symbolic activities that enmesh culture. Whether cultural sensitivity operates like a catalyst enabling the effectiveness of a standard therapeutic technique, such as modeling therapy in the present case, or whether cultural sensitivity itself is therapeutic, equipping youngsters in the fashion of anticipatory socialization to confront otherwise confusing demands, is an intriguing question warranting further inquiry.

CULTURALLY SENSITIVE THERAPY FOR ADULTS

The posthospitalization adjustment of the Hispanic chronically mentally ill and their utilization of aftercare services are timely research issues given the impact of the deinstitutionalization movement, which has resulted in the locus of care for the chronically mentally ill being moved from inpatient settings to the community at large (Rivera, 1986). Increasingly, families of the mentally ill are being asked to assume major responsibility for aftercare and are faced with enormous problems of trying to locate appropriate services for sick relatives in an environment of fragmentation of responsibility, insufficient financial resources, and inadequate support and rehabilitation opportunities. Consequently, many seriously mentally ill persons end up living a marginal existence and have to be readmitted to the psychiatric hospital only to be discharged once again. The fact that 85% of the patients discharged as a result of deinstitutionalization are located in the lower socioeconomic classes (Goldstein, 1981) adds poignancy to the problem. These observations hold particular significance for Hispanic chronically mentally ill (CMI) patients and their families since a substantial portion of the Hispanic population is economically disadvantaged. There is thus a pressing need to assess the requirements of Hispanic families who are playing a role in the care and rehabilitation of the discharged CMI Hispanic patient and to evaluate the impact of the discharged Hispanic CMI on the mental health and well-being of those living in the same household (Rivera, 1986).

Personal observation of a highly structured "psychoeducational" program emphasizing family intervention operating out of Bellevue Medical Center in New York City, as well as a study of the pertinent literature, suggests ways in which the design and delivery of this particular treatment approach might be modified to be more effective with and sensitive to the needs of Hispanic families who are increasingly being asked to bear the major responsibility for aftercare.

Rationale for a "Psychoeducational" Approach

Research of the past 50 years has implicated genetic and organic variables as well as a range of sociocultural variables as constituting important factors in the etiology, course, and outcome of chronic mental illness. A multitiered model of chronic mental illness has consequently emerged that encompasses biological, psychological, and environmental factors. Although the focus of research findings has been on schizophrenia, it is likely that these findings hold true for other chronic mental disorders.

There is general agreement that drug maintenance therapy constitutes one of the most important treatments for chronic mental illness. However, although drug treatment induces remission of psychotic symptoms for most patients, up to 40% experience relapse within one year after discharge (Hogarty et al., 1976). Therefore, drug maintenance therapy in and of itself has not stopped the "revolving door" pattern of discharge and readmission in psychiatric facilities. Although many researchers have underscored the role of genetic, biochemical, and anatomical factors in the transmission and manifestation of these disorders, justifying their theories with evidence of the effectiveness of somatic therapies, the role of psychosocial factors in influencing the cause and outcome of chronic mental illness has also been emphasized. Many researchers currently reject a purely biological explanation for the etiology and course of these disorders. Mednick (1958) was one of the first to propose a theory that schizophrenia occurs in individuals who are physiologically predisposed to this disorder when they are confronted with adverse and stressful environments. This is termed the diathesis-stress or vulnerability theory and it is currently the most strongly supported model for schizophrenic pathology (Meehl, 1962; Zubin and Spring, 1977; Gottesman and Shields, 1982).

Mednick's diathesis-stress model has provided a basis for developing a treatment framework termed a "psychoeducational" approach. At present, a number of different psychoeducational programs are described in the scientific literature (Leff et al., 1981, 1982; Anderson et al., 1980; McFarlane, 1983). Although programs differ with respect so specific components (e.g., extent of patient involvement, length of treatment, whether treatment interventions take place in the home or in the clinic), all programs have in common the fact that they attempt to integrate educational, behavioral, and supportive techniques to assist families in helping their chronically ill relative as well as themselves. Recognizing that approximately 65% of patients discharged from mental hospitals return to their families annually (Goldman, 1982) and that approximately 25% or 250,000 of this group are chronically mentally ill, proponents of the psychoeducational treatment model stress that families are the patient's and professional's most important allies in the rehabilitation process and, as such, the family's participation in treatment is necessary. At the crux of the psychoeducational approach is the overwhelming need expressed by families for more information and concrete advice concerning their relative's illness as well as the mounting evidence that the family's emotional environment can have a powerful impact, positive or negative, on the patient's adjustment to illness. The psychoeducational model also recognizes and incorporates into the services it provides research findings on factors associated with the course and outcome of chronic mental illness—factors such as the size and nature of the patient's social network and impact of life-event stress—and the importance of the family environment. A previous article by one of the authors (Rivera, 1986) reviewed recent research findings on these factors in non-Hispanic populations and speculated how such variables might have an impact on the Hispanic with chronic mental illness.

The Bellevue Hospital Family Support Group

In order to educate family members about CMI and its treatment, to help them develop their coping strategies, and to provide a more positive experience with mental health professionals, a psychoeducational workshop series, termed a Family Support Group, was offered to the relatives and friends of CMI patients at Bellevue Hospital Center. Consisting of ten 1½-hour sessions held in a multiple-family format twice a month, this workshop series had the immediate goals of providing families with information on the etiology, prognosis, and treatment of CMI (particularly schizophrenia); educating families about the importance of antipsychotic medications and their side effects; teaching skills in coping with psychotic symptoms; developing strategies to solve problems that arise out of living with a CMI individual; and introducing families to other community resources. Beyond the educational objective, another goal of the group was to provide a social support system for the families with the ultimate goal of reducing the frequency of relapse for the CMI patient and improving the patient's social functioning.

Families began attending the group at any time after the intake interview. Appropriate referrals to the group consisted of any relative or close friend of a CMI patient with a primary diagnosis of schizophrenic or manic-depressive illness. The group was not an appropriate referral for families of patients with an organic disorder such as Alzheimer's disease, alcohol or drug abuse, or major depression. Referrals were accepted from any hospital psychiatric inpatient or outpatient unit.

Families thought to be able to derive special benefits from the group were those who were very isolated and/or feeling overwhelmed in dealing with their ill relative, those who lacked general information about the relative's disorder, and/or those whose involvement with the patient was too intense and a source of stress for the patient.

The Family Support Group is different from family therapy in that this model recognizes that the family is not the focus of pathology. Therefore, goals and efforts of the support group remain focused on the patient. If family therapy focusing on systemic issues seemed indicated, families were referred to the hospital's Family Therapy Program.

Specific Interventions

Providing basic education about the nature, treatment, and prognosis of chronic mental illness was a fundamental component of the Family Support Group. Using schizophrenia as a model, family members were presented a historical overview of the illness. The DSM-III criteria for the diagnosis of the disorder and distinguishing factors between schizophrenia and other disorders such as manic-depressive illness and multiple personality were explained to workshop participants. Particular attention was paid to describing thought disorder, including delusions; ideas of reference and thought insertion; as well as hallucinations and the withdrawal, lethargy, and anhedonia that often accompany these more dramatic symptoms. The possible causes of schizophrenia were also addressed. Psychoanalytic and family interaction theories concerning the etiology of schizophrenia were briefly presented; participants were told there are no empirical data supporting such theories and that such views are outdated. The evidence for genetic transmission of schizophrenia was also presented to families during the workshop. Theories delineating the roles of biochemistry and environmental stress in the development and maintenance of symptoms were explained and the families were told that this model is strongly supported by available data. The impact of overstimulation in creating cognitive processing difficulties was emphasized as was the breakdown in the schizophrenic brain of a "hypothetical filter" that controls selective attention. This model of schizophrenic pathology was presented in lay language so that it could be easily comprehended. These explanations structured the management advice that was provided in later sessions.

Additionally, information about prognosis of the disorder was provided and family members were told about an axiom commonly voiced among psychiatrists in the United States called "the rule of thirds" (Torrey, 1983): one third of schizophrenics will not improve even with medication, one third will improve but not completely recover, and a final third will recover with no remaining symptoms. Schizophrenia was presented as highly treatable but not curable. Drawing an analogy to diabetes, families were told that schizophrenic symptoms could be controlled with medication and by learning to modulate stimulus input (stress) the way a diabetic learns to take insulin and modulate sugar intake. In this way, maintenance medication and stress identification and management were introduced as treatment strategies. The family's role in such treatment was then spelled out: to support medication and learn to monitor levels of stimulation in the home. The point that families are not to blame for schizophrenic pathology was stressed along with the family's role as a significant resource in the patient's recovery.

Families were also informed about the phases of schizophrenic illness and what to do in each phase. Families were taught that it is important for them to learn to recognize early warning signs and to call the patient's psychiatrist so that medication can be increased in order to avoid hospitalization. During the acute stage when hallucinations and other signs of thought disorder intensify, families were advised not to argue with the patient about such symptoms and to expect that hospitalization may be necessary even if the patient's medication is increased by the psychiatrist. During the residual phase of the illness, family members were counseled to arrange for an outpatient psychiatrist, to learn to recognize so-called negative symptoms of the illness such as lethargy and withdrawal, to give the patient "space," and to set realistic expectations while supporting small gains and setting limits. Family members were also advised of the importance of trying to continue with their own lives.

Finally, the educational component of the workshop entailed providing families with information about medications and their side effects. Families were lectured about how neuroleptic medication works and the varieties of medication available to treat psychotic symptoms, and were advised to expect a trial-and-error period that is usually necessary to find out which medications work best for each patient. Family members were also instructed how to recognize side effects of medications and were told about the existence of medications that control undesirable side effects. Finally, the limits of medication were discussed with family members (i.e., medication controls "positive symptoms" such as hallucinations and other signs of thought disorder but has no effect on "negative" symptoms such as apathy and withdrawal).

In addition to the educational component, efforts to enhance the communication, coping, and problem-solving skills of family members constituted another basic component of the Family Support Group. Accordingly, several workshop sessions focused on coping with troublesome symptoms and behaviors. For example, family members were instructed not to argue with patients about their hallucinations or delusions but instead to assist patients with reality testing by acknowledging that family members perceive things differently and urging the patient to divert his attention to more realistic concerns. Concrete advice was also provided about how to cope with a sick relative's lack of motivation, anxiety, depression, possible suicidal ideation, and aggression or violence. Additional workshops focused on fostering attitudes in family members that would promote the development of coping skills. The importance of taking a long-range view, making one change at a time, reaching consensus with other involved relatives, avoiding overinvolvement, and developing outside interests of their own was stressed to relatives. Behavioral techniques such as reinforcement, shaping, and time-out were described and examples of their implementation were provided.

Some sessions focused on improving communication among family members. Learning when to and when not to communicate (i.e., not when one is feeling upset) was stressed as well as the importance of selecting one problem at a time. General guidelines were provided to assist in managing verbal and nonverbal communications with the ill relative, including such suggestions as saying something positive first, identifying the specific behavior that one wants changed, saying how one would feel if the behavior changed, listening very carefully to what the ill relative says, and being brief and clear. Role-playing exercises in communication were also conducted within the workshop setting.

Specific strategies were provided to facilitate problem solving within the family. Families were taught to identify the problem and define it specifically, list all possible solutions without criticism, discuss each possible solution, choose the best solution or combination of solutions, plan how to carry out the best solution, review the implementation of the solution and praise everyone's efforts, and revise the plan if necessary. Role-playing exercises in problem solving were likewise conducted within the family support group sessions.

A final component of the workshop series was aimed at informing families about available community resources. Representatives from Friends and Advocates of the Mentally Ill (FAMI) spoke with the group about the history of the FAMI organization, its accomplishments, and the value of joining such a group. Additional guest presentations by social workers and other professionals provided information about day treatment programs, choosing a psychiatrist for medication, socialization groups and group psychotherapy, vocational rehabilitation, crisis teams in New York City, and negotiating with agencies like the Social Security Administration and the Health and Human Resources Administration for benefits.

Adapting the Family Support Group to Hispanic Families

Is the psychoeducational approach an appropriate treatment modality for use with the families of Hispanic CMI patients? It is generally accepted that there are values and choices implicit in all treatment approaches, as well as issues pertaining to cultural factors and dynamics, which must be taken into account when evaluating whether any traditional psychotherapeutic model meets the special problems and needs of a particular community. A large number of practitioners believe that mental health programs should be harmonious with the culture they serve. Is the psychoeducational treatment program outlined above culturally sensitive to the needs of Hispanics? If not, can this model be modified and adapted to provide a better "fit" to the cultural experiences of Hispanic patients and their families?

Before answering these questions however, the concept of cultural sensitivity needs to be addressed. Rogler et al. (1987) reviewed the relevant literature and examined how this concept was used by mental health practitioners and researchers in their work with Hispanics. Overall, three broad levels of cultural sensitivity were outlined by Rogler and his colleagues. The first involves rendering traditional treatment more accessible to Hispanic clients. The second consists of selecting a traditional treatment according to perceived features of Hispanic culture. The third and most ambitious level entails extracting elements from Hispanic culture to modify traditional treatments or to develop new therapeutic modalities. In the discussion that follows, the three levels of Rogler et al.'s cultural sensitivity model will be examined and considered in terms of their applications to the psychoeducational treatment model.

Level 1: Increased Accessibility

According to the cultural sensitivity framework established by Rogler et al., the first step in rendering psychoeducational therapy more culturally sensitive involves increasing the accessibility of treatment to Hispanic clients. At the lowest level, this consists of increased linguistic accessibility via the hiring of bilingual/bicultural staff, thereby overcoming the most blatant communication barriers existing between Hispanic clients and mental health staff. With respect to the psychoeducational approach, increased linguistic accessibility not only entails hiring bilingual/bicultural therapists who can be responsive to the marked differences in language domain among Hispanics (i.e., some rely on English exclusively, others use both languages equally, and some rely exclusively on Spanish), but also involves the issue of how to translate complex ideas from English into Spanish in a way that is comprehensible to a relatively unsophisticated population. Increased accessibility also involves the location and/or development of written and visual aids in Spanish that can be used as supplements to orally presented material. The Hope Family Project (Healing Opens Partnership Effects) is one example of just such efforts to make the profoundness of chronic mental illness understandable to socioeconomically disadvantaged Hispanic populations via culturally attuned media (McLaughlin, O'Brien, & Rosenberg, 1992). This project has developed a videotape that dramatizes both the shattering effect of a son's schizophrenia on a

Hispanic family as well as the hopeful effect education and support can have on the family and patient.

Beyond this minimal level of linguistic accessibility, increasing cultural accessibility also entails incorporating indigenous ethnic networks into the mental health system with the goal of reducing the cultural discrepancies between the two. In the case of psychoeducational therapy, this feature is an inherent component of the approach in that members of the patient's own family network are recruited as allies in the rehabilitation process. Family members are used as a means of modulating stimulation and stress in the patient's environment. Also, the fact that this treatment model asserts that families play a critical role in the treatment of CMI serves to increase the congruence between the psychoeducational treatment system and Hispanic culture, thereby being responsive to Level 2 of Rogler et al.'s cultural sensitivity model.

Level 2: Making Therapy More Culturally Appropriate

Level 2 of Rogler et al.'s cultural sensitivity framework entails rendering the selection of a treatment modality compatible with Hispanic cultural characteristics. In this respect, much has been written about the family's essential role in the institutional character of Hispanic society (Rogler and Cooney, 1984). Despite rapid social changes, Hispanic society at the root cultural level still centers on the family and its functions. Additionally, among Hispanics, the nuclear and extended family network often exerts a strong and pervasive effect on individual decision making (Fitzpatrick, 1971). The psychoeducational model does not sacrifice the family's authority for decision making and the overseeing of patient recovery. Rather than undermining the intricate pattern of Hispanic interpersonal relationships, the psychoeducational approach incorporates and mobilizes members and methods of the family system to further its own purpose.

At a more global level, Level 2 of Rogler et al.'s model asks the question, Is the treatment relevant to the context of Hispanic life? Observations and interviews conducted with family members of Hispanic CMI patients in treatment at a mental health clinic in the South Bronx reveal that many family members express a desire for more concrete information about schizophrenic illness and a need for learning appropriate techniques for coping with schizophrenic symptomatology. In this respect, the needs of Hispanic families caring for a mentally ill relative probably are no different from the needs of non-Hispanic families and relatives of the mentally ill. Consequently, the basic assumption of psychoeducational intervention that providing information to families is extremely important and valuable does not conflict with perceived Hispanic cultural characteristics and needs.

Despite the overall relevance of the psychoeducational treatment model in addressing the needs of Hispanic families caring for a mentally ill relative, are there other specific components and assumptions of the treatment model that are more or less congruent with traditional Hispanic values? For example, is the view, propagated by the psychoeducational model, of schizophrenia as a serious illness involving a biological vulnerability of unknown origin that makes patients particularly susceptible to stress from their environment, incompatible with Hispanic belief about causation of mental illness? Few studies have addressed the issue of whether their culture predisposes Hispanics to maintain different perspectives and values regarding the etiology and definition of psychosis (Rogler and Hollingshead, 1965; Dohrenwend and Chin Shong, 1967; Lubschansky et al., 1970; Rivera, 1985). Recent findings (Rivera, 1985) reveal that the concept of mental illness as the consequence of external stressors or as the result of brain dysfunction is not necessarily alien to the Hispanic perspective.

The psychoeducational treatment model also advocates the use of antipsychotic medication in the treatment of chronic mental illness and asserts that there are specific techniques that family members can learn to help in the management of a relative with CMI. Do such assertions coincide with Hispanic cultural characteristics? In this respect much has been written about the often-referred-to Hispanic expectation for a therapy that is instructive and provides tangible forms of intervention such as medication, direct advice, and immediate solutions as well as a therapist who is active (Sue, 1981). Psychoeducational therapy, with its emphasis on dispensing information, teaching coping skills, advocating medication, and providing very concrete behavioral instructions, meets these expectations.

Psychoeducational therapy also attempts to dispel the notion that families are to blame for their relative's mental illness and to dissuade the family from viewing the sick individual as malicious or malingering. The personal observations of one author, a Hispanic clinician possessing some experience working with families of the chronically mentally ill, reveal that Hispanic families are not immune to experiencing guilt and attributing their relative's illness to their own incompetency as parents, spouses, or children of the sick relative.

In a similar vein, recent findings (Rivera, 1985) show that Hispanics are as apt as non-Hispanics to view certain patient behaviors as "*mala-crianza y falta de verguenza*" (inconsiderate behavior and shamelessness) rather than identifying the behaviors as symptoms of the illness. Members of this population would therefore benefit from exposure to psychoeducational illness formulations.

On the other hand, one must question whether the democratic and egalitarian problem-solving paradigm proposed by the psychoeducational treatment model as a means of assisting families to approach problems in an organized fashion would be compatible with Hispanic family decision making. As Rogler and Cooney (1984) point out, the prevailing pattern of decision making in traditional Hispanic families is based on role segregation and stresses the superior authority and domination of the male and the subordinate position of the female. The psychoeducational decision-making model requires families to make decisions jointly, which contradicts the norms of role segregation and male superiority inherent in traditional Hispanic culture. It may be, however, that when families are emotionally anguished and overwhelmed, as is often the case when a CMI family member yields a disruptive and disorganizing effect on family life, traditional roles within the family are not strictly adhered to and there is no sharp segregation of conjugal roles in such families. Moreover, Rogler and Cooney (1984) found that in their Hispanic study group there had been a shift away from sharp segregation of conjugal roles toward more egalitarian task sharing and decision making. If this is the case, then the problem-solving approach proposed by the psychoeducational model may be implemented with Hispanic families. Alternatively, it may be that the egalitarian problem-solving approach espoused by psychoeducational intervention may have to be modified so that it does not clash with the values of traditional Hispanic families. Such modifications—either changing the treatment format or educating Hispanic patients and their families to accept the treatment—comprise Level 3 of Rogler et al.'s cultural sensitivity framework.

Level 3: Modifications of Psychoeducational Treatment

Thus far, any suggested changes in the psychoeducational approach have not involved any shift in professional goals, values, or conceptions of mental illness, nor any substantive changes in treatment format. However, Level 3 of Rogler et al.'s cultural sensitivity model does entail modifications in treatment format through the incorporation of Hispanic cultural elements. With respect to psychoeducational therapy, this might take the form of using certain ethnic characteristics in order to buttress the treatment modality. For example, it may be necessary to broach the subject of spiritism and encourage a discussion of spiritist beliefs and practices among workshop participants when providing Hispanic families with information about the causes of mental illness during an educational workshop. A number of investigators (Garrison, 1975; Lubschansky et al., 1970; Ruiz and Langrod, 1976) who have studied this system of indigenous psychotherapy have suggested that the greater the degree of mental illness evidenced by the Hispanic, the more likely he or she is to visit a spiritist. Consequently, the psychoeducational therapist can anticipate that a number of workshop participants may have sought the assistance of a spiritist for their sick relative at some point during the course of the illness. Moreover, when such beliefs are acknowledged by participants, they should not be discouraged and belittled by the therapist, but accepted as an alternative system of explanation and treatment since such beliefs are often part of a coherent system that many feel is as complex as the Western model (Garrison, 1975; Ruiz and Langrod, 1976). Additionally, the psychoeducational therapist might even encourage such practices, not as a substitute for professional assistance but as an addendum to traditional medications and interventions. The spiritist recognition of both "material" and "spiritual" causes facilitates the conflict-free use of both indigenous and professional systems of mental health care. The therapist's acceptance of spiritist beliefs and practices would be one example of using a specific and common element from the client's ethnic culture in order to complement and modify the provision of conventional therapy.

In a similar fashion, other aspects of the Hispanic explanatory model of mental and emotional illness could be incorporated into psychoeducational therapy. For example, it is often asserted that Hispanics do not make distinctions between mental and physical health (Padilla et al., 1975; Rosado, 1980). Keeping this in mind, the psychoeducational therapist working with Hispanics could easily modify explanations about the biochemical irregularities underlying CMI and present such an illness as an imbalance of a physiological condition and medication as a means of strengthening or balancing the physiological system, thereby creating a "fit" between participating families and the therapist as to the understanding and management of symptoms.

Closely related to issues of spiritism and ethnic explanations of causality are matters concerning proper diagnosis of chronic mental illness. Psychoeducational therapy provides relatives of the mentally ill with specific information about criteria used by professionals in making a determination of chronic mental illness. However, there are special issues regarding assessment and diagnosis of Hispanic clients that might also be addressed in a psychoeducational workshop. For example, a non-Hispanic clinician unfamiliar with the beliefs and practices of spiritism might attribute greater pathology than warranted to a Hispanic client who is immersed in the spiritist belief system. It can be argued that relatives of the Hispanic CMI have a right to know such facts. Also, relatives should be made aware that when a Hispanic client who speaks no English is assessed by an English-speaking diagnostician and an interpreter is used, interpreter-related distortions may give rise to important misconceptions about the patient's mental health status. Armed with at least some knowledge of the possible impact of language and sociocultural factors on psychiatric diagnosis, Hispanic family members can then play a more active role in obtaining an adequate psychiatric assessment for their sick relative.

Level 3 of Rogler et al.'s cultural sensitivity model entails altering treatment to match the characteristics of the Hispanic client's culture as well as sometimes providing elements that are missing from the culture and counteracting elements that may be overemphasized in the culture. Thus, with respect to the psychoeducational treatment model, the objective of modification in the approach might be to change culturally prescribed behaviors that lead to psychologically dysfunctional characteristics. For example, a number of clinicians working with Hispanic CMI populations have noted that Hispanic-American mothers, suffering a sense of emptiness in their lives, are frequently overinvolved with their psychotic offspring, particularly their sons. Because of the mother's unhappy circumstances, the sons become so important to them that many of these women have great difficulty setting any limits or standards of behavior for their ill offspring. They often extend themselves in making sacrifices and then feel hurt and rejected when the sons or daughters do not reciprocate. Based on their traditional upbringing within a culture that stresses the absolute self-sacrifice of the mother as a cultural ideal, as well as the established importance of children within Hispanic culture, it seems that becoming self-sacrificing mothers is the only fate available to them. This is a state of affairs that is often very damaging to the CMI son or daughter; studies in expressed emotion and the family environment have shown that overinvolvement leads to overstimulation, which is often associated with schizophrenic relapse and the necessity for rehospitalization. In such situations, the psychoeducational therapist may promote the idea that the "good" mother is also one who takes time for herself and engages in activities she enjoys as an individual. Such a therapeutic suggestion might be culturally revolutionary from the client's point of view, but it might also prove extremely helpful. In this way, the psychoeducational therapist would help these mothers to be more flexible and more aware of possible alternatives beyond their present, culturally limited coping spectrum so that they can have more choices regarding adjustment.

Another Hispanic cultural trait that might require transformation or modification through psychoeducation is that of *polychronicity*. Polychronicity refers to a culture in which several activities often occur simultaneously, i.e., several conversations, listening to music, watching television, dancing, etc., resulting in a high degree of noise and movement. In other words, a high noise level, multiple interactions, and movement have been posited to be culturally normal within many Hispanic families (Hardy-Fanta & McMahon-Herrera, 1981). Unfortunately, such an environment is often detrimental to individuals suffering from CMI; it is well documented that individuals with thought disorder are vulnerable to increased disorganization under conditions of overstimulation (Leff, 1976; Leff & Vaughn, 1981). Thought-disordered patients may become overwhelmed by all the activity and become more confused with this overload, manic patients may become increasingly energized, and depressed patients may become more withdrawn. The psychoeducational therapist may therefore have to devote increased time and attention to assisting Hispanic families in controlling the levels of stimulation in the home, thereby creating a home environment that is more supportive of the mentally ill relative.

Several Hispanic clinicians who work with CMI populations have also noted that there is a great degree of sharing of prescribed medications within Hispanic families. Leftover medication that has proven successful in relieving symptoms for one family member is often administered to another family member who displays similar symptoms without consulting a physician about the appropriateness of these procedures. This behavior may be a byproduct of the larger pattern of mutual help-giving that is very common among Hispanic nuclear and extended families (Rogler and Hollingshead, 1965). Hispanic CMI family members may be taking additional medication without their clinician's knowledge. The psychoeducational therapist working with Hispanic families may therefore have to spend considerably more effort educating family members about proper medication dosages and explaining possible dangers inherent in combining medications without consulting a physician. Considerable care should be taken not to disdainfully dismiss the family's misdirected help-exchanging efforts, as the pattern of reciprocal help is an important characteristic of Hispanic interrelationships. Moreover, the seductive pull of more medication is understandable in view of the frustration and disillusionment that standard treatment frequently offers.

Summary

I have described a program of intervention for CMI patients and their families that is in operation at Bellevue Hospital in New York City. Termed a "psychoeducational" program, it stresses the provision of information and the development of problem-solving skills by families in a structured manner. its goals include decreasing the distress and increasing the coping skills of family members as well as increasing the functioning of the CMI patient. An attempt has been made to ask and answer an important question about this model: "Will it work with Hispanic families?" The answer seems to be a qualified "yes," although only the actual implementation of the interventions described with Hispanic populations will bear this out. Additionally, specific suggestions have been made that are intended to increase the success of psychoeducational programs with Hispanic populations.

REFERENCES

Acosta, F.X., & Cristo, M.H. (1981). Development of a bilingual interpreter program: An alternative model for Spanish-speaking services. *Professional Psychology, 12*, 474–482.

Amato, A., Evans, R., & Ziegler, E. (1973). The effectiveness of creative dramatics and storytelling in a library setting. *Journal of Educational Research, 67*, 161–162.

Amor, R. (1969). *Afro-Cuban folktales as incorporated into the literary tradition of Cuba*. Unpublished doctoral dissertation, Columbia University, New York.

Anderson, C.M., Hagerty, G., & Reiss, D. (1980). Family treatment of adult schizophrenic patients: A psychoeducational approach. *Schizophrenia Bulletin, 6*, 490, 505.

Arbuthnot, M.H. (1976). *Anthology of children's literature* (4th ed.). New York: Lothrop Publishers.

Aspira. (1983). *Racial and ethnic high school dropout rate in New York City.* New York: Author, Career Education Program.

Bettelheim, B. (1977). *The uses of enchantment: The importance and meaning of fairy tales* (p. 14). New York: Vintage Books.

Brown, G.W., Birley, J.L.T., & Wing, J.H. (1972). Influence of the family on the course of schizophrenic disorders: A replication. *British Journal of Psychology, 122*, 241–258.

Brown, G.W., Monck, E.M., Carstairs, G.M., & Wing, J.K. (1962). Influence of family life on the course of schizophrenic illness. *British Journal of Preventive & Social Medicine*, 16, 55–68.

Bruner, J. (1986). *Actual minds, possible worlds.* Cambridge, MA: Harvard University Press.

Canino, I., Earley, B., & Rogler, L.H. (1980). *The Puerto Rican child in New York: Stress and mental health* (Monograph No. 4). New York: Hispanic Research Center, Fordham University.

Costantino, G. (1980). The use of folktales as a new therapy modality to effect change in Hispanic children and their families (Grant No. 1-RO1-MH33711). Washington, DC: National Institute of Mental Health.

Costantino, G. (1987). *TEMAS (Tell-Me-A-Story) Thematic Apperception Test.* Los Angeles: Western Psychological Services.

Costantino, G., Malgady, R., & Rogler, L. (1985). *Cuento therapy: Folktales as a culturally sensitive psychotherapy for Puerto Rican children* (Hispanic Research Center, Fordham University: Monograph No. 12). Maplewood, NJ: Waterfront Press.

Costantino, G., Malgady, R.G., & Rogler, L.H. (1986b). Cuento therapy: A culturally sensitive modality for Puerto Rican children. *Journal of Consulting and Clinical Psychology, 54*, 639–645.

Costantino, G., Malgady, R.G., & Rogler, L.H. (1988). *Technical manual: The TEMAS test.* Los Angeles: Western Psychological Services.

Costantino, G., Malgady, R., & Rogler, L. (in press). Storytelling-through-pictures: Culturally sensitive psychotherapy for Hispanic children and adolescents. *Journal of Clinical Child Psychology.*

Costantino, G., & Stiles, J. (1984). The Sunset Park Mental Health Center of the Lutheran Medical Center: Reorganization of a medical model mental health program into a cultural sensitive model for the delivery of mental health services to Hispanics. Unpublished manuscript, Lutheran Medical Center, Brooklyn, NY.

Derogatis, L.R. (1983). *SCL-90-R administration, scoring & procedures manual-II for the revised version.* Towson, MD: Author, Clinical Psychometric Research.

Dohrenwend, B.P., & Dohrenwend, B.S. (1969). *Social status and psychological disorder: A causal inquiry*. New York: Wiley.

Dohrenwend, B.P. (1966). Social status and psychological disorders: An issue of substance and an issue of method. *American Sociological Review, 31*, 14–34.

Faloon, I., Boyd, J.L., McGill, G., Strang, J., Moss, H. (1987). Family management training in the community. In M.J. Goldstein (Ed.), *New developments in interventions with families of schizophrenics*. San Francisco: Jossey-Bass.

Faloon, I., Boyd, J.L., McGill, C., Razoni, J., Moss, H.B., & Gilderman, H.M. (1982). Family management in the prevention of exacerbations of schizophrenia. *New England Journal of Medicine, 305*, 1437–1490.

Faro, S. (1939). *El folkorismo y su funcion social y politica* [Folklore and its social and political function]. Buenos Aires, Associacion Folklorica Argentina.

Fitzpatrick, J.P. (1971). *Puerto Rican Americans—The meaning of migration to the mainland*. Englewood Cliffs, NJ: Prentice Hall.

Freyberg, J. (1973). Increasing imaginative play of urban disadvantaged kindergarten children through systematic training. In J.L. Singer (Ed.), *The child's world of make-believe* (pp. 129–154). New York: Academic Press.

Friedman, G.A. (1958). A cross-cultural study of the relationship between independence training and achievement as revealed by mythology. In J.W. Atkinson (Ed.), *Motives in fantasy, action and society*. Princeton, NJ: D. Van Nostrand.

Gardner, R. (1971). *Therapeutic Communication with Children; The Mutual Storytelling Technique*. New York, Science House.

Garrison, V. (1975). Espiritismo: Implications for provision of mental health services to Puerto Rican populations. In H. Hodges & C. Hudson (Eds.), *Folk Therapy* (pp. 31–53). Miami: University of Miami Press.

Gittleman-Klein, R., & Klein, D.F. (1969). Proverbial asocial adjustment and prognosis in schizophrenia. *Journal of Psychiatric Research, 7*, 35–53.

Goldman, H. (1982). Mental illness and family burden: A public health perspective. *Hospital & Community Psychiatry, 33*, 557–560.

Goldstein, J.J. (Ed.). (1981). *New developments in interventions with families of schizophrenics*. San Francisco: Jossey-Bass.

Goldstein, J.J., & Kopekin, H. (1981). Stress and long-term effects of combining drug and family therapy. In M.J. Goldstein (Ed.), *New developments in interventions with families of schizophrenics*. San Francisco: Jossey-Bass.

Gottesman, I.I., & Shields, J. (1982). *Schizophrenia: The epigenetic puzzle*. London: Cambridge University Press.

Gurak, D., & Rogler, L.H. (1980). New York's new immigrants: Who and where they are. *Education Quarterly, 11*, 20–24.

Haberman, P. (1976). Psychiatric symptoms among Puerto Ricans in Puerto Rico and New York City. *Ethnicity, 3*, 133–144.

Hardy-Fanta, C., & MacMahon-Herrera, E. (1981). Adapting family therapy to the Hispanic family. *Social Casework, 135*, 138–148.

Hatfield, A.B. (1979). The family as partner in the treatment of mental illness. *Hospital and Community By Therapy, 30*, 338–340.

Hatfield, A.B. (1978). Psychological cost of schizophrenia to the family. *Social Work, 23*, 355–359.

Hogarty, G.E., Schobler, N.R., Ulrich, R.F., Meissare, F., Herran, E., & Ferro, P. (1979). Fluphenazine and social therapy in the aftercare of schizophrenic patients: Relapse analysis of a two year controlled study of fluphenazine decanoak and fluphenazine hydrochloride. *Archives of General Psychiatry, 36*, 1283–1294.

Holden, D.F., & Levine, R.R. (1982). How families evaluate mental health professionals, resources and effects of illness. *Schizophrenia Bulletin, 8*, 628–633.

Hollingshead, S., & Redllich, F. (1985). *Social class and mental illness*. New York: Wiley.

Howard, G.S. (1991). Culture tales: A narrative approach to thinking, cross-cultural psychology and psychotherapy. *American Psychologist, 46*, 187–197.

Jilek, A.L. (1976). The Western psychiatrist and his non-Western clientele. Transcultural experiences of relevance to psychotherapy with Canadian Indian patients. *Canadian Psychiatric Association Journal, 21*, 353, 359.

Kaplan, A. (1964). *The conduct of inquiry. Methodology of behavioral science*. San Francisco, CA: Chandler Publishing.

Klosinski, G. (1978). Report of a painting and fairy-tale therapy with a female anorexia nervosa patient. *Praxis der Kinderpsychologie und Kinderpsychiatries, 27*, 206–215.

La Fromboise, T.M., & Fink, S. (1990). *Use of traditional Chippewa storytelling with "at risk" elementary students*. Unpublished manuscript, Stanford University.

Lash, T., Segal, H., & Dudzinski, D. (1979). *Children and families in New York City: An analysis of the 1976 Survey of Income and Education*. New York: Foundation for Child Development.

Leff, J.P. (1976). Schizophrenia and sensitivity to the family environment. *Schizophrenia Bulletin, 2*, 566–574.

Leff, J.P., Kuipers, L., Berkowitz, R., Eberlain-Vries, R., & Sturgeon, D.A. (1982). Controlled trial of social intervention in the families of schizophrenic patients. *British Journal of Psychology, 141*, 121–134.

Leff, J.P., & Vaughn, C. (1981). The role of maintenance therapy and relatives' expressed emotion in relapse of schizophrenia: A two-year follow-up. *British Journal of Psychiatry, 139*, 102–104.

Lewis, O. (1966). The culture of poverty. *Scientific American, 215*, 19–25.

Lubschansky, I., Ergi, B., & Stokes, J. (1970). Puerto Rican spiritualists view mental illness: The faith healer as a paraprofessional. *American Journal of Psychiatry, 127*, 312–321.

Madrid, M.A. (1953). *The attitudes of Spanish-American people as expressed in their coplas or folk songs*. Unpublished doctoral dissertation, Teachers' College, Columbia University, New York.

Mair, M. (1989). *Between psychology and psychotherapy*. London: Routledge.

Malgady, R.G., Rogler, L.H., & Costantino, G. (1990a). Hero/heroine modeling for Puerto Rican adolescents: A preventive mental health intervention. *Journal of Consulting and Clinical Psychology, 58*, 469–474.

Malgady, R.G., Rogler, L.H., & Costantino, G. (1990b). Culturally sensitive psychotherapy for Puerto Rican children and adolescents: A program of treatment outcome research. *Journal of Consulting and Clinical Psychology* (Special Series on Treatment of Children), *58*, 704–712.

Malgady, R.G., Rogler, L.H., & Costantino, G. (1988). Reply to the empirical basis of ethnocultural and linguistic bias in mental health evaluations of Hispanics. *American Psychologist, 43*, 1095.

Mann, E.S., & Salvo, J.J. (1985). Characteristics of new Hispanic immigrants to New York City. *Research Bulletin* (Hispanic Research Center, Fordham University), *8*, No. 1–2.

Mason, A.J. (1921). Puerto Rican folklore. *Journal of American Folklore, 34*, 143–208.

McClelland, D.C., & Friedman, G.A. (1952). A cross-cultural study of the relationship between child-training practices and achievement motivation appearing in folktales. In G.E. Swanson, T.M. Newcom, & E.L. Hartley (Eds.), *Readings in Social Psychology*, New York: Holt.

McFarlane, W.R. (Ed.). (1983). *Family therapy in schizophrenia*. New York: Guilford Press.

McLaughlin, J., O'Brien, J., & Rosenberg, S.J. (1992). The whole family/la familia entera. New York: South Beach Psychiatric Center.

Mednick, S.A. (1958). A learning theory approach to research and schizophrenia. *Psychology Bulletin, 55*, 316–327.

Meehl, P.E. (1962). Schizotaxia, schizotypy and schizophrenia. *American Psychologist, 17*, 827–838.

Moscicki, E.K., Rae, D., Regier, D.A., & Locke, B.Z. (1987). The Hispanic health and nutrition examination survey: Depression among Mexican-Americans, Cubans, Puerto Ricans. In M. Gaviria, & J.D. Arana (Eds.), *Health and behavior: Research agenda for Hispanics* (pp. 145–159). Chicago: University of Illinois at Chicago Circle.

Myers, J.K., & Bean, L.L. *A decade later: A follow-up of social class and mental illness*. New York: Wiley.

National Puerto Rican Forum (1980). *The next step toward equality*. New York: Author.

Padilla, A.M., Ruiz, R.A., & Alvarez, R. (1975). Community mental health services for Spanish-speaking surnamed population. *American Psychologist, 30*, 892–905.

Paul, G.L. (1957). Strategy of outcome research in psychotherapy. *Journal of Consulting Psychology, 31*, 109–118.

Polcz, A. (1966). Puppetry in the psychodiagnosis and psychotherapy of children. *Pszichologicai Tanulmanyok, 9*, 625–637.

Rivera, C.J. (1985). *Perceptions of mental illness among Puerto Rican Americans.* Unpublished doctoral dissertation, New York University.

Rivera, C.J. (1986, Spring). Research issues: Post-hospitalization adjustment of chronically mentally ill Hispanic patients. New York: Hispanic Research Center, Fordham University, *Research Bulletin, 9*, 1.

Rodriguez, O. (1986, Spring). Overcoming barriers to clinical services among chronically mentally ill Hispanics: Lessons from the evaluation of Project COPA. New York: Hispanic Research Center, Fordham University, *Research Bulletin, 9*, 1.

Rodriguez, O. (1987). *Hispanics and human services: Help-seeking in the inner-city* (Monograph No. 14). New York: Hispanic Research Center, Fordham University.

Rogler, L.H., & Cooney, R.S. (1984). *Puerto Rican families in New York City: Intergenerational processes.* (Monograph No. 11). Bronx, New York: Hispanic Research, Fordham University.

Rogler, L.H., & Hollingshead, A.B. (1965). *Trapped: Families and schizophrenia* (2nd ed.). Huntington, New York: Krieger.

Rogler, L.H., Malgady, R.G., Costantino, G., & Blumenthal, R. (1987a). What do culturally sensitive mental health services mean? The case of Hispanics. *American Psychologist, 42*, 565–570.

Rogler, L.H., Malgady, R.G., & Rodriguez, O. (1989). *Hispanics and mental health: A framework for research.* Melbourne, FL: Krieger.

Rooth, A.B. (1976). *The importance of storytelling.* A study based on field work in northern Alaska. Stockholm, Sweden: Almqvist and Wiksell International.

Rosado, J.W. (1980). Important psychocultural factors in the delivery of mental health services to lower-class Puerto Rican clients: A review of recent studies. *Journal of Community Psychology, 8*, 215–226.

Ruiz, R. (1981). Cultural and historical perspectives in counseling Hispanics. In D.W. Sue (Ed.), *Counseling the culturally different: Theory and practice* (pp. 186–215). New York: Wiley.

Ruiz, P., & Langrod, J. (1976). The role of folk healers in community mental health services. *Community Mental Health Journal, 6*, 392–404.

Saltz, E., & Johnson, J. (1973). *Training for thematic fantasy play in culturally disadvantaged children: Preliminary results.* Center for the Study of Cognitive Processes, Wayne State University.

Scott, J., & Delgado, M. (1979). Planning mental health programs for Hispanic communities. *Social Casework, 60*, 451–455.

Smilansky, S. (1968). *The effects of sociodramatic play on disadvantaged preschool children.* New York: Wiley.

Special Populations Sub-Task Panel on the Mental Health of Hispanic Americans. (1978). *Report to the President's Commission on Mental Health.* Los Angeles: Spanish Speaking Mental Health Center, University of California.

Sue, D.W. (Ed.). (1981). *Counseling the culturally different: Theory and practice.* New York: Wiley.

Sue, D.W., & Sue, D. (1977). Barriers to effective cross-cultural counseling. *Journal of Counseling Psychology, 24*, 420–429.

Sue, S. (1988). Psychotherapeutic services for ethnic minorities. *American Psychologist, 43*, 301–308.

Sue, S., & Zane, N. (1987). The role of culture and cultural techniques in psychotherapy: A critique and reformulation. *American Psychologist, 42*, 37–45.

Szapocznik, J., Scopetta, M., & King, O. (1978). Theory and practice in matching treatment to the special characteristics and problems of Cuban immigrants. *Journal of Community Psychology, 6*, 112–122.

Toldson, I.L., & Pasteur, A.B. (1976). Beyond rhetoric: Techniques for using the aesthetic in group counseling and guidance. *Journal of Non-White Concerns in Personnel and Guidance, 4*, 142–151.

Torrey, E.F. (1983). *Surviving schizophrenia; A family manual.* New York: Harper and Row.

Trevino, F., Bruhn, J., & Brunce, H. (1979). Utilization of community mental health services in a Texas-Mexican border city. *Social Science and Medicine, 13*, 331–334.

Vaughn, C., & Leff, L. (1976). The influence of families and social factors on the course of psychiatry illnesses. *British Journal of Psychiatry, 129*, 125–137.

Weimer, S.R. (1978). Using fairytales in psychotherapy: Rapunzel. *Bulletin of Menninger Clinic, 42*, 25–34.

Westone, H.S., & Friedlander, B.Z. (1974). The effect of live, TV and audio story narration on primary grade children's listening comprehension. *Journal of Educational Research, 68*, 30–34.

Woutres, A. (1990). *Folk hero modeling with Black South African adolescents.* Unpublished manuscript, Vista University, Pretoria, South Africa.

Wright, G.O. (1954). Projection and displacement: A cross-cultural study of folktale aggression. *Journal of Abnormal Social Psychology, 49*, 523–538.

Zubin, J., & Spring, B. (1977). Vulnerability: A new view of schizophrenia. *Journal of Abnormal Psychology, 86*, 103–126.

AUTHOR NOTES

Correspondence concerning this chapter should be addressed to: Giuseppe Costantino, PhD, Clinical Director, Sunset Park Mental Health Center/Lutheran Medical Center, 514 49th Street, Brooklyn, NY 11220.

CHAPTER 10

HISPANIC DIVERSITY AND THE NEED FOR CULTURALLY SENSITIVE MENTAL HEALTH SERVICES

Robert G. Malgady, PhD

Professor of Quantitative Studies, New York University

"What has four legs, hair, hooves, and can be ridden?" My 6-year-old son's answer to this riddle is: "A horse." "Suppose," I then ask him, "the horse lost a leg, went bald, or refused to be ridden; would it still qualify as a horse?" My son says yes. When shown a picture of a four-legged, hairy, hooved pig, playfully being ridden by a child, my son informs me that this is not a horse, but a pig. How is it that even a 6 year old can distinguish between a horse and a pig, which have similar defining features, and can detect the concept of horseness, even when these same ostensive features are missing? I wonder about this because I cannot specify the essential defining features of the concept of culture. With the ease of identifying a concept such as horseness, we all seem able, after a brief personal interchange, to recognize individuals who come from a culture different than our own. Yet, it is difficult to specify an epistemologically satisfactory definition of culture.

Anthropologists have viewed culture most thoroughly, although cognitive psychologists would call their definition of culture "a fuzzy concept." For instance, LeVine (1984) refers to culture as a set of cognitions shared by members of a community. Such cognitions are of many types, including the intellectual, moral, aesthetic, and linguistic. We, as members of a society, become accustomed to certain values, beliefs, and behaviors on the part of other members of our society. These customs are more or less expected of individual members of a community because there is a formal (e.g., legal) or informal (e.g., moral) consensus on their correctness. When individuals from an extraneous culture unknowingly violate the customs of a community or society in which they find themselves, then empathic members of their host culture, recognizing their alien status, might excuse this deviant behavior. This is an everyday lay example of what is meant by being culturally sensitive.

I confess to having trouble with definitions of culture because, like the prospect of one day encountering a three-legged, bald, unrideable horse, I can think of too many exceptions to anthropological definitions of culture that increase their fuzziness. How large a group is needed to constitute a community or society? Are native-born members of a community or society who violate the social consensus still members of that culture? What are the necessary and sufficient criteria for distinguishing between cultures? To how many cultures can an individual belong?

The alternative to thinking loosely about culture leads quite naturally to what Howard (1991) has referred to as the "shreds and patches" concept of culture—the attempt to atomize culture into its discrete traits or dimensions. According to LeVine (1984), apparently this is not a currently popular approach in modern day anthropology. When culture is atomized into selective lists of customary values (e.g., democratic vs. republican), expected sex roles (e.g., female submissiveness vs. male-female equality), beliefs (e.g., fatalistic vs. internal locus of control), language (e.g., English vs. Spanish), and behavior (e.g., assertive vs. deferential), individuals' cultural profiles as native members of the same community will register many, if not all possible, permutations of these traits' values. Hence, the concept of a culture becomes superfluous.

The discomfort felt by anthropologists in trying to reduce culture to its essential defining features is not a new feeling. The philosopher Wittgenstein expressed it admirably as confusion engendered by a perceptual incapacity to separate similarities from differences:

> And the result of this examination is: we see a complicated network of similarities and criss-crossing: sometimes overall similarities, sometimes similarities of detail.
>
> Why do we call something a "number"? Well, perhaps because it has a—direct—relationship to other things we call (by) the same name. We extend our concept of number as in spinning a thread we twist fibre on fibre. And the strength of the thread does not reside in the fact that some one fibre runs through its whole length, but in the overlapping of many fibres. (cited in Pollio, 1974, p. 99)

Similarly, the overlapping and intertwining of the many fibers of a culture obscures their individual definitiveness, yet culture as a gestalt is detectable. As one atomizes the essential defining (necessary and sufficient) properties of any concept, such as the concept of culture, the distinctions between concepts are easily blurred. For instance, whiteness once was a defining attribute of a swan; however, a species was discovered that satisfied the concept of swanness in every way, except for the fact that it was black. Philosophically speaking, should the black swan constitute a new and distinct concept, or should blackness be admitted to the concept of swanness? A related, but more cultural anecdote occurred in a cowboy and Indian rerun I was watching the other day on TV, wherein an Indian refers to a black cowboy (without oxymoronic intent) as the "black white man." With atomization, even black and white boundaries separating cultures can become unclear.

Luckily, I am neither an anthropologist nor a philosopher. Like most psychologists (cf., Sue and Zane, 1988), I use the term *culture* loosely, more or less synonymously with the term *ethnicity*. I know enough not to use culture or ethnicity synonymously with race, but I hope that I am never asked to define what I really mean by culture. Therefore, despite the problem of definition, since we all seem to think we recognize a culture when we see one, I will presume there really are coherently organized webs of customs—more than shreds and patches—interlacing society's collective cognitions and behaviors.

This chapter discusses cultural bias in psychological assessment and psychiatric diagnosis, on the one hand, and the effectiveness of psychotherapeutic treatment for cultural minorities on the other. The theme of the *Festschrift* that occasioned this book was state-of-the-*art* Hispanic mental health research. However, I will suggest some hurdles that need to be posed and *scientifically* negotiated. The first hurdle is to determine whether a consideration of culture in mental health is worthwhile at all. Second, if a consideration of culture is worthwhile, what degree of culture specificity is necessary to enhance the quality of services delivered to Hispanics in this country? Third, is mental health policy prepared to be responsive to the answers to these questions?

THE FIRST HURDLE: IS CULTURE CONSEQUENTIAL TO MENTAL HEALTH CLINICAL SERVICES?

Several decades ago, scholars in the intelligence testing community in this country devised so-called culture-free and culture-fair IQ tests in their attempts to be sensitive to culturally marginated groups in our society, largely blacks. Psychologists rapidly apprehended the logical absurdity of attempts to create IQ tests that were free or void of culture. However, minorities have not fared any better, and indeed sometimes have performed worse, on culture-fair IQ tests, despite the best of both black and white intentions. Today, the norms of existing tests have, at times, been recalibrated to be fairer to members of other than the racially white, socioeconomically middle- and upper-class, English-speaking U.S. population. At other times, sometimes prompted by litigation, the tests have been abandoned altogether.

On the heels of the IQ testing controversy, allegations were raised in the 1970s about cultural "bias" against Hispanics, among other ethnic minorities, in personality assessment techniques, such as the MMPI (e.g., Padilla & Ruiz, 1975), and in psychiatric diagnosis (e.g., Del Castillo, 1970; Marcos, Alpert, Urcuyo, & Kesselman, 1973; Marcos, 1976). Much of this literature has been critically reviewed fairly recently (e.g., Lopez, 1988, 1989; Malgady, Rogler, & Costantino, 1987).

Similarly, as community mental health services to the poor, largely members of ethnic minority communities, were expanded following the civil rights movement of the 1960s, the mental health profession faced a related question regarding the appropriateness of standard psychotherapeutic techniques for members of other cultural groups. Claims were made that blacks, Hispanics, and other ethnic minorities did not gain access to clinical services in proportion to their mental health needs, and that after contact was made, they tended to drop out of treatment at a higher rate (Sue, 1988) or benefit less from treatment compared to their nonminority counterparts (Rogler, Malgady, & Rodriguez, 1989). Much of this literature has been critically reviewed by Rogler, Malgady, Costantino, & Blumenthal (1987). In both camps, mental health evaluation and treatment, the impetus of concern for culture was sparked by clinical observation among practitioners on the service delivery front and often by rhetorical argument on the academic front. There was very little scientifically sound empirical research to address the most fundamental question raised in response to a concern for cultural sensitivity: Does it matter? I believe that the bulk of the empirical evidence leans, though sometimes it seems almost imperceptibly, toward an affirmative answer to this question. As I mentioned earlier, fairly extensive reviews of the literature on these two topics are available elsewhere, so here I shall only briefly sketch the outline of this evidence and assume the affirmative as a premise to the second hurdle posed regarding Hispanic subcultural diversity.

In the area of mental health evaluation, including psychological assessment and psychiatric diagnosis, there is fairly convincing evidence that culture affects the scores an examinee receives on a psychological test and the impression of symptoms presented to an examining psychiatrist. On objective tests such as the Minnesota Multiphasic Personality Inventory (MMPI), more often than not Hispanics display selected profile differences, and more rarely differential factor structure, from the standardized norms (Malgady, Rogler, & Costantino, 1987). On projective test stimuli that have been developed with Hispanic culture in mind (Costantino, 1988), Hispanics not only evidence more self-disclosing projections of personality structure, but also the personality scales themselves have shown superior reliability and validity to standard projective tests, such as the Thematic Apperception Test (TAT) and Rorschach. To arrive at a firmer affirmative conclusion that culture is consequential to psychological assessment, cross-cultural studies are required that address rigorous psychometric criteria of test bias: differences in criterion-related validity coefficients, regression equations for predicting criterion-related validity indicators, and measurement non-equivalence in latent-trait item parameters. Virtually no research of this sort exists comparing Hispanics to non-Hispanics.

In the psychodiagnostic arena, research consistently has found that whether Hispanics speak English or Spanish, and whether the clinician is Hispanic or not, influence the mental health assessment (e.g., Marcos, 1976; Price & Cuellar, 1981), but whether or not Hispanics are overdiagnosed, underdiagnosed, or misdiagnosed remains unclear (Vazquez, 1982). There is substantially increased sensitivity regarding potential problems of psychological assessment and diagnosis of ethnic, linguistic, and cultural minorities in the latest version of *Standards for Psychological and Educational Testing* (1985), published jointly by the American Psychological Association, American Educational Research Association, and the National Council on Measurement in Education. Compiled by a national panel of psychometric experts, these technical standards are advisory in nature, "formulated with the intent of being consistent with the APA's Ethical Principles of Psychologists (1981)" (p. vii). In no way, however, are these recommendations to be construed as establishing cultural minority assessment policies.

Other evidence that standardized psychological scales and psychiatric diagnostic criteria are biased against members of other cultures has often been rendered in medical anthropological circles (e.g., Kleinman, 1991; Good & Good, 1986). Armed with rich examples of psychiatrically consequential behavior observed by anthropologists to be customary in other, usually non-Western societies, the argument is that a given behavior deemed pathological in Western psychiatric culture may be quite normal in another culture, and vice versa. The anthropologists' examples are dramatic eye-openers, countering notions that psychiatric diagnostic criteria are cross-cultural universals and, probably rightfully, challenging the medical reality of an institution such as the *DSM-III-R* (*Diagnostic and Statistical Manual of Mental Disorders, Third Edition, Revised*, 1987). These culturally conflicting anecdotes, however, do not directly inform more service-oriented issues, such as the extent to which *DSM-III-R* misdiagnosis occurs among members of the cultural minority, or show how such bias might be corrected once it is assessed. If the psychiatric customs demanded by the *DSM-III-R* are in such conflict with the customs of other particular cultures, we need to demonstrate empirically the limits of accurate psychiatric diagnosis with cultural minorities.

There is more reason to believe that culture is consequential to the treatments that Hispanics receive in clinical settings. First of all, there is evidence that Hispanics underutilize mental health resources relative to epidemiological estimates of their population needs (Rodriguez, 1987). Thus, even if standard psychotherapeutic treatment modalities were equally effective in attenuating symptomatology with Hispanics as with nonminority clients, culturally sensitive methods would be necessary, as the proverbial saying goes, to "lead the horse to water." Unfortunately, a second problem is that once led to the water, the horse often doesn't drink: Sue (1988) reports that more than half of ethnic minority clients, Hispanics included, drop out of psychotherapy after the first session. Cultural sensitivity, once again, is required to maintain Hispanics in the therapeutic situation. Rogler's metaphoric cultural sensitivity pyramid refers at its first level to the creation of special Hispanic clinics within Hispanic communities, with Hispanic ambiance, support of Hispanic cultural traits, and Spanish-speaking service personnel (Rogler et al., 1987). The literature documents that such culturally sensitive efforts to increase the accessibility to and cultural proximity of standard treatment services result in increased utilization and decreased attrition (Rogler et al., 1987).

Once the horse is led to water and persuaded to drink, however, a concern beyond the proverb is the quality of the water itself. Scaling Rogler's pyramid, the second level of culturally sensitive treatment involves considering the perceived cultural characteristics of the Hispanic client when selecting from the standard battery of available therapeutic interventions. Highly familial Hispanics might be excellent candidates for a family therapy (e.g., Ho, 1987; Szapocznik et al., 1978, 1989). Recent migrants with little or no English language skills may be excellent candidates for psychoeducational pretherapy interventions designed to prepare them for what to expect in the treatment process (Ruiz and Casas, 1981). Third-generation, English monolingual, middle or higher socioeconomic status Hispanics may fare as well as their non-Latino neighbors without any special consideration of culture, despite their Hispanic surname and heritage.

Reaching the pinnacle of cultural sensitivity, efforts have focused on bringing culture directly into the therapeutic modality. Examples from our National Institute of Mental Health-sponsored work include the use of folktale characters with very young children (Costantino, Malgady, & Rogler, 1986), pictures of inner-city Hispanic families and urban settings with older children and younger adolescents (Costantino, Malgady, & Rogler, in press), and historical biographies of Hispanic "heroes" with older adolescents (Malgady, Rogler, & Costantino, 1990a, 1990b). These casts of cultural characters were presented as role models in modeling therapy interventions with high-risk and borderline *DSM-III-R* youngsters. Compared to standard group therapy techniques, untreated (equal attention) control groups, and school-based dropout prevention programs, we have consistently documented favorable treatment outcomes, such as decreased anxiety, phobic, and conduct disorder symptomatology, and increased self-esteem and ethnic identity, with use of cultural infusions into modeling therapy. These and other promising treatment outcome studies (e.g., Szapocznik, Kurtines, Santisteban, & Rio, 1990) involving second- and third-level cultural modifications of therapy strongly support the proposition that culture is indeed consequential to the effectiveness of psychotherapeutic intervention (Kazdin, 1993).

Some interesting questions that are prompted by successful treatment outcome studies on Hispanic cultural sensitivity invite inquiry as to why cultural sensitivity enhances treatment benefits. Some researchers have suggested that culture indirectly influences outcomes by facilitating the treatment process (Sue & Zane, 1987). Sue and Zane speculate that matching minority clients with minority clinicians has a "distal" effect by enhancing the client-therapist relationship, moving the client toward therapeutic goals; whereas it is the culturally enhanced therapy process, in turn, that impacts "proximally" on treatment outcomes. They and their colleagues at UCLA's Asian-American Mental Health Research Center are currently engaged in testing their hypothesis regarding ethnic (as a proxy for cultural) matching by conducting therapeutic process analyses of minority clients in the Los Angeles area (Zane, 1992, personal communication).

Another question that remains to be addressed regarding why

culture is consequential to treatment outcomes is related to Sue and Zane's thinking. Do first-, second-, and third-level cultural adjustments to standard treatment modalities merely open the therapeutic doors, or is there therapeutic value to cultural sensitivity itself that rubs off on the client throughout the treatment process? Whether cultural sensitivity attenuates the cultural distance between client and therapist, enabling a proven therapeutic technique to work effectively; whether cultural sensitivity forms a ground surrounding the therapeutic figure; or whether cultural sensitivity becomes part of the figure itself, are issues that remain unaddressed in the literature. By seeking answers to questions such as these, research on the effectiveness of culturally sensitive treatment techniques moves closer toward science and away from art.

THE SECOND HURDLE: HOW CULTURE SPECIFIC DO WE NEED TO GET?

Presuming that culture is consequential to mental health evaluation and treatment, even without quite knowing why, a cause for hesitation in disseminating culturally sensitive services to the Hispanic population is this population's sociodemographic and, supposedly, *sub*cultural diversity (e.g., Gurak & Rogler, 1980). Discourse on the theme of Hispanic diversity usually begins with a litany of sociodemographic population parameters.

According to the 1990 census (United States Bureau of the Census, 1991b), problems with its accuracy notwithstanding, Hispanic residents in this country number somewhat more than 21 million, comprising about 8.6% of the United States population. Relative to the 1980 census, this figure is an increase of about 2.2% in proportionate representation. More dramatic than per-capita representation, the proportion of Hispanic householders in the United States increased by 68% since the last census. The distribution by national origin is 63% Mexican, 11% Puerto Rican, 5% Cuban, 14% Central and South American, and 7% "other" Hispanics. Becoming increasingly more geographically provincial, Hispanics comprise slightly more than 12% of the population of the state of New York and 24% of New York City. Both state and city distributions by national origin are similar: about 50% Puerto Rican, 4% Mexican, 3%

Cuban, and 43% "other." These figures do not include the vast number of illegal aliens or "undocumented" status residents, nor the 3.5 million residents of the United States Commonwealth of Puerto Rico who constitute a population double the size of New York City's Hispanic population. Census estimates specific to the Hispanic population in the United States (United States Bureau of the Census, 1991a) provide additional insight into Hispanic sociodemographic diversity. However, the Census Bureau does not report separate population figures for Dominicans, who constitute a significant portion of the Hispanic population of New York City and the state of New York. According to other sources, Dominicans are the most rapidly growing immigrant group in New York City public schools, outnumbering the influx of the next largest incoming group of youngsters—Jamaicans—by more than a 2-to-1 ratio (New York City Division of Public Affairs, 1992; New York City Board of Education, 1992).

The census's five categories of Hispanic origin are nearly equivalent to each other and to non-Hispanics in male/female distribution with 49% to 52% females, and there is a consistently high rate of urban residence (83% to 97%) across groups (U.S. Bureau of the Census, 1991a, 1991b). Mexicans, Puerto Ricans, Central Americans, and South Americans are considerably younger (median = 24 to 28 years old) than Cubans (median = 39 years old) and "other" Hispanics (median = 31 years old). The rate of married status is lowest among Puerto Ricans (51%) and highest among Cubans (62%), with the remaining groups being similar to non-Hispanics (54% to 58%). A dramatic difference is in the rate of single female-headed families: The Puerto Rican rate (43%) is more than double the Cuban and Mexican rates (19%), and 1 ½ times the rates of other Hispanics (27%) and Central and South Americans (26%). Cuban families are smaller in size (median = 2.81 persons) than non-Hispanic families (median = 3.13 persons). Puerto Rican (median = 3.37 persons) and other Hispanic families (median = 3.38 persons) are larger, whereas Central and South American (median = 3.81 persons) and Mexican (median = 4.06 persons) families are the largest.

Educationally, Cubans (61%), Central and South Americans (60%), and other Hispanics (71%) are most likely to complete high school or above, although all at a rate well below the 80% non-Hispanic rate. Mexicans and Puerto Ricans are least likely (44% and 58%, respectively).

Unemployment rates are distinctive, with the rate for Mexicans and

Puerto Ricans running 4% higher than the rate for non-Hispanics, Cubans, and other Hispanics. There are striking occupational differences among the groups. Whereas non-Hispanic men are most likely to be engaged in management and professional jobs (27%), only Cuban men follow this modal pattern (26%). The remaining Hispanic groups are far more likely to be employed as operators, fabricators, and laborers: Mexicans, at the rate of 32%; Puerto Ricans, 25%; Central and South Americans, 31%; and other Hispanics, 23%. In contrast, women in four of the five Hispanic groups are most likely to be employed in technical, sales, and administrative support positions at rates (38% to 48%) similar to the non-Hispanic modal rate of 45%; the exception is Central and South American women, employed at a 35% rate in service occupations (U.S. Bureau of the Census, 1991a, 1991b).

Median household income of all Hispanic groups is less than that of non-Hispanic households ($30.5K in 1990 dollars). Cuban ($26K) and other Hispanic ($25.5K) median household incomes are the highest, followed by Central and South Americans ($23.5K) and Mexicans ($22.5K). Puerto Ricans exhibit distinctively the lowest median household income ($16K), almost half that of non-Hispanic families. This income pattern mirrors the distribution of below-poverty-level families, ranging from only 17% among Cubans (compared to 12% among non-Hispanics) up to 41% among Puerto Ricans. Household income figures are somewhat deceptive because, separately, male and female Puerto Rican workers have median incomes comparable to or higher than most other Hispanic groups. The greater apparent poverty of Puerto Rican households, as opposed to individuals, derives largely from their lesser likelihood of having two income earners.

Thus, the major social, demographic, and economic distinctions among the five Hispanic groups can be summed up as follows. Cubans and other Hispanics are the oldest, best educated, and best off financially; they have the smallest families and are least likely to be headed by a woman. Cuban men singularly are most likely to be in higher socioeconomic status occupations. Puerto Ricans and Mexicans are the youngest, least educated, poorest, and have larger families. Puerto Rican households singularly are far most likely to be headed by a woman.

What are the consequences of this type of diversity for the provision of culturally sensitive services? With regard to age diversity, there is probably a far greater need for mental health evaluation and treatment services for children and adolescents among Mexican Americans and

Puerto Ricans. Well over a third of the population of these two groups is under 18 years old, compared to less than a fifth of the Cuban-American population. Income and education patterns, tending to be correlated with service utilization and to portend general mental health risk, suggest that Puerto Ricans and Mexican Americans may be at higher risk of mental disorder and yet less likely to use community mental health resources. There are probably also economic implications for service systems researchers regarding payment and insurance options. However, a far more interesting figure is the prominence of female-headed households among Puerto Ricans—up to twice the rate of other groups (the male-head rate is no different from Cubans or non-Hispanic families). Apart from the economic burden, this probably is a salient feature that must be taken into consideration in therapeutic interventions involving members of female-headed Puerto Rican families. Some of our own research with adolescents found, quite serendipitously, that culturally sensitizing modeling therapy by presenting biographic stories of Puerto Rican heroes is particularly effective with adolescents who lack a parental figure in their household (Malgady, Costantino, & Rogler, 1990).

None of these sources of Hispanic diversity appearing in census reports, however, stem directly from *cultural* differences between the groups. As difficult as it may be to operationally define what is meant by culture, it is even more difficult to operationalize *sub*cultural differences. I know of no reference source that describes the cultural diversity of Hispanic subgroups stemming from different national origins. Nonetheless, trying to play the role of an amateur anthropologist, I conducted some interviews with about a dozen Puerto Ricans, attempting from my etic perspective to discover how various Hispanic subcultures stereotypically differ. The most consistent patterns I could detect, coming from lay persons and professionals alike, were that all groups were readily distinguishable by a native Spanish-speaker according to their accent, certain particular idiomatic expressions, and music and food preferences. I doubt that accent, music, and food preference differences are very consequential to mental health treatment or evaluation. However, to the extent that idiomatic expressions bear relevance to the disclosure or failure to disclose psychopathology, being idiomatically attuned to the client is essential to accurate psychological assessment and psychiatric diagnosis and to first-level culturally sensitive intervention.

Another characteristic of possible consequence is race. Latin American Hispanics, regardless of subgroup, vary widely across the racial spectrum from white to black. My Puerto Rican informants were of the impression that Dominicans living in the United States were more likely to be black and were generally darker in skin color than the other groups. There is an extensive body of literature of psychotherapy with Afro-American blacks (see Sue and Zane's, 1987, review), which might be generalizable to black Dominicans, or a black member of any other Hispanic subgroup for that matter. So here, too, no special innovation or modification of current treatment intervention strategies seems warranted on consideration of race.

I was also informed of a variety of other, seemingly inconsequential, characteristics. The Puerto Rican cultural informants reported that Dominicans tend to giggle a lot, act immaturely, and are less conscious about time than other Hispanics. Cubans, I was told, are extremely achievement and status oriented, to the point of appearing supercilious to other Hispanics. European Spaniards, who fall in the "other" Hispanic category, will go out of their way to avoid being confused with Mexicans, Puerto Ricans, or Dominicans, and insist that they are "Spaniards" not "Hispanics." Puerto Ricans reported themselves as being proud, appearance conscious, and nurturant.

This experience leaves me with the feeling that little cultural fine tuning may be necessary for mental health services that have been demonstrated to be effective with one or another Hispanic group. Sensitivity to the language, racial, and broad cultural traits of Hispanic culture in general is probably sufficient, although this speculation has not been empirically tested. The most relevant subcultural diversity appears to be lodged in family structural, educational, and socioeconomically patterned differences between nationalities. Attempts to identify subcultural differences, moreover, amount to specifications of shreds and patches of culture (Howard, 1991), not the more transcendent fibril quality of cultures that anthropologists detect.

To scientifically address the hurdle of Hispanic diversity, two types of research studies of mental health clinical services need to be conducted. One type of research should take culturally sensitive techniques that have demonstrated effectiveness with one Hispanic group as a point of departure for replication with other Hispanic groups. The major goal of such studies would be to determine the simple generalizability, in a statistical sense, of evaluation and treatment techniques across Hispanic subcultures. Research of this type might seek answers to questions such as: Do family therapy techniques, developed and tested with Cubans in Miami (e.g., Szapocznik et al., 1978, 1989), also demonstrate favorable treatment outcomes with Puerto Ricans and Dominicans in New York City and with Mexican Americans in Los Angeles? Do treatment outcomes of cultural storytelling in modeling therapy, developed with Puerto Ricans in New York City (Costantino, Malgady, & Rogler, 1986; Malgady, Rogler, & Costantino, 1990), replicate with other Hispanic subcultural groups? As mundane as this fundamental research problem is, there is a simple need to establish the breadth of generalizability of culturally sensitive clinical services that are known to be effective.

The second type of research promises to be more interesting. Once there is evidence that culturally sensitive techniques replicate uniformly or fail to replicate with certain Hispanic groups, there is a need for comparative research. In the study of treatment outcomes, research of this type would include multiple Hispanic groups in the same study, attempting to assess the interactive effects of treatment and Hispanic diversity. This is especially challenging because of the wide geographic diversity of the major Hispanic enclaves in this country. The principal question to be addressed by this research, broadly stated, is: Are there differences between Hispanic groups in responsiveness to particular culturally sensitive techniques? The ultimate goal of comparative Hispanic studies would be to situate evaluation and treatment techniques in their complete social, demographic, and cultural contexts. In the study of mental health evaluation, research of this type would seek to determine how measurement parameters (e.g., norms, reliability and validity coefficients, factor structures, latent-trait item characteristics, and psychodiagnostic criteria) vary as a function of Hispanic subcultural membership. In the study of mental health treatment, research of this type would seek to determine how treatment outcomes of culturally sensitive modalities (e.g., symptom severity ratings, time to relapse, rehospitalization rates) vary as a function of Hispanic subcultural membership. Both are interactive research questions involving Hispanic diversity, subsumed under the broader question of the degree or extent that modifications of status quo clinical services need to be made on behalf of Hispanic clientele. If empirical studies demonstrate that Hispanic diversity is consequential to mental health evaluations and treatments, this is likely to prompt ad hoc explorations into the reasons why.

THE THIRD HURDLE: IF HISPANIC DIVERSITY MATTERS, ARE WE PREPARED TO DO ANYTHING ABOUT IT?

A state-of-art review of both the scientific and anecdotal evidence on the general question of whether or not Hispanic cultural sensitivity is an important consideration in the delivery of clinical services would almost certainly conclude the affirmative. The development for Hispanics of separate psychological assessment techniques and test norms (e.g., Costantino, 1988), the promise of new culturally sensitive psychodiagnostic criteria in the forthcoming *DSM-IV* (e.g., Fabrega, 1991), and the initiation of special Hispanic mental health programs in community mental health settings (e.g., Rodriguez, Lessinger, & Guarnaccia, 1993) suggest that mental health public policies and service systems are in accordance with this affirmative conclusion.

The state of art and science is such that most studies have not included more than a single Hispanic nationality or subcultural group. Hence, little or no information is available on either the cross-subcultural generalizability of research findings or, theoretically more intriguing, potential moderating effects of subcultural group membership on such findings. When sufficient literature becomes available subjecting Hispanic subcultural diversity to the same scientific scrutiny as generic Hispanic or nationality specific foci, an affirmative answer that subcultural diversity is consequential to the delivery of mental health service may prove to be a formidable (and perhaps insurmountable) pragmatic hurdle for federal, state, and local mental health policy makers and their service systems' procedures.

Suppose that culturally sensitive mental health assessment and treatment services need to be even further sensitized—subculturally sensitized. Is this going too far, expecting too much from an already overburdened system? For Hispanics alone, there might be a need for separate considerations for the five major subcultures (hopefully not all 20 or so nationalities). In regard to assessment, standardized instruments such as the MMPI might have five distinct Hispanic norms tables, factor structures, reliabilities, and criterion-related validity indices, each probably broken down further according to the usual age and sex demarcations. In regard to diagnosis, there might be five distinct Hispanic sets of exceptions and additions to *DSM* diagnostic criteria. In regard to mental health treatment, standard therapeutic modalities would need not just to be culturally sensitized, but subculturally slanted in five distinct ways to accommodate diverse Hispanic clients. Needless to say, the effectiveness of such subculture-specific treatment modalities would have to be evaluated and, if found effective, mental health workers would need to be trained in these new techniques. The effort and cost of such treatment outcome research, retraining of current mental health professionals, and graduate education of prospective professionals indeed would pose a severe economic challenge to the mental health services system.

Now further suppose that parallel advances were being made by our colleagues specializing in mental health issues confronting members of Asian-American, black, and Native-American cultures, each of which has even more subcultural groups than Hispanics. The level of cultural specificity may well reach unmanageable proportions. Admittedly, empirical data to confirm my assertions are lacking, but my speculative conclusions are as follows:

1. Within major ethnic groups, such as Hispanics, it is difficult to specify narrower subgroup differences that are cultural in nature and that are likely to be consequential to mental health evaluation and treatment outcomes.
2. Any attempt to specify narrower subgroup differences is likely to reduce to an exercise in "shredding and patching" Hispanic subcultures into discrete traits, thus doing violence to the essential nature of the concept of culture in its richest philosophical and anthropological senses.
3. Statistically speaking, the magnitudes of generic culturally rooted differences between the major ethnic groups—though often significant—pale in comparison to other qualifiers such as age, sex, education, and socioeconomic status. Hence, the magnitudes of special cultural differences within the major ethnic groups—if significant—are likely to be even paler.
4. The resources that would need to be mustered to act affirmatively in response to subcultural diversification of mental health services are probably not likely to be forthcoming.
5. Therefore, mental health research and clinical services resources probably would be more wisely spent by searching for and developing appropriate courses of action for dealing with the cultural commonalities among Hispanic (and other ethnic groups') nationalities, not their cultural diversities.

REFERENCES

American Psychiatric Association. (1987). *Diagnostic and statistical manual of mental disorders* (3rd ed., Revised). Washington, DC: Author.

American Psychiatric Association. (1987). *Diagnostic and statistical manual of mental disorders* (3rd ed., Revised). Washington, DC: Author.

American Psychological Association. (1985). *Standards for educational and psychological testing*. Washington, DC: Author.

Costantino, G. (1988). *The TEMAS thematic apperception test*. Los Angeles: Western Psychological Services.

Costantino, G., Malgady, R.G., & Rogler, L.H. (1986). Cuento therapy: A culturally sensitive modality for Puerto Rican children. *Journal of Consulting and Clinical Psychology, 54,* 739–746.

Costantino, G., Malgady, R.G., & Rogler, L.H. (in press). Story-telling through pictures: Culturally sensitive psychotherapy for Hispanic children and adolescents. *Journal of Clinical Child Psychology*.

Del Castillo, J. (1970). The influence of language upon symptomatology in foreign-born patients. *American Journal of Psychiatry, 127,* 242–244.

Fabrega, H. (1991, April). *Cultural and historical foundations of psychiatric diagnosis*. Paper presented at the National Institute of Mental Health Conference on Culture and Diagnosis, Pittsburgh.

Good, B.J., & Good, M.J. (1986). The cultural context of diagnosis and therapy: A view from medical anthropology. In M.R. Miranda & H.H. Kitano (Eds.), *Mental health research and practice in minority communities: Development of culturally sensitive training programs* (pp. 1–27). Washington, DC, NIMH, Minority Research Resources Branch, Division of Biometry and Applied Sciences.

Gurak, D.T., & Rogler, L.H. (1980). New York's new immigrants: Who and where they are. *NYU Education Quarterly, 11,* 4.

Ho, M.K. (1987). *Family therapy with ethnic minorities*. Newbury Park, CA: Sage Publications.

Howard, G.S. (1991). Culture tales: A narrative approach to thinking, cross-cultural psychology, and psychotherapy. *American Psychologist, 46,* 187–197.

Kazdin, A.E. (1993). Adolescent mental health: Prevention and treatment programs. *American Psychologist, 48,* 127–141.

Kleinman, A. (1991). *Rethinking psychiatry*. New York: Free Press.

LeVine, R.A. (1984). Properties of culture: An ethnographic view. In R. Shweder & R. LeVine (Eds.), *Culture theory: Essays in mind, theory and emotion* (pp. 67–87). Cambridge, England: Cambridge University Press.

Lopez, S. (1988). The empirical basis of ethnocultural and linguistic bias in mental health evaluations of Hispanics. *American Psychologist, 43,* 1095–1097.

Lopez, S.R. (1989). Patient variable biases in clinical judgment: Conceptual overview and methodological considerations. *Psychological Bulletin, 106*, 184–203.

Malgady, R.G., Rogler, L.H., & Costantino, G. (1990a). Hero/heroine modeling for Puerto Rican adolescents: A preventive mental health intervention. *Journal of Consulting and Clinical Psychology, 58*, 469–474.

Malgady, R.G., Rogler, L.H., & Costantino, G. (1990b). Culturally sensitive psychotherapy for Puerto Rican children and adolescents: A program of treatment outcome research. *Journal of Consulting and Clinical Psychology (Special Series on Treatment of Children), 58*, 704–712.

Malgady, R.G., Rogler, L.H., & Costantino, G. (1987). Ethnocultural and linguistic bias in mental health evaluation of Hispanics. *American Psychologist, 43*, 228–234.

Marcos, L.R., Alpert, M., Urcuyo, L., & Kesselman, M. (1973). The effect of interview language on the evaluation of psychopathology in Spanish-American schizophrenic patients. *American Journal of Psychiatry, 130*, 549–553.

Marcos, L.R. (1976). Bilinguals in psychotherapy: Language as an emotional barrier. *American Journal of Psychotherapy, 30*, 552–560.

Padilla, A.M., & Ruiz, R.A. (1975). Personality assessment and test interpretation of Mexican Americans: A critique. *Journal of Personality Assessment, 39*, 103–109.

Pollio, H.R. (1974). *The psychology of symbolic activity*. Menlo Park, CA: Addison-Wesley Publishing Company.

Price, C.S., & Cuellar, I. (1981). Effects of language and related variables on the expression of psychopathology in Mexican-American psychiatric patients. *Hispanic Journal of Behavioral Sciences, 3*, 145–160.

Rodriguez, O. (1987). *Hispanics and human services: Help-seeking in the inner city* (Monograph No. 14). Bronx, NY: Hispanic Research Center, Fordham University.

Rodriguez, O., Lessinger, J., & Guarnaccia, P. (1993). The societal and organizational contexts of culturally sensitive mental health services: Findings from an evaluation of bilingual/bicultural psychiatric programs. *Journal of Mental Health Administration, 19*, 213–223.

Rogler, L.H., Malgady, R.G., Costantino, G., & Blumenthal, R. (1987). What does culturally sensitive mental health services mean? The case of Hispanics. *American Psychologist, 42*, 565–570.

Rogler, L.H., Malgady, R.G., & Rodriguez, O. (1989). *Hispanics and mental health: A framework for research*. Malabar, FL: Krieger.

Ruiz, R., & Casas, M.E. (1981). Culturally relevant and behaviorist counseling for Chicano college students. In P.P. Pederson et al. (Eds.), *Counseling across cultures*. Honolulu, Hawaii: East-West Center.

Sue, S. (1988). Psychotherapeutic services for ethnic minorities. *American Psychologist, 43*, 301–308.

Sue, S., & Zane, N. (1987). The role of culture and cultural techniques in psychotherapy: A critique and reformulation. *American Psychologist, 42,* 37–45.

Szapocznik, J., Kurtines, W., Santisteban, D.A., & Rio, A. (1990). Interplay of advances between theory, research, and application in treatment interventions aimed at behavior problem children and adolescents. *Journal of Consulting and Clinical Psychology, 58,* 696–703.

Szapocznik, J., Rio, A., Murray, E., Cohen, R., Scopetta, M., Rivas-Vasquez, A., Hervis, O.E., & Posada, V. (1989). Structural family versus psychodynamic child therapy for problematic Hispanic boys. *Journal of Consulting and Clinical Psychology, 57,* 571–578.

Szapocznik, J., Scopetta, M., & King, O. (1978). Theory and practice in matching treatment to the special characteristics and problems of Cuban immigrants. *Journal of Community Psychology, 6,* 112–122.

United States Bureau of the Census (1991a). Current Population Reports, Population Characteristics, March. Washington, DC.

United States Bureau of the Census (1991b). 1990 Census of Population and Housing, September, Summary Tape File 1A. Data User Services Division, Washington, DC.

Vazquez, C. (1982). Research on the psychiatric evaluation of the bilingual patient: A methodological critique. *Hispanic Journal of Behavioral Sciences, 4,* 75–80.

AUTHOR NOTES

Correspondence concerning this chapter should be addressed to: Professor Robert Malgady, Program in Quantitative Studies, 735 East Building, New York University, Washington Square, New York, NY 10003.

HISPANIC MENTAL HEALTH RESEARCH AND PRACTICE: WHERE DO WE STAND NOW?

Robert G. Malgady

Five years ago, outstanding issues and research problems in the Hispanic mental health literature were organized by Rogler, Malgady, and Rodriguez (1989) according to a five-phase framework. The first phase organizes research on the emergence of mental health problems. The second phase concerns use of clinical services, particularly the issue that Hispanics are underserved. If services are used, the third phase focuses on sources of possible cultural bias in the assessment process. After a mental health evaluation or diagnosis has been rendered, the fourth phase concerns the development and outcomes of culturally sensitive treatment interventions. The last phase involves the outcomes of post-treatment services and factors influencing either the readjustment to the community or relapse and rehospitalization of Hispanic patients.

These five phases are integrated, not only by the natural sequence of events they represent—from the emergence of a mental health disorder through the discharge and subsequent fate of the mental patient—but also by the underlying concept of how culture and the acculturative process shape the course of mental illness. The chapters in this book invite us to revisit the five-phase framework in the context of these two broader, integrative themes.

The first collection of chapters represent the most current thinking, by authoritative sources in a variety of disciplines, about the acculturative process and how crossing cultural barriers has an impact on the emergence and treatment sequence of mental illness.

From Professor Harwood's anthropological perspective, the usual theories of acculturation have mistaken geographic boundaries as markers of independent cultures. As he aptly points out, modern day immigrants are highly diverse in their relative immersion into American culture. They do not arrive in this country with an American cultural *tabula rasa*.

Viewing acculturation as a highly dynamic and fluid concept, Harwood challenges us to develop more appropriate measures of acculturation in order to study its role in the mental health process. The challenge is to represent both the etic and emic views from the host society and the society of origin, respectively, and to assess individuals' own cognitions and emotions regarding their multiethnic environment. Another contribution of Professor Harwood's chapter is the suggestion that cross-cultural mental health research needs to consider how individuals appraise their own feelings about their ethnic identities, values, and beliefs. How they cope with such feelings has a direct bearing on their mental health.

Professor Padilla's chapter makes a related observation about the literature on psychosocial development of children and adolescents. A mistake in the socialization literature, according to Padilla, is the assumption that children are socialized into a single culture. The consequence of this assumption is that biculturality traditionally has not been identified as variable and therefore was seen to be irrelevant to the study of the socialization process. Padilla argues that, in order to better understand the socialization process, we need to assess children's coordinate positions on a bicultural grid. Like Harwood, he too stresses the need to assess positive or negative regard (affect) for each culture as well as immersion into the cultures (competence).

Padilla also contributes to our understanding of a complex process by delineating four family structural situations that follow diverse pathways toward dual culture socialization. His two principles of assimilation—by invitation and ethnic protection—represent organizing concepts in the field. Another unique idea in Professor Padilla's chapter is that the "motives" behind bicultural adaptation vary with an individual's generational status, from survival value among first-generation immigrants, to bridging family and host society conflicts in the second generation, to a protective motive in combatting discrimination in subsequent generations.

Where Professors Harwood and Padilla stress the need to assess the cognitive and affective orientation of immigrants and their offspring to the culture of origin and the host culture, Dr. Cortes reaffirms the need for acculturation measurement scales to bear an isomorphic relation to the conceptual definition of biculturality. A critical limitation of extant measurement scales is the overrepresentation of language items, which psychometrically impugns the scales' content validity. Acculturation, as all these authors write, is more than simply English language acquisition. Moreover, the typical forced-choice response format of most acculturation measurement scales juxtaposes the two cultures competitively as mutually exclusive, thus undermining the scales' construct validity.

Cortes shares Padilla's thinking regarding the variety of social and interpersonal factors that may mediate whether or not acculturation leads to adaptive or maladaptive outcomes. Cortes strongly advocates multiple measures of both acculturation and mental health outcomes and stresses the necessity of studying the dynamic process of their relationships longitudinally across the lifespan of the immigrant and his or her offspring.

From the first three chapters and the new directions charted for research, a paradigm emerges for research on the fundamental question of the relationship between acculturation and mental health. This paradigm is portrayed in Figure 1. As the figure illustrates, the authors suggest the need to assess multiple dimensions of acculturation to the culture of origin prior to (or more realistically upon) migration as well as at their preconditioned acculturation to American society. Multiple measures should be assessed in both major domains, cognitive and affective. Intervening between the levels of bicultural involvement—and necessarily the distance between cultures—are myriad psychological, social, economic, and situational factors. Depending upon the particular array of mediating variables, an individual's bicultural profile impacts differently—favorably or unfavorably—on mental health outcomes. The model also rather ambitiously proposes that this dynamic cycle ought to be traced longitudinally over time for individuals and across subsequent generations and permutations of diverse ethnic mixtures. The model also corresponds to Sue and Zane's (1987) hypothesis that ethnic and cultural factors have an indirect or distal effect upon mental health outcomes, as mediated by process variables that are proximal to these outcomes.

The model derived from the first three chapters, though based largely on research with Hispanic populations, is not uniquely Hispanic. It applies generically to any immigrant or ethnic minority group where the person's conception of and feelings about a second, nonnative culture are modified.

Professor Ruiz first focuses on one Hispanic subgroup, providing us with an informative overview of the history of Cuban migration to the United States. He exposes us to an emic view of the binding force of traditional Cuban cultural values, such as dignity, respect, love and familism, and the origins and practices of folk healing (*santeria* and *brujeria*). He concurs with the preceding authors that acculturation can have positive or negative mental health consequences, depending on "the strength of the personality." He later highlights the diversity of Cuban Americans, Puerto Ricans, and Mexican Americans in terms of two socioeconomic factors: income and education.

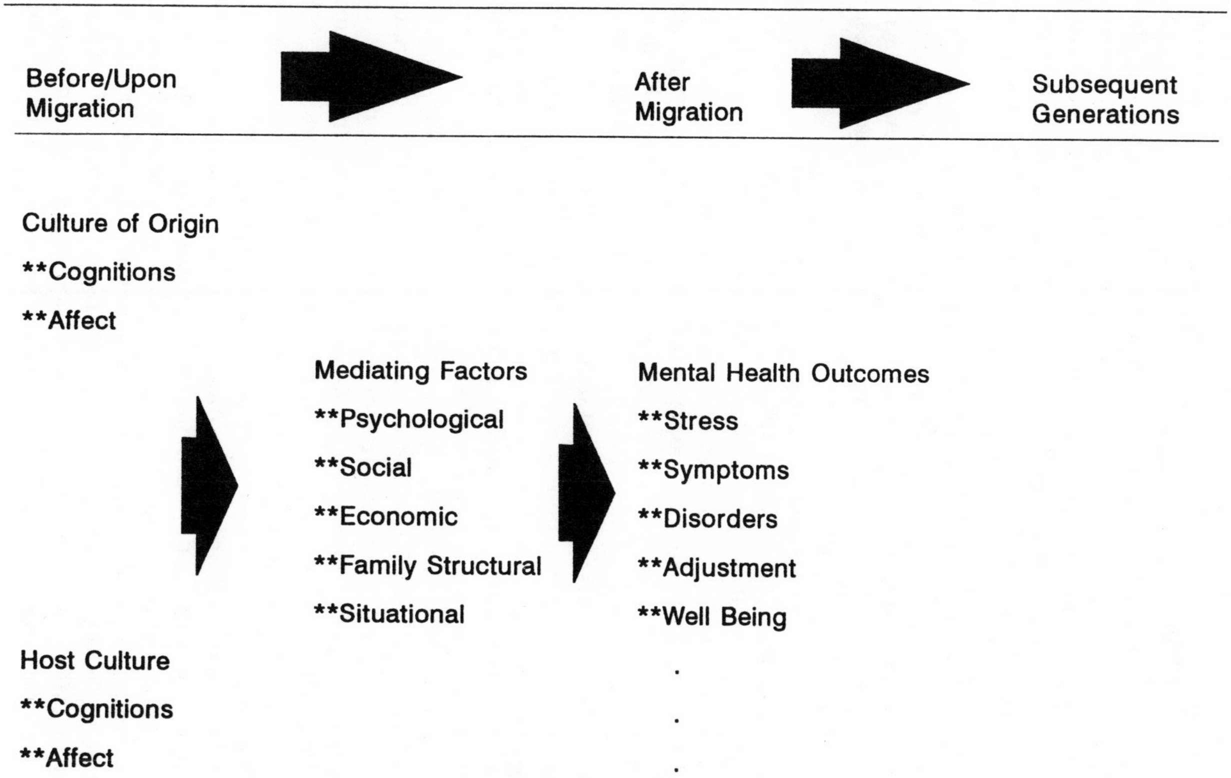

Before/Upon Migration → After Migration → Subsequent Generations

Culture of Origin

**Cognitions

**Affect

Mediating Factors	Mental Health Outcomes
**Psychological	**Stress
**Social	**Symptoms
**Economic	**Disorders
**Family Structural	**Adjustment
**Situational	**Well Being
	.
	.
	.

Host Culture

**Cognitions

**Affect

Figure 1. Mediated relationship of biculturality to mental health outcomes.

In the acculturative process, however, Ruiz argues that Cubans have used a different model than other Hispanic groups; they have used an integrational model of adaptation as opposed to assimilation, separation, or marginalization. They seem to be adept at retaining their Cuban cultural heritage, while successfully adapting to interaction with the host society. Indeed, according to Ruiz, Cuban culture reciprocally has altered American culture. From the standpoint of a practicing psychiatrist, Professor Ruiz offers culturally sage advice on factors affecting Cuban-American patients' attitudes toward and expectations of mental health care and treatment compliance. This dialogue delivers what is referred to in chapter 10 as a clear discourse on how cultural factors are relayed into assessment and treatment. Unfortunately, what we still need is similar emic psychiatric advice from other Hispanic subcultures for comparison.

Professor Roberts provides insight into the prevalence of depression and associated risk factors among Mexican-American youth. This chapter is particularly useful because there are virtually no reliable epidemiological data on Hispanic youth in this country. Another contribution of Roberts' study is its cross-cultural emphasis, comparing Mexican-American with non-Hispanic white youth. His results, moreover, are consistent with the literature comparing Hispanic and white adult rates and risk of depression. Nonetheless, his research leaves us with the lingering question of whether observed differences between Hispanics and whites in prevalence rates and risk odds ratios of depression are attributable to ethnicity (culture) or socioeconomic status. Roberts points out that, among other factors, acculturation and ethnic identity need to be included in future epidemiological studies of mental health comparing different ethnic groups. Certainly more studies, not only of depressive symptomatology but also clinical depression, are needed in order to determine, in Roberts' words, "how ethnocultural background constitutes a unique risk for such dysfunction."

In the concluding chapter of the first section of this book, Professor Salgado de Snyder calls our attention to a much neglected topic in the migration and acculturation literature. She demonstrates the active role played by women in the decision-making process of immigration by men and the increased stress they face as single household heads and economic providers in their spouses' absence. She also documents changing immigration trends indicating that, while the previous norm was for Mexican women immigrants to accompany their husbands, recently there has been an influx of single immigrant women seeking better employment opportunities. She also introduces the distinction between voluntary and involuntary (imposed by male authority) female immigrants, their differential receptivity to acculturation, and their symptoms of mental illness, particularly depression.

The chapters by Harwood, Padilla, Cortes, and Roberts relate primarily to the first phase of the Rogler et al. (1989) framework: the role of stress accompanying both the migration experience and the acculturation process in psychological well-being or the emergence of mental disorders. Ruiz's guidance in chapter 4, particularly his advice on how cultural considerations can be used to attract and maintain Cubans in treatment, is related to the second phase of the framework: utilization of services. The second section of this book, chapters 7–10, pertain to mental health assessment, treatment, and aftercare, the last three phases of the framework.

For the past two decades, Commissioner Marcos has confronted the problem of how language and cultural distance between patient and clinician perturb the psychiatric diagnostic interview. His contribution to this book, like Ruiz's sage advice regarding psychiatric treatment of Cubans, maps the terrain for clinicians dealing with limited English-proficient clients. Marcos' work provides us with directions for clinical practice and future research. He shows us how the patient's attitude toward the clinical situation, motor and speech activity, affect and emotional tone, and sense of self constitute a psychiatric anagram to be unscrambled by the psychiatric examiner.

Very few empirical studies of the language and diagnosis problem are in the literature. As Marcos informs us, those studies that are available are equivocal. The lack of research on and empirical clarity of this problem is ironic because accurate psychiatric diagnosis is a prerequisite to the accurate estimation of epidemiological prevalence and risk of psychiatric disorders, to appropriate psychotherapeutic and psychopharmacologic intervention, and to clinical judgments about post-discharge aftercare. Without challenging the veracity of the diagnostic system itself (e.g., DSM-III-R), accurate psychiatric diagnosis across the language barrier is indeed the most fundamental problem in psychiatric practice and research because it defines the unit of analysis.

In chapter 8, Professor Szapocznik and his colleagues, Professors Kurtines and Santisteban, present one of the most sophisticated programs of theoretically based scientific research on culturally sensitive psychotherapeutic interventions for Hispanic children and adolescents. For many years, Cuban Americans have been the focus of this programmatic research on Structural Family Therapy, which is rooted in structural systems theory. This chapter relates the authors' most recent and ongoing efforts to extend this seminal work to Nicaraguan, Colombian, Puerto Rican, Peruvian, and Mexican-American families. Perhaps one of the most creative aspects of their significant breakthroughs in psychotherapy theory, research, and practice is how they are able to promote family therapy without the family present (One-Person Family Therapy). The studies described are also scientifically exemplary because they compare treatment retention rates and behavioral outcomes of Structural Family Therapy to standard child treatment modalities (psychodynamic therapy) and to a nontherapeutic recreational activity control. Future research needs to direct attention to the therapeutic process in order to understand the interpersonal mechanisms by which culturally sensitized therapy, such as the structural systems-based therapies, promote behavioral change.

Whereas Szapocznik, Kurtines, Santisteban, and Rio focus on a program of culturally sensitive psychotherapy for Cuban Americans, Drs. Costantino and Rivera concentrate on cultural treatment modalities for Puerto Ricans in chapter 9. This work uses material indigenous to Puerto Rican culture—folktales, heroic biographies, and family scenes—presented through a storytelling modality in role modeling therapy for children and adolescents. The examples provide clinical guidance on how to adapt cultural material to therapeutic functions and how age-appropriate modalities are critical to this process. Much like the work of Szapocznik and his associates, Costantino and Rivera's work has been extended to include children of diverse Hispanic origins in their treatment outcome studies. Their methods of culturally sensitizing psychoeducational treatments for seriously mentally ill Hispanic adults are theoretically rooted in Rogler et al.'s (1987) three-tiered framework of cultural sensitivity. Once again, the challenge posed by the promising findings on cultural treatment adaptations that "work" with Hispanic children, adolescents, and adults is the need for process studies. We need to resolve the proximal/distal hypothesis of whether or not culture is directly linked to treatment outcome or indirectly linked through its facilitation of the therapeutic process.

In the last chapter, my discussion of Hispanic diversity touches on the work done by many of the preceding authors on assessment and treatment issues involving Hispanic culture. While there is still much research needed to determine more precisely the role of culture in the diagnosis and treatment of mental disorders, this chapter attempts to sketch out what the end of our search might hold in store for us.

The clinicians contributing to this book have offered state-of-the-art knowledge on how cultural and language barriers can be crossed in the psychiatric diagnostic interview and in subsequent psychotherapeutic treatment interventions. Their suggestions are based on first-hand empirical research and application in clinical settings. The new directions for research provided by the authors chart pathways, some of them interconnecting, toward achieving a scientific understanding of the nature of culture from a multidisciplinary perspective; the behavioral, emotional, and cognitive processes involved in acculturation; the cultural link to mental health or illness; and the role of culture in assessment and treatment of mental disorder.

Given the unprecedented volume of contemporary migration streams from Latin America and other non-English-speaking countries, coupled with a Hispanic population (and more generally a linguistic and ethnic minority population) growing at a more rapid rate than the white, English-speaking majority, the mental health assessment and treatment issues confronted by the authors in this book promise to increase in salience in the years to come.

REFERENCES

Rogler, L. H., Malgady, R. G., & Rodriguez, O. (1989). *Hispanics and mental health: A framework for research.* Malabar, FL: Krieger.

Rogler, L. H., Malgady, R. G., Costantino, G., & Blumenthal, R. (1987). What does culturally sensitive mental health services mean? The case of Hispanics. *American Psychologist, 47*, 565–570.

Sue, S., & Zane, N. (1987). The role of culture and cultural techniques in psychotherapy: A critique and reformulation. *American Psychologist, 42*, 37–45